DANCING AT THE EDGE OF DEATH

The Origins of the Labyrinth in the Paleolithic

By Jodi Lorimer

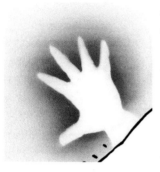

Jodi Lorimer
1711 SE 40th Av
Portland OR USA 97214

Illustrations: Ben House

ISBN 0 9578329 5 8

Kharis Enterprises Publishing

A Division of Kharis Enterprises Pty Ltd ABN: 61 831 018 044
8 Parkdale Court Robina Queensland Australia 4226
Phone: +61 7 55 930 360 *Fax:* +61 7 55 930 367
E-mail: info@kharis.com

ACKNOWLEDGEMENTS

A friend asked me, when the years of writing this book were at an end, how I kept at it for so long. For one thing, I was pestered to resolve the central questions that got me started in the first place. And I discovered that, if I let it go for a while as life intruded, I missed it and it missed me. Together, I, and my constant companion, the Process of writing, saw it through to completion. So first I must thank the Process that encouraged and prodded me to keep on. I used to believe that it was easy for the likes of Joseph Campbell, a handsome, intelligent, well-connected and well-financed white male, to be cavalier about his philosophy of 'following your bliss'. Yet as the writing of this book continued, I discovered paths opening, books appearing and people entering my life who offered help and support. One pivotal and utterly unexpected such person was Julie Forbes who, for reasons still unclear, donated money to my cause after knowing her for maybe an hour. This allowed me to focus intently for over a month on the work and get a considerable distance down the road.

Staring at photos in books can only inform one of so much. Although I have toured some decorated caves available to the public many, like Lascaux, are closed to all but the very few. I received patient, professional answers to my questions concerning Paleolithic cave art from the unfailingly gracious Jean Clottes. His comment to me of 'bon courage' to complete my book meant more than he could know. I have been fortunate to benefit from extended, fascinating and occasionally hilarious emails from David Whitley on the subjects of shamanism, cave art and his theory of genetic mutation. A special debt of gratitude goes to Jim Keyser, our energetic and brilliant cave tour guide and wine connoisseur. He has loaned me invaluable books, given advice and information, shared spirited lunches, and conspired to seat me next to Jean Clottes at dinner, for which I am eternally grateful and yes, Jim, I owe you big time. I thank Mike Taylor of the Oregon Archaeological Society for sharing photos and personal experiences of his journeys into many important caves and for reading some of the text.

I reserve a special gratitude for the deep and abiding encouragement from my sister, Barbara, who patiently endured a million pages of dreck and still felt the book was worth writing. Her

unswerving faith in me has been a secure anchor in the high winds of life. Yes, Grandmother was right. My husband, Michael Sweeney, has grown with me through the writing as we have found our way down our own marital labyrinth and into the light. He has supplied love, books, critiques, praise and energetic anthropological discussions, challenging me to defend my ideas and tighten up flabby thinking. I thank my children, Davin and Faye, for their love and support while Mom pursued her personal obsession, and my brother, Doug, for his affectionate support.

Carolyn Winkler dropped what she was doing on a sloshing wet Sunday afternoon to teach me not to fear Keynote software. And I owe a sincere debt of gratitude to the readers and cheerleaders; Sandra Waldren, Jean Casper, Melissa Coe Grewenow, and Judy Chambers. Ladies, your abiding friendship and invaluable assistance at difficult bends in the road kept me going when little else did.

Jeff MacDonald faithfully tolerated my latest labyrinthine discoveries over years of mushroom hunting in the Oregon woods, until he finally convinced me to present to the annual convention of the Society for the Anthropology of Consciousness, moving my ideas from vanity project to public forum.

Thanks also go to Ben House for his dedicated work on creating the wonderful illustrations. He understood and appreciated the subtleties and nuances of the art innately and has added some marvelous grace notes to the final work.

The furry companionship of the kitties, Selkie, Bosco and Lyra, made those chilly 5am mornings devoted to writing infinitely more cozy. Although their critique was thin, the support was undeniable, despite the occasional tap dance on the keyboard.

Finally, my thanks to Mark Viney. For years as our houseguest, we have enjoyed his amazing tales of growing up in Australia, having each foot in different worlds. I never suspected he would be the person to carry this twinkling of an idea into the material world.

I wouldn't have made this journey without all of you.

CONTENTS

THE MYTH OF THESEUS

Theseus was born the son of the Snake and of the Bright Sky. Of the Goat and of the Sea, in a time when the long thin fingers of myth were entwined firmly in the locks of history, so that one believed itself conjoined with the other. And, in truth, it makes no difference, for what we believe, is. Those who told and re-told the story of Theseus down the years believed his father descended from the line of Erechtheus, those ancient fathers of Athens from the heather flanked mountains who wore golden amulets of snakes and kept a sacred serpent in their place of worship. The serpent with the man's head spoke the wisdom of the oracle and the people of Athens followed her bidding. Theseus's mother was one of the many descendants of Pelops, powerful king of the Peloponnesus, and she was called Aethra, the Bright Sky. Some believe Theseus's father was Aegeus, a mortal and king of Athens who, despite dire warnings from the oracle, bedded Aethra and got her with child. But others know that later that night, while Aegeus lay in dreams of love and wine, bright Aethra waded into the inviting summer sea where the god Poseidon surged into her and planted his divine seed. And so, in Theseus was brought together the deep Earth secrets, the brilliant light of the sky, and the beauty and torment of the sea. He was both son of a king and god, securing his path to heroism.

Aethra, not wanting it bandied about that she consorted with either gods or rival kings, kept the identity of her child's father quiet, though her father may have mentioned the name of Poseidon to one or two close friends. But before he returned to Athens, her lover Aegeus secreted a sword of the house of Erechtheus, its hilt entwined with the family's sacred snake, and a pair of sandals in a hidden hollow of rock called the Altar of Strong Zeus, instructing her that, when his son was strong enough, he should lift the great rock, lay claim to the sword and shoes, and make his way to Athens to be recognized by his father, the King. Aegeus then returned alone to Athens and his regal duties.

With such a triple helping of nobility surging in his veins, Theseus couldn't help but grow to be strong, quick, beautiful and brave and soon he and his mother were standing before the great rock where she confessed his parentage. He easily lifted the stone, claimed the gifts his father had left for him and set out for Athens. As true heroes will, he scorned the far safer route by sea and elected instead to go overland, through a thicket of murderers and thieves that infested the road and were a plague to honest travelers. In this, and other ways, he was to follow in the footsteps of Hercules, his personal hero and distant cousin. His mother pleaded with him not to wade into a land infested with brigands and bandits but, being a hero, he would have none of it. Hercules had earlier rid the land of many of the thieves, but some had escaped and continued to plague good people. Theseus took it upon himself to finish the job. Besides, it just wouldn't look good for the noble son of Athens to take the easy way out.

Guided by glorious intent, he made his way to Athens. He killed a notorious bandit with his own club and, deciding that he liked the looks of the weapon, kept it with him as his own. He tossed another brigand off a cliff, another he whipped in a wrestling match. One especially foul creature named Sinnis he gave a dose of his own medicine. Sinnis was massively strong and was known by the locals as Pine Bender for his habit of asking passers-by to help him in this curious pastime. Then, once the treetop was bent to the earth, Sinnis would let go, sending the unfortunate traveler on a short flight to death. Or, even worse, Sinnis would tie one arm to one bent tree and the other to a different bent tree and release the trees like catapults to hurl parts of the hapless traveler in opposite directions. And, believing it was the duty of blue bloods to likewise rid the earth of especially nasty creatures, Theseus sought out and destroyed the Crommyonian sow. Having killed all the villainous men and animals that needed it, Theseus entered Athens with a heightened sense of his heroic nature.

He stopped to bathe and, dressed in a long robe with his long hair plaited, he entered Athens. A group of stone masons working on the roof of the temple of Apollo saw only his delicate beauty and mistook him for a girl. And like construction workers everywhere, expressed their frank admiration and asked why he was walking about unescorted. To demonstrate that he was no mere girl, Theseus unyoked the oxen from their cart and tossed one of the alarmed animals in the air as high as the temple roof. It was the first of many

adventurous encounters he was to have with cattle.

It must be told that back before Theseus was born, Aegeus had promised the sorceress Medea that he would protect her from her enemies if she in turn would cast a spell that would bring him a longed-for heir. He had stood by his promise. When Medea, on the lam for having spontaneously combusted her philandering husband Jason's new bride, showed up on Aegeus' doorstep in her chariot drawn by winged serpents, Aegeus took her in, married her and raised her sons. Having the witch of Colchis so near the throne of Athens caused no end of factional fighting in the city, for she had two sons and, as far as anyone else knew, Aegeus was without a blood heir. Medea turned the divisive politics to her advantage whenever she could to ensure her sons' futures.

It was she who first recognized Theseus, the young heir come to claim his throne; for it was her magical spells that helped to create him and she knew her work. Her own sons, now also come of age, were in line to inherit the crown of Athens and she was not about to let this come-lately foil her plans. Theseus, as was the custom with travelers, was invited to court for a feast of welcome. Unleashing her considerable wiles and making use of the factional tensions abroad in the city, she easily convinced the aged Aegeus to have Theseus, whom she had represented to the King as a dangerous stranger, killed at the banquet. She arranged for a poison cup of wine, poison being one of her fortes, to be delivered to Theseus at the table and waited eagerly for him to drink. Theseus, despite his strength, beauty, heroism and intelligence, decided in all humility, that it would be too brazen to reveal himself too openly and rather wanted his father to recognize him on his own. So, in a show of cutting his meat, he drew forth the sword of the house of Erectheus and sliced at his dinner. Aegeus, catching site of the sword in the young man's hand and the tainted wine in the other, leaped to dash the cup to the floor and welcomed his son and heir to his new life in Athens. The city erupted in celebrations the like of which had never been seen; garlanded oxen were slain and multitudes fed, fires lit on all the altars, the temples of all the gods were knee-deep in gifts, and the glorious exploits of the young Theseus were sung till what cows were left came home,

Aside from the sons of Medea, who were closely guarding their fortunes, Theseus had cousins in Athens who fully expected to inherit the throne upon the death of Aegeus. They were seriously distressed to see this upstart appear from nowhere and snatch away

their dreams of wealth and power. Dividing into two forces they rallied troops and set upon a course of civil war. But an informant in their ranks revealed their plans to Theseus and the uprising was quickly put down by Aegeus and his noble son. Theseus, to cement good feelings among the people of Athens and boost his popularity ratings even higher, made his way to the plains of Marathon where a monstrous, fire-breathing white bull, said to belong to Poseidon, was wreaking havoc upon the countryside. It was said that the bull had killed hundreds of men, including, some said, Androgeus, the son of Minos, King of Crete. Others say Androgeus was murdered most treacherously. As with the previous monsters and evildoers, the bull was quickly subdued and then led in captivity through the streets of Athens where it was later sacrificed to the glory of the Sun god Apollo. Medea, meanwhile, cast a magic cloud of invisibility around herself and stole away into the night.

The story of Theseus must take a turn in another direction for a moment, south to Crete, where yet more bulls appear on the landscape of myth like pins on a map. Crete was a beautiful island kingdom made rich by its swift fleets of ships that traded all manner of goods from Egypt to the Pillars of Hercules. Graceful, dark-skinned beauties with flowing curls and bare breasts, and lean handsome men who danced and feasted in airy palaces, were ruled by the legendary King Minos and his queen, Pasiphae. Zeus, Minos's father, had taken a shine to the maiden Europe and, disguised as a great white bull with jeweled horns, carried her on his back over the sea to Crete, where she bore him three sons. Later, after Zeus abandoned her, Europe married the reigning king of Crete who raised her sons as his heirs in his painted palace. Minos rose to power in Crete after the death of his adopted father, and banished his two brothers, Sarpedon and Rhadamanthys. King Minos and Pasiphae had a daughter named Ariadne, a pure and innocent blossom. Yet this part of the story is about her brother. Her half-brother Asterios, actually, whose name means 'star', how he came to be, and how he was killed by Theseus.

Minos, ablaze with his new power, dedicated an altar to Poseidon and boasted that the god would answer whatever prayer he sent to them. He prepared everything for a sacrifice, then asked that a bull be sent from the sea as proof of his right to rule. Poseidon, god of horses, earthquakes and the sea, sent the mighty King Minos a fabulous bull. A magnificent white bull appeared on the shore of Crete, boiling out of the waves like a small mountain of foamy

10

spindrift. Never before had there been seen such a creature of beauty and Minos, seized by greed, couldn't bring himself to slaughter it, but sent it to run among his own herds and sacrificed another, inferior bull instead. Poseidon had a reputation for having an excitable temper, as would be expected of the god of earthquakes, and this affront to his sanctity and generosity would not go unpunished. He fixed Queen Pasiphae with an unnatural lust for his beautiful bull.

There lived in Crete a remarkable man named Daedalus who was gifted with the talent of being able to manufacture the most marvelous things, only one of which was a magnificent dance floor inlaid with an ingenious pattern, for the princess Ariadne. Pasiphae sought him out and begged his help in allowing her to satisfy her lust for this bull from the sea. Daedalus built for her a beautiful hollow cow in which she could stand concealed and be serviced by the white bull. She became pregnant from this unnatural act and later gave birth to a monstrous child with the body of a man and the head of a bull. He was named Asterius, Of the Starry Sky, but was known as the Minotaur.

King Minos vowed to hide both the beastly child and his Queen's indiscretions away. He called for Daedalus and told him to build a place to house the Minotaur away from the eyes of man. The famous artificer created the Labyrinth, a building whose inner pathways were so convoluted and involved that the unwary who entered would soon be utterly lost and never find their way out to the light of day again. And at the very center of this maze was kept the Minotaur.

Minos, still seething over the murder of his son near Athens, had ever since, waged perpetual war on Athens. It was a time of great strife for Athens; the gods lay waste the countryside and the rivers dried up. The oracle was consulted, and it was decided that to appease Minos would also lift the curse of the gods that devastated their land. A delegation was sent to Minos, who demanded that seven of Athens's finest young men and seven finest young women be sent to Crete as tribute for his son's murder every nine years.

The time for the tribute to be sent rolled around, and Theseus, keen to help relieve the sufferings of the people of Athens, offered himself as one of the seven young men. When Aegeus decided he could not talk him out of it, Theseus and the rest of the 13 young people were put aboard a boat and sent on their way to Crete amidst much piteous lamentation by the people of the city. The boat was

rigged with black sails and it was agreed that, if Theseus should be successful, kill the Minotaur and end the tribute, they would change the sail to white for the return trip as a signal of their safety.

Upon arriving at the fair isle of Crete, they were met by King Minos and his retinue, including Queen Pasiphae and the princess Ariadne. One look at the noble and beautiful Theseus, and Ariadne was in love. Throwing all caution and familial devotion to the wind, she contrived to see Theseus in private, promising to save him if he would take her with him to Athens when he escaped. He promised to marry her and she presented him with a ball of thread, or, a clew, and some say, a sword. The thread he was to tie to the lintel of the Labyrinth and unwind it, as he found his way into the depths of the Minotaur's lair. Once he had slain her half-brother the monster, he was to follow the magic thread back to the entrance and escape.

All went according to plan and Theseus slowly made his way into the dank, fetid depths of the Labyrinth till he could hear the rumbled mutterings of the hungry creature turning in his small space and smell the rancid ferment of past feasts. Armed with the sword, Theseus hacked off the head of the bellowing Minotaur and made his way back to the clear upper air, following the thread of Ariadne. He and his companions stove in the hulls of Minos' famous navy and, with Ariadne in hand, sailed to the island of Naxos. There they made sacrifices to the god Apollo, feasted and celebrated their victory with dances. Ariadne, exhausted with the day's events, fell into a deep sleep. When she awoke, it was to see the Athenian ship, the black sail filled with wind disappearing across the sea. She had been abandoned.

In his excitement, Theseus had forgotten the promise he'd made to his father to change the black sail to white, should he be successful. Old Aegeus, watching the sea each day from the cliffs, spied the black sail returning and, in his grief over his lost son, threw himself into the ocean, which is, to this day, called the Aegean Sea. Theseus and the youth of Athens returned to a confusion of wild grief at the loss of the king and a wild joy that the mission was successful and the horrible tribute to Minos at an end. Libations were offered to the gods in gratitude for their return and preparations were made for a dolorous funeral for King Aegeus. Theseus, however, had sealed his future with the people of Athens and accepted the crown as their king.

CHAPTER 1

HOW WE BEGIN

"This is the story of how we begin to remember
This is the powerful pulsing of love in the veins
This is the story of how we begin to remember
These are the roots of rhythm and the roots of rhythm remain."
Paul Simon, ***Under African Skies***

Young boys flung out of the sky from flaming chariots or blasted from the backs of winged horses. Another spiraling to his death in the purple sea on broken wings. Mountains made of glass and forests of silver, copper and gold, spinning wheels and flaming iron shoes. As a child, my heart lived in this fairytale land alive with myth. I was thrilled by legends roiling with serpents and strangling vines, stepsisters who cheerfully lopped off toes to fit glass slippers, children eaten by wizened crones and fathers snatched away by magic.

My own father was thrown from his chariot when he was 40 I was one, shot through the windshield of a truck, leaving him incapable of a normal life but well able to teach me the ethics of poker and the philosophy of Nietzsche; "What does not destroy me makes me stronger." His momentary swerve to miss the oncoming young driver rooted an Accident at the center of our lives around which we wove our family legend, making straw into gold.

We grew up in a land that had been seamed with gold, where nuggets as big as your head washed out of the river banks with the spring rains and desperate men from all over the world slogged and fought, drank, gambled and died and a few got rich. Mark Twain spun his yarn about jumping frogs filled with buckshot in a cabin just over the river. A mysterious old hermit named Vince lived across the field in a hovel with a pack of nervous feral cats. He made knife blades from old files and fitted them into whittled handles. He never washed, made hundreds of gallons of wine from

grapevines he'd brought from Yugoslavia at the turn of the last
century in barrels big enough to fit four kids, kept his meager food
safe from vermin in a suspended cage and was the endless subject of
terrifying stories from my older brothers. Joaquin Murietta, either a
wronged Chilean miner or vicious Mexican criminal, depending on
your point of view, hid out from the law in a house at the top of our
driveway. His partner in crime, Three Fingered Jack, was, however,
undeniably a psychopathic killer who invented uniquely cruel ways
of slaughtering Chinese miners.

Joaquin and Jack rode through my dreams on smoldering horses,
flaming capes streaming out behind and Vince, haggard and gaunt,
materialized around dark corners. I grew up knowing monsters
tromped the earth in seven-league boots and it was wise not to
attract their attention. The only certainty was uncertainty. This was
confirmed in my high school years when my mother also went
through the windshield of a car, recovering but adding another
stratum to the 'Luck of the Lorimers' legend. And yet again in the
strange days of the Vietnam war, my oldest brother was flung from
the sky like a later-day Icarus and not expected to survive the crash
of his helicopter, his injuries eerily reminiscent of my father's. The
Army thoughtfully sent his flight helmet home, carefully cleaned
but split down the middle. Our family stumbled unaided through the
emotional minefields of his partial recovery.

That children fell from the sky was no surprise to me. I wanted to
know what they did once they landed.

The Accident became the central metaphor of our family's life.
We examined potential scenarios of what-ifs, as a way of probing at
the sensitive tissue of who we were, and the scar tissue of who we
were not. Certainly we were different from all the families we knew.
Like all children, we ran our lives through the filter provided by our
parents, and theirs before them, a legacy of quarreling with fate.

We rarely saw our paternal grandparents, but knew Dad was
keenly suspicious of his minister-father's Baptist convictions and
had an abiding love for his gentle, clairvoyant mother. Dad was
handsome and resembled his heroes, F. Scott Fitzgerald and Jack
London. He reveled in testing authority; he built boats, drank like
the sailor he was, became a communist and tried pot before it was
illegal. My mother defiantly lowered her family's Catholic flag, a
standard they'd carried for centuries. She refused to attend church
and Holy Names Academy, nicknamed Homely Dames for the ugly
uniforms. She loved dancing and Big Band music and her dark

complexion and curly hair passed as dubious-enough in Seattle's mixed-race nightclubs. Not surprisingly, my parents eloped. They raised us on a liberal spiritual diet of my mother's Christian mysticism and Dad's combined humor, unease with the Bible, and a philosophical challenge to define our values. At the time, I was pretty sure none of my friends had these conversations with their parents.

We four children came to decide, given our Dad's good looks and penchant for strong drink, it was a blessing that he had been partially blinded and left unable to drive, yet he could still quote Nietzsche chapter and verse. That which had not killed him had made us all stronger. We made a virtue of near tragedy. The Accident, swooping in from nowhere, forced us to reflect on the value of pain and its many categories. The subsequent accidents began to look like a curse, making the virtue of tragedy harder to defend.

In mythology, children who fell from the sky were generally where they didn't belong in the first place, having gotten there through ignorance and pride. Bellerophon should never have tried to fly Pegasus to the home of the gods, as if he himself were an immortal, and Phaeton, stamping his little foot, demanded to drive the chariot of the sun and went down in flames. Others, like Hansel and Gretel, were good children who did what they were told and yet were abandoned in an enchanted forest. Occasionally, these falling children landed bent, but not broken to find themselves launched on a perilous journey of self-discovery into a personal enchanted forest of the soul. Along the labyrinthine path dubious friends gave them 'gifts' and, suffering more, they learned to distinguish those having value. Gradually approaching the fearsome center of meaning they encountered a dragon guarding the treasure and fled, only to be drawn back to the core where they learned that pain tempered with courage and compassion becomes integrity.

'Accident' doesn't assume divine intention. Enlightment is momentary, but the journey is eternal. How do people endure the harsh trials life gives them and continue on in the wake of devastation? By putting one foot in front of the other and each day moving a little farther along the path we must walk. We must live expecting the unexpected; find a way of healing and acceptance of what comes. From shattered glass we assemble a mirror for the soul.

For me, the resonant strangeness and joy that mythology gave me provided a structure upon which to hang the maps of my personal

journey, for underpinning these stories with no happy ending was an emotional wisdom I did not find elsewhere. The Greek labyrinth of my childhood story was a fearsome place where one could lose one's soul, devoured by a beast. However, there was an Ariadne in the wings, a woman who held the secret to escaping certain doom. It was possible to survive the challenge at the Center and follow Ariadne's golden thread back to life, emerging strong and victorious. Gradually I have come to understand that the journey is a much larger experience of traveling an unfamiliar route, requiring great courage. Humans have a hunger for life and an illogical determination to survive. The symbol of the labyrinthine journey underlies these life odysseys, and the odysseys reinforce the symbol, both personal and legendary, as a cartography of spirit, giving form and purpose to suffering with a promise of healing and peace.

THE DEMENTED GRANDMA

I like to think of mythology as the demented grandma, born in ages past and now consigned to the dark basement of the modern mind. The family on the main floor, busy with their everyday lives, can hear her moving about, singing at odd hours of the night, sometimes quite beautifully. In the morning, there are signs that she has visited upstairs while they slept, leaving strange mandala paintings and the unsettling vaporous whiff of midnight ceremonies. Worse, she is liable to make startling and undignified appearances at inappropriate times. Up she rises from the basement, festooned with cobwebs, wild haired, and draped in floating skirts and sparkling shawl. She circles the dinner table, embarrassing everyone, uttering esoteric poetry and sexual innuendo that the adults know are true but can't admit in front of the children. Yet, truth be told, they secretly enjoy her performances. They break up an otherwise predictable evening. There's something about her they like, but they just can't quite put a finger on it. She is interesting, after all, a little scary and astonishingly insightful with a laser-like intensity that can be disconcerting. It is whispered that she's crazy like a fox. One child in particular, usually the youngest, takes to sneaking down the stairs to listen to Grandma's stories, despite being told explicitly not to.

In exploring the symbolism of the labyrinth, I, the youngest, was enticed down the basement steps to listen to Grandma's stories, and wandered into a labyrinth of ideas where each twist and turn revealed another mystery. The children who fell from the sky landed

and grew up. Their lives are the eternal journey through the avenues of the labyrinth. I have sought the origin of the labyrinth back through time, following the winding path to the center. How and why has the mythic symbol of the labyrinth so vigorously rematerialized in the modern world? In what form have the ideas of the ancients come down to us? Encompassing a ponderous breadth of spiritual power, the labyrinth has endured across time and cultures attracting significant contemporary imagery along the way, yet the core mystery remains eternally meaningful. What makes it such a potent psychic generator?

I began this journey simply enough. While reading the newspaper one morning, an article appeared over the rim of my coffee cup about a group of workshop participants at an Episcopalian Retreat Center walking a labyrinth. There was a photo of quiet-bodied people, sock-footed and reverential, some with scarves, some with talismans, eyes closed in prayerful silence, wending their way along the candle-lit circuitous path of a purple labyrinth.

My personal acquaintance with the labyrinth was from a childhood book of Greek myths. It was a dangerous puzzle where one needed to be an armed hero and have a magical guide to escape being eaten by the vicious creature, half man, half bull, that dwelt at its heart. The fact that the story danced around how the Minotaur had come to be through the 'unnatural passion' of the Queen of Crete sent up my child's red flag that grown-ups weren't being quite square with me. There must be more here than meets the eye. And there was entirely too much focus on the golden boy, Theseus, as if we were being distracted from the real story with a 'pay-no-attention-to-the-man-behind-the-curtain' ploy. Mysteries were wrapped in enigmas here with no true happy ending. The finale in which Theseus claimed the crown of Athens didn't resolve the emotional turmoil of blood and misery that lay at the heart of the tale; a history of cannibalistic sacrifice, an abandoned princess and a king who hurled himself off a mountain into the sea in despair. There was definitely a demented grandma somewhere in the basement.

The Minotaur's tale of gruesome murders and the implied peculiar sexual proclivities that created him did not easily translate that morning over coffee into a reverential Sunday activity of choice. What was going on here? What possible connection could there be between these peaceful Episcopalians and a ravenous mythological beast? The answer must lie at the heart of the

labyrinth, the experiential goal for the Sunday walkers and both prison and home for the Minotaur. Thus began my journey to find the origin of the labyrinth, to explain how two such divergent ideas as peaceful meditation and hideous death could coexist in one symbol that it is both graphic symbol and metaphorical path of life's journey. I invite you to follow in my footsteps to the heart of the mystery along a path that joins science with mysticism. There we will discover that the source and self-generating power of the labyrinth lies at the borderland separating life and death, in the hands of healing shamans of the Paleolithic.

SYMBOLS OF THE DEPTHS

At the heart of the mystery is the nature and definition of a symbol and its vital place in culture. Billions of dollars have been spent and committees exhausted to consciously invent immediately recognizable brand images for large corporations. But a mythological symbol is a very different animal.

A symbol can be a term, word or image we might know from our everyday lives which, beneath an apparently simplistic surface, carries within it layers of deeper secrets that can never be fully defined. Its ultimate truth is paradoxical, both somewhere deep inside our being and far beyond our rational awareness where we discover experiences beyond those our reasoning mind can grasp. A symbol embodies within itself opposite principles in equal measure, a mystic koan like the sound of one hand clapping that causes our reason to rebel against it, but our imagination to reverberate. At its deeper levels, the symbol acts like a crucible, a churning dynamic of repelling energies, generating perpetual metamorphoses that boost us out of normality and into the realm of the divine. Through the marriage of mystical contradiction, transcendence beyond the constraints of the material world is attained.

All spiritual paths have symbols that reveal Greater Truths through this resolution of opposites; the Hindu mandala squares the circle, the Chinese Yin-Yang contains the dark passive female principle and the light active male principle divided by a sinuous line. Each part holds within it a bit of the other, as everything contains an opposite. The Star of David unites two triangles, one representing the male principle and one the female, among other interpretations. The labyrinth is also a dualistic symbol divided by left, or right-hand turns, or the journey inward, followed by the journey out. At the heart of all these dynamic symbols lies a still

center, the transcendent union of opposites where all motion ceases.

The unconscious releases its fantastic vapors continually and we cannot ignore these persistent phantasms whose power is able to frighten or entrance us. Sometimes this happens spontaneously through illness, dreaming or other rapturous states. When it does, the unbidden manifestation of a symbol in one's life, appearing like a fiery angel at the gates of consciousness, can provoke overwhelming emotion and personal transformation; the 'Saul-on-the-road-to-Damascus' experience. We find ourselves drawn to an image and may suddenly see it everywhere. I was captivated by the unexpected appearance of a labyrinth in my local newspaper and launched on this investigation. Perhaps we have a recurring dream that insists on appearing in our sleep. A picture pours unbidden onto the canvas or an unexpected metaphor materializes in our writing. Symbols operate of their own volition, a miracle apart from our conscious selves, yet one that tugs at our deepest needs with both an intimacy we've never experienced before and one that unites us with the realm of universal truth.

Emerging charismatic leaders often reveal a symbol representative of their newly inspired authority. Arising as the remedy for the ills besetting a people during a time of painful historical upheaval, the symbol's spiritual and psycho/social content, propelled by the leader's conviction and power of personality, is adopted by an entire society. It is incorporated in to the society through rituals and ceremonies that respond and appeal to those people who interpret its message for the masses. History is transformed as a result. This book will show this was true of human society in the Paleolithic, when the labyrinth first coalesced into form.

Consider the religious and socio-cultural impact of the Christian cross and its influence, for good and ill, over the last 2000 years, beginning with the crucifixion of Jesus. The cross was originally a brutal form of prolonged execution employed liberally by the Romans and others before them. With the death of Jesus, however, this simple conjunction of a vertical and a horizontal line became a symbol of suffering, forgiveness, martyrdom, and the achievement of spiritual transcendence. Carried to a mystical level, it represents the opposing principles of the universe, the material world and the spirit world, with the intersection being the unification of these opposites, the spirit-journey of the Glory Road by which all souls meet in God. Medieval iconography emphasizes the dualistic nature of the cross by adding equal and opposite images; lions and lambs, and the bloodied body of Christ at the moment of translation into radiant spirit wreathed with lilies and roses.

The swastika is found in many ancient cultures around the world from Central Asia to pre-Columbian America. Its implications are numerous, but traditionally it is a solar symbol, indicating the passage of time and the enduring spiritual power of life. Now, however, the swastika, chosen by Hitler as the insignia for his nationalistic Nazi Party, reverberates with the horrors of the Third Reich.

The labyrinth in Western symbolism is commonly known not only as the lair of the Minotaur, but also as the pattern that decorates the floors of medieval Christian cathedrals all across Europe, most famously Chartres Cathedral in France. There was a brass plate at its center in centuries past, some say with a minotaur on it, but it has long since disappeared. Chartres' classic design has become the template for endless numbers of labyrinths elsewhere. During the Middle Ages, walking the labyrinth of the cathedral was representative of having made the rigorous journey to the holy city of Jerusalem, itself a symbolic paradise where the saved soul was seen as a 'new city'. The pilgrimage was a sacrificial journey to the sacred center of Christendom, where the pilgrim was met by the Holy Spirit and cleansed of sin. The actual, physical pilgrimage, though embraced by many, was often beyond the financial or physical capabilities of others and walking the cathedral labyrinth was a soul-cleansing facsimile.

How, then, can a labyrinthine symbol so easily contain both monster and god at its center? What spiritual, experiential metaphor links these paradoxical visions across the vast gulf between them and has done so for people all over the world? And what is the process by which symbols make themselves known in the world? From what dimension do they surface in our lives to shatter a bulwark of old beliefs or to knit together the fabric of a new spirit, arising like gold cloth woven from straw in the space of a night?

SPIRITUAL CUBISM

Symbols connect our intellect with the lush forests of imagination because they emerge from a well of archaic emotion. They demand that the ignored dream that woke us, sweating in the night, be lifted into consciousness. Although often less terrifying in the clear light of day, sometimes the dream is still disturbing. It hovers, a nagging

phantom of unease that only we can see, a messenger bearing important information. It must be brought to consciousness, the phantom released.

Our rational intellect alone is incapable of giving shape to this phantom. We can only express the true emotional terror or rapture a symbol triggers through art, which both provokes and releases intense feelings. Art allows us to view the Mystery from a multitude of angles simultaneously, becoming a sort of spiritual cubism, revealing facets that make no logical sense yet disclose great secrets to our non-rational selves. The image of the Minotaur originates in the labyrinths of the Paleolithic and has survived a multiplicity of incarnations since. George Frederick Watts' painting of "The Minotaur", a fairly modern interpretation, is a case in point. A creature with a bull's tail and head and a powerful human torso, is pressed against a bare stone balcony, looking out across a wide, misty sea. Under his bestial hand lies a small, dead bird. His mouth is partly open as in a sigh. His small horns, tufted with curls, are not dangerous. His expression conveys deep despair. This is not the ravenous beast of legend, but an earthbound creature, tormented by isolation and a mindless jealousy of the little bird that has the wings to escape this place. He bears a resigned misery and is worn out with longing. In a moment, the viewer is struck viscerally by layer upon layer of meaning, where the intellect requires the above paragraph to explain. For those of us familiar with the monster in the depths of the Cretan labyrinth or the flagrantly sexual incarnations of Picasso's, by comparison, Watts' image fills us with pity.

The mythology of a people is a compendium of metaphors of these transcendent moments describing the workings of their universe and how it all came to be. Their culture and stories express a body of mystical revelations that become a tribal encyclopedia. An ill-starred love story between a princess and a dashing hero is a sweet fairy tale, often with moral warnings about the dangers of looking for love in all the wrong places. But throw in a labyrinth and a Minotaur and we are transported to the land of legend. Tie this story to others in a cycle of tales that reflect prismatically back and forth on each other and the deeper realms of myth open up. The presence of a symbol casts a spiritual aura around all involved, transforming players on a stage to metaphors for much larger forces moving in the universe. A mere story is elevated to ritual drama.

MERCURIAL MYTHS

Interpreting a mythic symbol such as the labyrinth and its transformation through time is the result of involved cultural processes. Each society places its unique stamp upon it, provided the symbol remains relevant. Yet a precise definition of myth remains elusive. Scholarly dogfights argue that myths are ritual narratives, moral dogma, mnemonic devices, pure entertainment and more. All are probably right to some degree, contributing facets to mythology's hall-of-mirrors complexity.

The universal character of myth, its archetypal energy, is the imprint of the human spirit. If we were to choose a metaphor to explain the mythic process, it would be the god Mercury. The ancients observed the planet Mercury's habit of racing through the sky and associated it with speed and mutability. The god's qualities of eloquence, cunning and volatility are all qualities of mythic consciousness.

The pursuits of medieval alchemists, attempting to bridge the divide between the mystical and the scientific, ran counter to the powerful Catholic Church and so were couched in elaborate metaphor. They associated the planet Mercury with quicksilver, categorizing this paradoxical silvery solid that flows like water as a transmutation-substance. Their aim was to change matter from the impure base to the pure superior, from the mutable to the eternal. Mercury's (both the chemical and the god) capacity for transformation made it an essential ingredient. Ultimately, their goal was to find the 'philosopher's stone'; the personal mystical experience of God. Enduring life's hardships with grace and dignity was the spiritual counterpart of the alchemical crucible, burning away the superfluous psychic elements to reveal the incorruptible 'golden center'. This idea parallels the metaphoric journey into the labyrinth as the pilgrimage to the higher self. The capacity for transformation was key to enlightenment.

An energetic, youthful god, Hermes/Mercury was the patron of communication, and is credited with helping to create the alphabet and invent music, for what is myth without story and song? His statues were called 'herms', named for his earlier incarnation, the Greek Hermes. With the god's head at the top of the statue and an erect phallus on the front, herms represented sexual potency and fertility generally. Herms were placed at crossroads to mark places of transition or boundaries, and to assist travelers on their journeys. As the god of boundaries, he is the one best able to reset or

transgress those boundaries he defines through creative communication. In the same way, myths explore moral and spiritual boundaries and the penalties for transgressing them, to help guide us through the labyrinthine journey of life.

The coexistence of boundary and transgression produces an inherent restlessness. Just as myths are never resolved, nor should they be. Revelation is their purpose, not resolution. This constant motion arises not from perpetual discontent, but from a polarity of life's energies and the vital communication between the two. The cross, mandalas, the labyrinth, the Star of David, and others symbolize this. The sparking from one pole to the other, the surging of dynamic energy between equal but opposite life experiences, virginity/sexuality, creation/destruction, life/death, is the vital engine of human consciousness. To come to a wise decision requires that we explore the options. Mythology's examination of ethical and spiritual complexities helps us to do that. These dynamic metaphors of life experience result in the constant human yearning for the magical Center, the stasis of a healthy spirit at contented rest.

Mercury is a shamanic deity whose mythic responsibilities parallel the spiritual specialists of tribal peoples. Decked out like a superhero in winged sandals, helmet and flowing cape, he can fly between all three realms of existence. Not only does he carry messages from Olympus to the middle world of humans, but also escorts souls to, or more rarely, back from, the underworld of the dead. As a sacred shaman, he embodies the concept of healing as a return to balance of the individual and the spiritual wellbeing of the people. Bearing his magic wand, the caduceus, a staff entwined with snakes and a pair of wings on top, he guides the human psyche through visits to the land of dreams and of the dead and provides them with survival tools. Hansel and Gretel lost their breadcrumb trail, but found the courage to survive through Mercurial trickery, deluding the cannibal-witch into believing Hansel was too thin to eat. Those who learn the ways of these mythic realms return to this plane with newfound wisdom and, by healing themselves, contribute to the health of their society. Those who do not remain trapped in these other worlds, or return broken and, literally, dis-spirited, suffering the consequences of their lack of mythological street smarts.

Myths and shamans, like Hermes/Mercury, facilitate communication between the levels of human consciousness and the multiple worlds of being by using all the resources at hand,

23

including trickery and illusion, revulsion, illness and fear, to kick us off our comfortable conscious track and awaken us to the deeper mysteries of being. The substance of Mercury is aptly named; a perfect, magical silver ball that is impossible to grasp, beautiful and poisonous. Attempt to pick it up and it breaks into a hundred other perfect silver balls. This is the very nature of myth. The ephemeral raw materials of the deep psyche emerge into consciousness and take solid form in the construct of a myth.

THE DRAW OF THE MYTHIC

Mythology is the sacred literature of a people, an encoding of identity that establishes a seamless, multi-faceted relationship between the individual and the physical and spiritual worlds. It is the device by which change is rendered intelligible and meaningful. Ritual enacting myth allows people to participate in transformation and resolve anxieties associated with change. Myths have a fascinating and necessary way of transforming over time, adapting to a changing world to meet the needs of the society that relies upon it. If a myth does not adapt it dies, or becomes an anachronism, an artifact of a bygone era no longer possessing transformative power. Some myths, the key to their symbol system lost, appear to us like inscrutable visitors from another planet. Others, like those recently deciphered from the Mayan culture, emerge from a cocoon of lost language to take wing in our imagination. They have been literally carved in stone right in front of our eyes, and now reveal a beautifully complex world of gods, demons and heroes astride a magical landscape.

Still other myths are disguised by layers of time and cultural adaptation. We perform illogical, expensive, time-consuming and peculiar activities, but have forgotten or ignore the compelling myths that dictate them. We carve squash and light them with candles. We dress our children like the living dead and hand out candy on our doorsteps to other horrifically attired strangers wearing masks, unthinkable on any, but the sacred day. We give evergreen trees an honored place in our homes once a year, and hang small models of winged spirits, shiny balls, toys and white-bearded men from their branches. We risk life and limb in inclement weather to clamber on to rooftops, to fix a deer by our chimneys and string electric lights in the rain. We place groups of plastic people and farm animals in a sacred arrangement on our lawns. We feast or fast at certain times of the year as dictated by the phases of the moon on ritual foods that echo the legendary migrations of ancient people. In the spring we string trees with images of rabbits and chickens and hide colored eggs to be found by children. These activities, at whatever mythic level we understand them, have a personal, spiritual, familial and cultural resonance to which we respond. Illogical on so many practical levels, we follow an interior logic of a more convoluted variety and do them anyway. It just feels right and somehow necessary. It is the unnamable mercurial drive towards health that calls us to it, seeking a peaceful center of balance and wellbeing.

We grasp at vestiges of sacred energies that once consumed the lives of our ancient forebears to tap into the magic we feel is there. People in increasing numbers are walking labyrinths because this experience has just such a resonance. Grace Cathedral in San Francisco has created a cottage industry, supplying labyrinth paraphernalia to those who come to walk their mystical stone paths. Chartres Cathedral has been pressed by modern-day pilgrims to remove the pews that cover their labyrinth on Fridays, much to the dismay of the local Catholic ladies who consider this an encouragement to pagans . Ancient turf labyrinths are being dusted off and replanted, mail-order portable labyrinths painted on canvas are obtainable on line and others have appeared in schoolyards. You can contract to have one built in your yard, and Amazing Maize Mazes have been sculptured in cornfields as family entertainment. In Santa Fe, New Mexico, a labyrinth outside the Folk Art Museum was built so as to create an echo for those who speak aloud at its center. Prisons rent portable labyrinths and cancer wards have installed them in meditation gardens. Ephemeral labyrinths are drawn on beach sand to be taken later by the waves. And the Episcopalians offer labyrinth walks at their churches on special occasions.

THE LABYRINTHINE JOURNEY

Why do we do these things? Most simply, because they make us feel good. Many people are unaware that deeply embedded in the fun of children running through a maze is the pre-Christian mystical experience of the labyrinth, the ancient layers of resonance. Those of us who can't sit still to meditate find that swinging around the loops of the labyrinth puts body and mind in synch and allows thoughts to relax. The experience of walking the labyrinth is a physical meditation, a kinesthetic connection with a spiritual

destination. There is the feeling of participating in a mystery, finding peace in a chaotic world, one that links us to another time of stories and powers we no longer can name.

Beyond the sense of participatory joy lies the dark frontier of terrible necessity. Life drives us through illness, accident, war, rape and other terrors to seek out a deeper sense of 'health', one that reintegrates a shattered psyche or a devastated culture. To remain alive and functioning, one must find one's soul again. It has become lost in the chaos of a larger 'illness' and inner peace and balance must be regained.

The Tarot deck is a symbolic narrative of the labyrinthine journey, each card representing a different kind of life-experience. It is divided into two parts; the Minor Arcana that survives with some changes as our standard poker deck, and the Major Arcana, suppressed by the Catholic Church in the Middle Ages as a tool of the Devil. Laying out the cards of the Major Arcana in order and in the shape of a figure eight, the upper half are sun cards with the heads all fanned upright, symbols of one's relationships in the conscious world. The Fool, card number zero, is Everyman embarking upon his life's quest. His first encounter is with card number one, Hermes/Mercury, the Magician who stands at the entryway, the boundary between the flesh and spirit. The Magician manipulates his considerable powers to create illusion, an important metaphoric tool in the shamanic shed that the Fool must decipher. Yet he also offers magical survival tools for the Fool's use. The Fool is the embryonic Parsifal of medieval legend. Leaving the protective womb of home and mother, he must learn to distinguish Truth from Illusion. Thrilled with the adventure and innocent of the dangers of life, he is oblivious that he is stepping off a cliff. In fact, he is about to fall out of the sky and into the labyrinth.

Further down the path the Fool encounters other symbolic characters that represent relationships and experiences in the external conscious world. The appearance of The Hermit warns the Fool that an internal journey is about to begin. Alone, with his staff and lantern, the Hermit shows the way to life's deeper secrets. At the point where the cards cross in the center of the figure eight, at the spinning Wheel of Fortune, they become moon cards, reversed with heads turning inward. The Fool's journey will demand that he sacrifice outmoded and limiting life ways and confront painful realities. The Death card heralds transformations in behavior and belief, so that he may be led into the deeper realms of the

unconscious towards spiritual awakening. Eventually he transcends to the cards of the celestial realms, the Star, Moon and Sun. The final card is the Universe or the World card; indicative of the integration of opposites that transcends the duality of paradox. It is the card of completion and peace and echoes the incorruptible philosopher's stone. But of course, the figure eight is the symbol of infinity and we must return once again to the card of the Fool, but as a wiser fool, to learn a different life's lesson. The labyrinth is an eternal spiral.

RESONANT MEANING

A myth is creative in the most basic, self-animate sense. If a story can be easily pigeonholed and resolved it isn't a myth. Although many myths, particularly popular Greek myths, have apparently been set in stone by publishers of the last 100 years, a closer examination of the sources reveal complex layers of interpretation. The gross simplification of myths, their 'Disneyfication', has led to interpretations that sanitize the mysteries right out of them with cute characters and happy endings. Even so, the Disney version of the medieval Welsh masterpiece, the *Mabinogion*, called "The Black Cauldron", was still too upsetting to many; its version of the horned god Cernunnos disturbed conservative Christians. Making Zeus's rape cases palatable to children has produced displays of writer-acrobatics, despite mythologists' protests that these are not, and never were intended to be, children's stories. Nor were many fairy tales. A survey of the genuine Grimm Brothers' collection reveals baby stealing, hideously painful trials and cannibalism concealed behind sugarcoated gingerbread walls.

The women's movement and the revival of goddess worship has stimulated a re-examination of traditionally testosterone-laden myths and produced some fascinating reinterpretations. Female scholars have gained entrance to the Holy of Holies, library archives, whether or not they have their menstrual periods, and are challenging hide-bound assumptions. No longer shackled to the paradigms of Judeo-Christian male-dominated scholarship, these new explorations of ancient texts have presented a different kind of logic. Works by Elaine Pagels, Barbara Tedlock, Jane Ellen Harrison, Marija Gimbutas and Elizabeth Barber, among many, have provided significantly different feminist interpretations of these ancient works, inspiring many of their male counterparts to reconsider assumptions as well. Whether or not one agrees, their

arguments provide a valuable counterpoint to traditional interpretations. Figures from Medusa to Mary Magdalene and topics such as witchcraft and midwifery have been re-evaluated from a feminist perspective. Ariadne, portrayed in Greek myth as the traitorous, love-besotted girl who aids the heroic Theseus in killing the Minotaur, was originally a goddess of ancient Crete and part of a much older tradition appropriated by the Greeks. Appreciating the story from the point of view of the Cretans gives it a very different perspective, an historical echo, recounting a mythic version of the people of the great goddess being overtaken by the conquering Greeks, as did happen. The Minotaur as well has an earlier incarnation not so easily dismissed as a monstrosity.

RECOMBINANT MYTHOLOGY

In his marvelous book *The Marriage of Cadmus and Harmony* Robert Calasso introduces the mutable nature of myth by leading five different sections of the first chapter with "But how did it all begin?" He implies no simple Big Bang at the origin, which then spooled out in a tidy storyline. Rather, myths are mutable tales shared in oral traditions hundreds of centuries before the written word fixed them on a page.

The Grail cycle is one such mutable collection of myths that appears on the shadowy borderland between oral and written stories when literate Christians pushed inexorably into the homeland of Celtic culture. At the heart of the legends is the battle between the old religion of Druidic nature-worship and the new mind-set of Christianity. The clash between these two world views with humanity caught in the center is what gives the stories their magical/dangerous edge. If belief is the core of being, whom does one believe? The love triangle of King Arthur, Guinevere and Sir Lancelot is the focal point, but spinning off from this hub are the legends of the Lady of the Lake, the Fisher King, Parsifal, Sir Gawain, Mordred, Merlin and Morgan La Fey. Like Helen, Paris and Menelaus in the *Iliad*, these lovers are but instruments in the greater battle between rival gods and clashing cultures.

The myths intersect, overlap and merge their luminous imagery, revealing multiple facets not possible to see in a single tale. Variations are both inevitable and vital. Through ages of translations and transcriptions in frigid monasteries, muddled by mistakes and purposeful editing, we are left to decipher the meanings through the foggy distance of time.

The Grail, for example, is either described as the cup that Jesus used at the last supper or that caught his blood as he died on the cross. But pre-Christian legend describes it either as the god Bran's magical drinking horn, or the banquet platter of King Rhydderch, both of which miraculously fill with whatever food or drink a person desires. The Grail is also paraded through the palace of the dying Fisher King as a mystical lesson for the Tarot Fool, Parsifal, who doesn't get it at the time. It is sought by knights of the Round Table but never found. Only Parsifal, after much suffering and penance and Sir Galahad, a knight of pure spirit, are granted visions of the Grail. The Monty Python version, however, takes the story to a level of brilliant silliness. The success of Dan Brown's *The DaVinci Code*, bears witness to the magnetic power of intersecting two momentous symbols, the Grail and the cross. Through the telling and retelling of the story of the Grail, what began as a cycle of Celtic myths is refracted into a far-reaching prism of imagery, having at its center the Holy Grail, the Ultimate Desired Object. Calasso's question of 'How did it all begin?' may as well be 'How does it all continue?'

SYMBOLIC THOUGHT

Symbols and myths have awakened in humans a sense of awe from the very beginning, showing us the wonders beyond the mundane world as if parting a veil to reveal a treasure hidden in plain sight. This book will be a journey down ancient pathways into the heart of the labyrinth. Our guides will be the shamans of the Ice Age, who ventured into the winding deep caverns of the earth to merge with spirits. They did not invent the labyrinth. Their shamanic Argonauts of the spirit discovered it, exploring the frontiers of the human capability to hallucinate and ecstatically enter into a fecund world of power.

Archaeology has revealed the making of simple sacred spaces dedicated to ceremonial activity as long ago as the era of Neanderthals. Then, about 35,000 years ago, the creation of what we consider representational art appears to have exploded across the mental and physical landscapes of humans like us. Time frames for similar awakenings differ in other parts of the world, but the focus of this book will be Western Europe. In the Upper Paleolithic this eruption in the human capability for symbolic thought was recorded for over 200 centuries as cave paintings, portable sculptures, engravings, bas reliefs and personal adornments. They made

elegantly decorated clothing and wore animal teeth and beads. We can assume that they had body painting, carved wood, painted hides and objects made of perishable feathers, fur and natural fibers. But these fragile items have not survived. The even more ephemeral arts of song, poetry and stories are lost to us forever, although musical instruments survive to attest to their existence. In the far reaches of some deep caves the patterned footprints of youths appear fresh, as if they had just left. And there are dancing minotaurs painted on the walls of mind-altering subterranean chambers.

What compelled people over 30,000 years ago to explore caverns miles underground? Even today with guides, battery-powered lamps and sophisticated climbing gear it can be a frightening experience. Imagine entering a vast cavern where no one had ever been before carrying a burning brand or a small tallow lamp that may illuminate only a few feet of this enormous space. Navigating slippery floors, narrow passageways and climbing chimneys would have required two hands at times and one hand needs to hold the light. There may well be bears, wolves or other predators nearby. The floor may have collapsed up ahead. We marvel at their courage and determination. Why relentlessly pursue such a dangerous practice and then leave magnificent images on the walls that perhaps very few, if any, people would see? To touch the sacred. The surface of the earth was covered in miracles; of springs bursting from rock, animals, plants, and life of every kind, all of it beholden to the earth. To enter the earth's deep places was to come close to the generative power that made that life possible, to communicate with and try to know it somehow.

As we'll see, the hallucinatory capability of the modern human mind, coupled with an expansive and curious intellect, expressed in metaphoric language and art, gave form to the amorphous spirit world. The visions of other worlds beyond this one were actively sought out and relationships with its inhabitants nurtured. The Paleolithics were refining religion, and at the heart of this pursuit lay the metaphor of the labyrinth. It spontaneously emerged during this efflorescence of spirit and art requiring a consensus of interpretation, a codification into society as representing the route to significant psycho/spiritual processes. The symbol's power is such that for tens of thousands of years it has continued to accumulate accretions of meaning, like a coral layering on sub-aqueous life forms through time, and yet at bottom it remains unchanged. The potency of the symbol as the transformative generator of spiritual energy has retained its integrity as well as its paradoxical nature. A modern labyrinth walker is able to be not only comfortable, but uplifted by a symbolic journey to the Center where an ancient walker faced down the Minotaur, bloodied by his feasting on the broken youth of Athens. From tales of Osiris to Herodotus, Dante and Umberto Eco to Jorge Luis Borges, a film named *Labyrinth* with David Bowie slipping through MC Escher's impossible architecture, and another, *Pan Labyrinth* setting the god Pan in counterpoint to Franco's Spain, the labyrinth symbol adapts to the needs of the culture in which it arises.

It appears in a variety of guises; a tomb, a holy place of worship, a building so constructed as to entice one to enter, but to deter one from leaving, the abode of monsters or gods, the land of the dead to which one must have a guide. But always as the gateway to Otherworlds, parallel universes of spirit. It has been quartered into the seasons, bisected into masculine and feminine principles, and broken into lunar cycles. Whatever form it takes, it is simultaneously supreme artistry and utter chaos, the crucible of creation and of destruction, the path of ignorance and of enlightenment, a dynamic process and a static form.

Implicit in all of the tales of the labyrinth is the idea of seeking out, whether by choice or fate, that which is contained at the heart of the labyrinth. One is compelled to enter by an illness that has taken over one's soul. A healing, a restoration of self, requires that the ego be relinquished and the spirit embraced by confronting the Power at the center. By discovering the central mystery the paradoxical nature of the labyrinth is resolved in a moment of epiphanic transcendence. Should the seeker survive this transformative journey to confront the ultimate challenge, he re-emerges, healed and profoundly changed, into his own world once again, bearing the treasures of wisdom to share. We owe this visionary process to our Paleolithic forebears, as we will see.

To claim to grasp a symbol or a myth in its entirety in any state besides divine revelation is to declare it dead, so this book is just another foray into the wilderness. I rather present a line of reasoning and interpretation following the evolution of an ancient metaphor into the modern day. How can its reach be so vast, so ancient and yet so modern? Why are labyrinths once again, after centuries of hibernation, reappearing in our midst, ancient anachronisms that seem so familiar, and so comforting?

THE PARADOX PERSPECTIVE

It is important to mention a significant distinction at the outset between a maze and a labyrinth. A maze is generally described as multicursal, that is, having many paths, and designed with more than one entrance, sometimes more than one exit, and there are dead ends along the way that force the walker to backtrack and try another route. A maze is designed to confuse. The path to the exit is random. A labyrinth, on the other hand, is unicursal, with one entrance that leads down a single path to a center and back out to the exit by the same path. The challenge of a labyrinth lies not in the route, but in overcoming the difficulties of the journey itself, the courage to persist along a singular pathway to the heart of a mystery, and to re-emerge from the experience a changed being. Labyrinths have been created in a wide variety of forms, but they are always precise.

The labyrinth is the perfect embodiment of a paradox; a concept seemingly contradictory or opposed to common sense that defies expectations, and yet one that is perhaps true. By creating what are essentially two different 'landscapes' a multi-faceted metaphor is revealed. That a labyrinth can be simultaneously both chaos and ultimate order, terrifying and beautiful, debilitating and inspirational, makes it a symbol of exceptional dynamism. It all depends on your perspective.

Imagine yourself walking inside the narrow corridors of a labyrinth. Perhaps you've done this in a garden. Your vision is limited on all sides. As you walk you are constantly changing direction, making now a tight turn to the right, now a long-looping turn to the left. The sensation is that you must be getting closer to the center because the turns are tighter. But then you feel yourself taken all the way out to the edge again and imagine that you'll never get there. It is impossible to make any logical sense out of the path you are following because you can only see what is right in front of you. This is all great fun. Being disoriented and 'lost' for a short time is titillating entertainment, as long as rescue is guaranteed.

But imagine that the walls are impenetrable stone. A low ceiling drops down from above so there is no escape over the walls. There is little light. You have no idea how big this place is or how long it will take you to get through. As you swing back and forth along the senseless corridors, you begin to wonder if you'll ever get out. Is there a center? And, if so, what is in the center? Are you going in circles? Will you survive? Impatience gives way to choking

claustrophobia and an overwhelming sense of chaos. Perhaps you've been deceived and wonder if you are headed for some hideous ordeal, if it is only to endure the terror of entrapment. A steadying hand on the wall comes away wet with slime. The dankness grows. Water is dripping somewhere. The rotten smell of something dead whiffs up from the stone floor, and from way down inside the walls emerges the muffled grumble of something large heaving slowly about. Now, THIS is the stuff of myth.

But let's change perspective again. You are the cunning Daedalus, creator of the Cretan labyrinth, who was imprisoned within its confusing walls. You have built a brace of wings from wax and branches and seagull feathers to escape from this trap of your own device. And as you rise, your great wings beating the salt sea air of Crete, you look down one last time on the walls of your former jail and marvel at your own ingenuity. How beautiful a shape it is! How regular the pattern, how harmonious the form. It is a creation of great artistry that depicts a grand sense of order, one that can only issue from the divine. Choosing a careful path to preserve your delicate wings, a path between the heavy mist below that could soak the feathers and drag you into the crashing waves, and the wax-melting heat of the sun above, you escape what would have been sure oblivion, buoyed by the epiphanic joy of ultimate freedom attained. This, too, is myth.

Ambiguity is the labyrinth's central nature. It is always unstable, changing its personality and ours as we change perspective. Ambiguity doesn't settle well with us, because it doesn't settle at all. It's a messy, non-linear way of being that challenges the Creation-Existence-Armageddon model of the Judeo-Christian tradition. Like a psychic nuclear reactor, the labyrinth generates creative emotional and psychic processes in whatever guise it appears. It is continually breeding new versions of itself that demand we revisit our categories and redefine what the symbol means to us in our time. And, as we will explore, the experience of the labyrinth is not only ancient, it is hardwired into the brain structure of the earliest humans, biologically indistinguishable from us, who first recognized its ineffable potency.

In pre-literate antiquity, the labyrinth design and its cousins, the spiral and the meander, were symbols that occurred worldwide in rock art and weaving patterns, on pottery, and was scrawled as ancient graffiti on a wall in Pompeii. From the Near East to New Grange in Ireland, and from the American Southwest to Siberia, the

labyrinth pattern is one of the oldest symbols in the history of mankind and one of the most universal. To understand the significance of this mythological symbol requires that we dig into the very core of human experience and tread the paradoxical paths of belief and biology, history and myth, and discover where they cross over into transcendence, at the Center.

FOLLOWING THE PATH

We begin at the beginning of modern humans in an ice-bound Europe about 35,000 years ago. What allowed them to succeed where the resident Neanderthals did not? What made our ancestors quintessentially human and ferocious survivors? Mythically, how did these early adventurers, tumbling out of the hot blue skies of Africa, manage to land on their feet in the frozen valleys of France? The key was a brilliant combination of biology and curiosity, facility and adaptation that, through art, expressed metaphor. Metaphor, in turn, enhanced culture, and culture created more complex symbolic art. This sparking between survival in a harsh environment and artistic expression created the emergence of the labyrinthine idea as soul-journey, a fusion of purposeful outer and inner vision.

Consider every chapter another course along the journey deeper into the labyrinth. To reach the center we must first explore the emergence of modern humans and human thought. We'll examine altered states of consciousness, shamanism, tribal culture and mystical architecture. 'Seeing' in a multitude of ways will be explored, for what we 'see', our perspective, is what we believe. One of these explorations will be the nature of altered states of consciousness and the natural human capability to hallucinate. Another is our awakening to the brilliance of ancient peoples. The discipline and courage of Paleolithic shamans to train themselves to enter trance states and navigate hallucinatory Otherworlds set humankind on a spiritual path we continue to pursue today. The artists of those times have left us their codices on the walls of caves. Finally, grasping the Hermit's lantern, we'll follow these shamans into the lightless depths of these ancient cathedrals. This is where Ice Age shamans conversed with spirit animals, brought them through the veil separating the worlds and fixed them on the walls. And in Lascaux, the Queen of Paleolithic caves, we'll journey with them through the appropriately named Axial Gallery, itself a paradox, as an axis is a straight line around which figures rotate, and

finally journey to the heart of the mystery where god and monster meld.

Can one symbol represent so much? Why has it endured through the whole history of humankind, emerging into consciousness in one form, only to sink and re-emerge later in new cosmic clothing, like a magnificent fish breaking the surface of a pond to consider us thoughtfully before sinking once again as we drop our net?

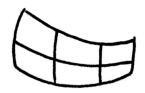

CHAPTER 2

PREHISTORY DISCOVERED

*"...while the higher forms of religious faith pass away like clouds,
the lower stand firm and indestructible like rocks."*
Sir James George Fraser

*"Very deep is the well of the past. Should we not call it bottomless?
The deeper we sound, the further down into the lower world of the
past we probe and press, the more do we find that the earliest
foundations of humanity, its history and culture, reveal themselves
unfathomable."*
Thomas Mann, Joseph and His Brothers

SEEING IS BELIEVING

How, and even if, one sees the journey of the labyrinth, is a
matter of perspective. The walls of our assumptions keep us to a
path whether we are aware of it or not. To pursue the origins of the
symbolic labyrinth and to address the question why it is re-emerging
today, we must imagine our way backward in time. Reflecting on
our historical prejudices reveals how far we've come in a relatively
short time; how intractable bias has crumbled in the light of
undeniable proof, entirely restructuring the way we perceive history
itself and ancient peoples. Our modern world is tamed literally
almost to death, whereas Ice Age people were inextricably bound to
a now-vanished wild world, a landscape teeming with herds of
enormous animals. We share with them the labyrinthine experience
as a fundamental part of our humanity. But first we needed to
believe that such a world, and such humans, once existed.

It is 1660 and a party of friends is spending the day exploring the
limestone cave of Niaux in southern France. One of the men, Ruben
De la Vialle, follows a path into a dark gallery enclosed by smooth
grey walls. To record the moment, he writes his name in florid script
near paintings of a bison and an ibex. In fact, the surface of this

that. Swarms of eager tourists packed up their lunches and lamps and tromped through Lascaux, blissfully unaware they were obliterating the delicate archaeological record on the floor of the cave. By 1960 it was apparent that the increased warmth from the open air, the infiltration of microbes and even the very breath of visitors was conspiring to destroy the now world-famous paintings. Molds were growing on them. The cave was sealed by the government to all but the most important visitors from the French Ministry of Culture and their guests, air locks and chemical footbaths were installed, and a precise replica was built nearby for tourists to visit.

CHAUVET

By the time Chauvet was found by three French speleologists in 1994, significant lessons had been learned. Remarkably, the cave was discovered in an area popular for tourism and caving in the limestone escarpment above the Pont d'Arc in France. Its entrance sealed in antiquity by scree, it had lain literally under the feet of countless vacationers until spelunker Jean-Marie Chauvet and two friends, purposely exploring the escarpment for caves that may house Paleolithic art, noticed a draft emerging from among the stones. They removed rocks until the opening was wide enough to enter. Inside, they found themselves poised on a ledge and lowered themselves into the dark with a rope.

Chauvet and his fellow explorers descended into the most spectacular painted cave found in modern times. As if under a fairy-tale enchantment, where the substantial cliff face shimmers and gives way to a fantastical landscape, so the sunlit modern world evaporated as they entered an ancient, sparkling wonderland. Pillars of limestone and frozen calcite waterfalls appeared in their lamplight. Great wings and flutes of stone unfolded down the walls. Fragile formations of snowflake delicacy told them they were the first humans to enter this magical cavern in countless centuries. Displayed on gallery walls, tucked into recesses and sketched on stalactites were some of the most stunning Paleolithic paintings ever found. The explorers were keenly sensitive about contaminating the environment and inadvertently destroying information. They restricted their exploration to a minimum and were careful to walk in each other's footprints so as not to disturb the floor. They *were seized by a strange feeling. Everything was so beautiful, so fresh…Time was abolished, as if the tens of thousands of years that*

separated us from the producers of these paintings no longer
existed. It seemed as if they had just created these masterpieces.
Suddenly we felt like intruders. Deeply impressed, we were weighed
down by the feeling that we were not alone; the artists' souls and
spirits surrounded us. We thought we could feel their presence; we
were disturbing them.'
(*The Mind in The Cave*, David Lewis-Williams)

The explorers immediately contacted Jean Clottes of the Ministry of Culture, a gracious man who is generous with his knowledge. He did not really believe the significance of the phone call, fearing this was another case of forgery, a modern charlatan drawing "Paleolithic" images for fun and profit. He was reluctantly pulled away from family Christmas festivities to investigate. But once inside the cave, high on a curtain of calcite that suspended from the ceiling, he found an owl, drawn with a finger in the light crust of decayed limestone. Beneath the owl, the floor had fallen away, collapsed ages ago into a deep pit. No one could have gotten to the ceiling to make this image for millennia. Clottes knew the art was genuine. The pristine condition of the cave convinced them they were the first to enter in tens of thousands of years. This was one of the most exciting discoveries of the century. The cave was sealed immediately to all but a very few select visitors. When undeniable dates determined the oldest use of the cave to have been about 32,000 BP the result was an astonishing realignment of attitudes about ancient humans and their creative potentials. Here was sophisticated art to rival Lascaux, using techniques thought not been invented until the Renaissance.

Chauvet is an unequalled laboratory for Paleolithic studies. Investigations of the cave are proceeding extremely slowly and carefully with every attempt to minimize the impact on the cave environment, as impact translates into potentially lost information, a lesson well learned from Lascaux. In the age of sophisticated computer software, DNA research and other scientific investigative techniques, the potential to recover information is unparalleled. The floor of the cave has been covered by a raised metal walkway. No excavation of the floor has taken place and none will for years to come. Artifacts on the surface have been photographed where they were found, carefully removed, studied in the lab and returned to their original resting places to await future research. The study of Paleolithic art and the awareness of its significance in the deeper understanding of the human story has come a long way indeed. The

very thought of touching a painting without observing the proper procedure is inconceivable, let alone scratching your name next to one. Posted outside many of the caves still accessible to the public is the ubiquitous sign "ne touché pas" reiterated emphatically by every tour guide. Chauvet offers the opportunity to discover information about our Paleolithic ancestors in ways never before dreamed.

Up to the present almost 300 sacred caves have been found in France, some with only a few images and others decorated throughout. In the 17th and 18th centuries antiquarians and collectors began to realize that hunting for buried treasure in the tombs and monuments of ancient people would help them reconstruct a history of the past if they did it methodically. The careful removal and documentation of stratigraphic layers of soil allowed for relative dating of the artifacts embedded in it. Archaeology began to develop as a discipline about the time of Darwin and de Sautuola. Archaeological research is traditionally, by necessity, a destructive process; pigments must be scraped off to determine the materials used to create the paintings, a floor has to be excavated layer by layer to reveal the artifacts under it and their relationship to one another, charcoal and parts of bones are ground up and subjected to chemical analysis.

But traditional archaeology is undergoing transformations. With the pace of technology and science moving at breakneck speed, all caution is being observed to avoid destroying any part of a site or artifact. Future research methods may perhaps discover a way to learn what we need to know and yet still preserve them largely intact. Clottes has suggested that perhaps eventually DNA may be recovered from remnants of saliva in the paint. The artist who took powdered pigments into his or her mouth and applied it to the wall by spitting may have perhaps left behind genetic traces. These might reveal information about the individual artists, such as their age, sex and genetic makeup. The very careful and nondestructive research techniques being employed at Chauvet endeavor to wring as much information out of the site as possible while still preserving it for future science.

Imagine what was lost at Lascaux and Niaux and the dozens of other painted caves trampled by hordes of ignorant thrill-seekers. The prehistoric entrances to many of these caves had collapsed as a result of thousands of seasons of freezing and thawing, which sealed and preserved the interiors. This left them undiscovered for eons and completely undisturbed. Refrigerated at a relatively constant

temperature and humidity, the caves appear to modern discoverers as if the ancient people had just departed moments ago, leaving the cold ashes of their fires, their tools and even their footprints behind in the moist clay floors. Attempts to educate the public about the delicacy of cave sites notwithstanding, some modern discoveries have still been damaged. The unwitting discoverers of Le Reseau Clastres trampled the floor in 1970 and the entire village wandered through the cave of Covaciella the day it was discovered.

The people who painted Lascaux were there about 18,600 BP (Before the Present). Chauvet was a spiritual center to its people 14,000 years before that. Our world is almost as distant in time from Lascaux as Lascaux is from Chauvet. Charcoal found in the cave has revealed that it was visited as early as 32,000 years ago. It is the oldest painted cave yet found and closest in age to the time modern humans arrived in Europe from Africa. There was a second period of use dated to about 27,000 BP. During each of these two intervals, paintings were made over a fairly brief stretch of time. Significantly, even at the earliest date, the artistic techniques demonstrated in Chauvet, the use of perspective and surface preparation for example, are equally complex as those employed at Lascaux, painted thousands of years later. There is no such thing as progress when it comes to art. Time is plastic. These people, who were biologically identical to us, arrived here with the techniques and talents to create magnificent art. More importantly, they also possessed the inner vision and desire for symbolic representation nested into a cultural context. This context, which we'll explore, integrated the subject and the act of creating the art into the landscape of the subterranean, labyrinthine cave and, simultaneously, into their cultural and spiritual landscape as well.

TIME TRAVEL

Stand on a busy city street corner and try to imagine away the mark of man; erase the buildings, the noise and traffic grids and envision the rolling contours of the natural land. Looking through this reverse lens of antiquity, the modern world melts and fades. The asphalt that paves 10 lanes of highway in a smooth, controlled ribbon of commerce lets loose its tidy sidewalks and oozes into a lakebed, disguising itself with a deceptive sheen of rainwater that invites thirsty creatures into a tantalizing trap.

As a child, I gazed with fascination at the pictures in my book about the Ice Age, thrilled at the savage spectacle and struggling to

imagine what that world had been like; that it had actually existed somewhere. Their beards and coats clotted with black ooze, these strange creatures thrashed, roared and agonized with exhaustion as tar pulled them into a treacherous pit. Mastodons, giant sloths and horses, caught in the tar-bed, looked like a convenient meal to prowling saber-toothed cats, patient buzzards with12-foot wingspans and a pack of dire wolves. But the predators, like their intended meals, all succumbed to the treacherous asphalt and yielded up their bones to science thousands of years later. These wild-eyed ancient beasts emerged from their strange tomb into the center of what some may consider to be a similarly treacherous area in the heart of today's downtown Los Angeles, Rancho La Brea on Wilshire Boulevard, populated in our time some would say by different predators and different prey.

The disconnect between the world of these creatures and my own collapsed in an instant. On a trip to Los Angeles with my mother, we drove by the La Brea Tar Pits, housed in a museum on this very busy street. The untamed primeval world of gigantic, bloodstained beasts was now utterly domesticated by restaurants and office buildings. Here is where this wild place had been that leaped off the pages of my book and captivated my imagination; right under our feet. Defleshed and stained by the tar, their remains allow the images, a fossilized palimpsest, to bleed through of a time when animals ruled the world and humans were a snack food.

If we were to slip through a time warp into what is now downtown London during the Upper Paleolithic, a period of time from 40,000 to 11,000 years ago, we would find mammoths bathing in the Thames and spotted hyenas circling a wounded woolly rhino on what would one day become Fleet Street. Shaggy bison would be wandering the site of the future National Theatre and herds of small, swift horses would be seen lunching on the eventual grounds of Buckingham Palace.

Artists' renderings of the vanished world of the Ice Age appear to our modern techno-charged sensibilities like illustrations for a sci-fi quarterly. Longhaired men girded in furs gut a gigantic bison with stone knives while women strung with heavy necklaces of shells and animal teeth carve a bloody haunch into strips to dry over a fire. Bundles of dried meat are lowered into storage pits dug into the permafrost. Other muscled men, seated around a fire, wield bone hammers and chip flint into leaf-shaped blades while older children look on. Other children dressed in beaded leather carry a bowl of

food to a gray-haired crone seated by a fire. They sit near a circular structure built of thousands of giant interlocking mastodon bones. It has a Gothic arched doorway made of two ivory tusks. The structure is covered with hides, and inside a huge painted mastodon skull stands, empty eye sockets staring outward to the daylight. In the distance, a massive glacier pushes slowly towards them down the mountain. Everything about this world is gigantic and raw, as if seen through a colossal wild lens. How could such a strange world have been here, right where we stand today?

In North America, the continent was empty of people until relatively recently. One of the oldest sites discovered in the New World is Monte Verde in Chile. Artifacts and bones, sealed under a layer of peat that had grown over them, dated the site securely to 12,500 BP. There is conjecture over a possibly much earlier occupation that some believe may be as old as 33,000 years, but it remains highly controversial. Beringia is recognized as the emigrant highway for the pioneering Paleo-Indians who originated in northern Asia and traveled to North America. What used to be called the 'land bridge', a misnomer that implied a narrow isthmus surrounded by crashing icy waves, was really a vast, ice-free landmass that linked Siberia and Alaska. The Paleolithics would have never known it was a 'bridge' of any kind. The seabed of the Bering Strait was exposed during the last glaciation when the sea levels were at their lowest. People who hunted the herds of mammoth, horse and caribou unwittingly colonized North America by following the herds. It is also assumed they used boats, traveling along the coastline, but any evidence of living sites now lies under the ocean. How the Paleo Indians got as far south as Chile by 12,500 BP if they came by way of the Beringian land bridge is the subject of on-going discussion in the archaeological world. Dates from ancient sites elsewhere have yet to line up with any congruency. Having made the crossing on to the American continent when the sea level was low enough to do so, it is calculated that to travel the 15,000 kilometers to Monte Verde and arrive by 12,500 BP they would have had to cover the entire distance in 2000 years. That's practically warp-speed considering they were on foot or hugging the coast in tiny boats and raising children along the way.

It is amply clear, however, that humans, wherever they went, exhibited a global genius of creative adaptability and exploitation of new ecosystems. Whether hunting seals from skin-covered boats or caribou on land, the tools, techniques and organization were

invented and put to use. Huge and peculiar animals the newcomers had never seen before had exclusive dominion over this vast American landscape, almost impossible to imagine in our world stuffed with humans. They came upon New World camels, lions called smilodons armed with canines almost eight inches long, a giant plated armadillo called a glyptodon, a beaver the size of a bear and teratorns, carnivorous birds bigger than condors. The slow-moving giant sloths with long claws at the ends of its shovel-like paws towered over the tallest man.

Today, humans infest the planet like a virus. Our numbers and pollutants are altering the very chemistry of the earth and changing the weather. Glaciers from Greenland to Antarctica are melting at an alarming rate and the earth's temperatures are creeping up. Islands in the Pacific are submerging under rising sea levels, forcing populations to move to higher ground. Governments are ironically squabbling over control of untapped oil fields revealed by the melting of the ice cap, the very substance that is largely causing the devastation of the planet. Drought, followed by fierce fires, destroys vast areas. Animal species go extinct every day as delicate wetlands are drained and ecosystems ploughed under for housing developments. Lumber companies and farmers are surgically removing the 'lungs of the world', the Amazon jungle. The accelerated decimation of the planet's wild places at our hands leads us to be too easily wowed and comforted by the vision of only a few hundred birds circling a wetland, the small remnants of flocks that once darkened the sky with their wings. The heavy hand of the industrial world has nature in a death grip, little realizing or caring how fragile our future is.

Modern urban dwellers are remote from the wild natural world and dependent on products that endanger its very survival. The extent of many people's involvement with the animal kingdom is limited to carefully sliced and cellophaned parts in a grocery store cooler, and their pets, which they dress in clothes and jewelry as if they were odd little children. As humans dominate the land, pressing further into the wilderness, inconvenient animals fall by the way. Brushes with the untamed animal kingdom are pesky and sometimes dangerous invasions of our sedate lives. The perpetrators must be brought under control; the alligator on the Florida golf course, bears rummaging in the garbage behind Sac's in Whistler, and the cougar that stalks the runner. Programs to reintroduce wolves, grizzly bears and lynx to their native habitat have been met with stubborn resistance by the people who inhabit the fringes of these lands. Bison that wander out of Yellowstone Park in search of forage are liable to be shot by ranchers. The Biblical injunction that man have dominion "over all the earth and over every creeping thing that creepeth upon the earth" has been taken to the bank. The message is clear; we are masters of the earth and we will subdue it at our will, even if it kills us.

We have drifted so far from the natural world that it is beyond our imagining to know how it feels to have to kill to eat every day; to make the necessary weaponry from rocks and sticks, to know your quarry so intimately, to know its habits, its quirks, its anatomy, its family, and perhaps to have watched it grow for a season or two until you know it personally. Then, after careful planning, you track it and feel the spear enter the flesh, watch its eyes see you, grow wild then slowly glaze with death, smell the creature's body and hear the sound it makes as you empty it of blood, and love it for feeding you. The intimacy shared with this animal is complete. You take its hide, its teeth, bone and sinew and fashion warm clothing for your child. The animal is not then just a part of your life. It is your life and the lives of your family, inseparable, as are all the other creatures you have slain and eaten and transformed into the necessities of survival. It is your kin. You share the same animating principle with these animals, a deep kinship of spirit. Killing an animal to maintain your life then becomes a ritual sacrifice. The animal dies so you may live.

The inhabitants of Ice Age Europe were still tens of thousands of years away from the idea of dominating animals. There was nothing tame in their world. The dog, probably the first domesticated animal, did not become so until about 10,000 BP, and like dogs everywhere, probably were drawn to the garbage. Everything that was, was organic. The Pleistocene, the geological era that ended about 12,000 BP with the last Ice Age, was home to a rich mixture of species with no parallel in our world today. We can barely begin to imagine the staggering numbers and variety of wild creatures our earliest ancestors in Europe lived among, fought with, and depended upon for existence. Nor how that sea of animal life they swam in colored their dreams, informed their songs and helped define them as human, different from but utterly dependent upon their relationship with the wild natural world.

It is into this remote world of early humans and shaggy beasts that we must go in search of the origins of the labyrinth, peeling

back the layers of time to reveal our common humanity, to touch these ancient minds. The artful, geometric structures we know as a labyrinthine form is a product of the Neolithic mind, one informed by the plotting of fields and structuring of houses and cities. We will pass beneath that to the wild, organic world of the Paleolithic and the bedrock concepts underlying these later structures. The journey will take us not only into the deep vaults of painted caves, but also down the neural avenues of brain structure. And, in the gray matter, we'll find that not much there, really, has changed; only the outward clothing of culture.

The Paleolithic ancestor of the Minotaur of Crete dances across the walls of deep caves, one of our most ancient and enduring archetypes. In Crete, an earthy bull-god who was once the powerful consort of the Great Goddess, was conquered by Zeus, the bull-sky god of the Greeks and banished to a labyrinthine prison. Yet today, the Minotaur endures in legend, literature and art. What is the nature of this creature that he has such a powerful hold on our imagination?

CHAPTER 3

LAIR OF THE MINOTAUR

"Navidson quickly does an about face and returns to the doorway. Only now he discovers that the penny he left behind, which should have been at least a hundred feet further, lies directly before him. Even stranger, the doorway is no longer the doorway, but the arch he had been looking for all along... He has no idea which way to go, and when a third growl ripples through that place... Navidson panics..."
House of Leaves, Mark Z. Danielewski

DANCE OF LIFE

At the heart of the legendary labyrinth dwells a beast, the Minotaur, a liminal creature caught between worlds in the process of transformation. He is always male, having the head of a bull and the muscular body of a man. In Greek myths he never runs loose in the upper air chasing nymphs nor slakes his thirst in a sun-dappled spring, droplets falling from his curly beard. He doesn't roam the gilded halls of palaces or quaff wine at a noisy banquet. He waits alone for his food or his murderer.

He is a creature of darkness, eternally imprisoned at the subterranean Center. Trapped by mythic device, forever awaiting his inevitable doom at the hands of the cocky hero. The Greek Minotaur is a cannibal, the child of unnatural passion, wild and ravenous. It is this surging bestiality, teetering on the thin divide separating the lusty creation of life and the insatiable hunger to destroy it, that makes him a fascinating danger to our orderly lives. The Minotaur is caught, belonging nowhere but here at the interface between life and death, a tragic monster plagued with unnatural hungers, a mythological metaphor of the raging animal urges of killing and consuming that we humans strive to contain. Unwelcome by human society, he cannot endure the light of day. Yet even trapped in his prison he is a worthy opponent for he knows every twist and turn of

his dungeon. Hunted down by a hubris-struck hero, his inevitable slaughter is a testament to heroic self-important valor and our own reflected glory. The Minotaur at the center of the labyrinth is both what is sought and what is feared; the ultimate challenge to Greek glory and soul survival of the hero-king.

From a different perspective, Picasso first created his minotaurs as frolicking drinking buddies of Zeus. They are portrayed too as lovers of elegant women who admire them while they sleep peacefully on the ladies' rumpled, flower-curtained beds. The obvious virility in a massively muscled animal and Picasso's lusty taste for bullfighting and women must have inspired the frank sexual imagery, for there is nothing in the Greek myth to suggest the Minotaur was anything but a sterile cross-breed. Picasso makes him a potent sexual predator, carrying a bare-breasted swooning woman off to her violent (yet desired) fate. Eventually, the darker profundities of the myth emerge in his art. As an image of war-warped humanity during the devastation of WWII, the Minotaur appears as an indomitable juggernaut, a destructive force of relentless human nature before which the innocent can only hope for peace and surrender. Yet in Guernica the Minotaur has evolved again; he is removed from the chaos of humans, hovering above the fray of humanity. A natural force of creativity and regeneration, he implicates necessary destruction, but is not its agent. This is much closer to the ancient truth. Picasso has tracked the Minotaur back to his origins.

This morphing of the personality of the Minotaur is the nature of mythic consciousness; those reverberant nodes around which are spun legends, giving them form. Moving backward in time from Picasso's multi-faceted creature, through the supernatural Gothic devils of the Middle Ages to Crete, we encounter a multiplicity of renderings. Another step back into remote time, and we find yet another incarnation; the Minotaurs of the Paleolithic are dancing, foot upraised, arms held out, amidst a vibrant swarm of animals. This man/bull knows the secret of slipping from one world to another, from the world of waking life above to the mysterious world of spirit below. Transforming from man to spirit animal and back again, an incarnation of potency, he is a conduit of spirit information. He is a shaman who has mastered the art of metamorphosis in the deep mysteries of the labyrinthine cave. This Minotaur is no aberrant perversion of nature, no fearsome cannibal. Exactly the opposite. He has merged with the animating forces of his world, the animal gods, the fount of life and power, and become a healer.

MINOAN STORIES

But something happened along the way after the Paleolithic and before the Chartres labyrinth stood proxy for the spiritual journey to Jerusalem, putting a stop to this easy metamorphosis; the Greeks. Crete 4000 years ago was a rich, graceful island of elegant painted palaces with great fleets of fast ships, no defending walls, golden diadems and goddesses with poppy crowns. Their palaces were crowned with great stylized horns, in Egypt the hieroglyphic symbol for 'horizon', and so, gateway to the sacred sky. Early Cretan myths tell of Io and Europa, women-who-were-cows, carried off by the sky/bull god, Zeus. Europa was taken on his powerful bull's back through the ocean waves to Crete where she bore his sons, among them King Minos. The women's names signify they are moon goddesses and natural consorts to the sun god. Ariadne was no love-struck girl, but Crete's great goddess, 'bright shining one'. A tablet from the palace of Knossos declares her sanctity. Where all the gods are given offerings of honey, the 'mistress of the labyrinth' is a given greater portion. She wore the horns of the moon and, as Mistress of Animals, answered the peoples' honeyed prayers for fecundity. Ceremonies celebrating fertility were observed out in the open under the oak trees of Gortys, with the sacred coupling of the moon/cow priestess and the sun/bull god, Asterius.

Minos, the 'moon's creature', was not one king but many kings, whose name was a title and who bore responsibility as priest/consort. Very few names of Cretan kings besides Minos have come down to us. They left us no monuments of crowned and bearded men on thrones, no paintings of military triumphs with enchained slaves. Instead their palace walls were decorated with murals of graceful youths, swallows, dolphins, goddesses and worshippers. It would appear they were not interested in being personally remembered. The imagery and echoes of distant myths are rife with maidens and bulls, their transformation from gods to humans and animals and back again as fluid as the leaps of bare-breasted women who vaulted over charging bulls in the sunny arena of Knossos.

Echoing stories of the distant past in ancient Crete, Ariadne was a princess in Homer's *Iliad*, and he wrote about her labyrinth. It was a patterned dancing floor out in the open air where dark-eyed young

men and maids grasped a rope and danced, the better to follow the intricate pattern. At the Center, the focal point of this ritual dance was a fecund blessing of procreative power. This image, a promise of life's fruitfulness, was worthy of being hammered by the god Hephaestos into the glorious shield Achilles carried into bloody Troy. How did it all become so dark, forced out of the life-giving sun and into the grim depths of a maze-prison?

As Mycenaean Greeks supplanted Cretan culture, the legend and its players took on new incarnations. King Minos chose to secure his power by demonstrating his affinity with the god Poseidon, in itself a vainglorious display. Minos would offer back to Poseidon the god's own bull, a magnificent animal, if he would make it manifest. In response, a perfect white bull emerged from the waves, striding in through the spindrift. Poseidon offered it up so generously to Minos, a great gift given with the easy confidence of a sacred pact. Yet the earthly king failed to uphold his part of the bargain. He kept the excellent bull among his herds and substituted a lesser animal. The sacrifice, the vital link between man and god, was broken. From this betrayal spins a skein of mythic treachery down the ages. The great goddess reappears in later tales, incarnated yet diminished in the guise of wronged and deserted princesses who die by their own hand, hung, self-sacrificed to pay the debt to the betrayed god; Pasiphaë, Ariadne and Phaedra, whose names all speak of luminosity.

The Great Goddess, originally a Cretan incarnation of Pasiphaë, a moon goddess, is diminished, becoming Minos's queen. She is made to pay for his greed. Fixed by the god's curse, she lusts, not for the god as in more ancient days, but for his perfect bull. Poseidon, originally a god of Crete, but becoming more Greek by the minute, chooses her, a blameless incarnation of the great goddess, to suffer for the crime. No longer powerful and free to couple in the sunlight with the bull/god, her desire to blend with the god is made depraved by a curse; she must hide in a contraption built by Daedalus to conceive, instructed by the clever smith how to open the trap door and slide her long legs into the wooden hollows of a fabricated cow to slake her desperate thirst. To her eternal shame, she gives birth to the Minotaur, a perversion of both god and man.

Monsters are omens. Life is out of balance and the insolent hero, Theseus, strides on to the stage. In other myths he captures bulls, kills bulls, and throws them as high as a temple roof. He doesn't

belong in this myth. Or, rather, the myths of Crete have been reformed to accommodate his conquest of their goddess. He is an interloper, neither god nor bull. He is a Greek imperialist who has come to conquer Crete and steal her stories. The sun/bull god is driven underground, to become a vile creature. Ariadne is reduced in the Greek telling from great goddess to love-besotted, treacherous girl who helps slaughter her half-brother and betray her father. She is abandoned by the self-obsessed hero for whom she has given up everything. Her open-air communal dance floor where young people courted in a complicated erotic dance of life is closed in, transformed into a place where the fruit of the queen's shameful behavior is hidden. The rope, which used to lead springtime youths in a dance of love, has become a magical thread unwinding in the darkness, from the portal to the black center and back. Where life used to beat at the heart of the labyrinth it has become a fearsome place of death. Poseidon has claimed his sacrifice.

The Minotaur, banished to a living death and a diet of virgins, had a name. His name and true identity have been lost through the ages. He is remembered only as a monstrosity. He is Asterius, of the sun or of the starry sky, the astral/sun/bull, not at all the proper name for a creature confined in a dank prison. In a previous mythic generation he was King Minos' adoptive father, marrying Europa after Zeus abandoned her on Crete. But no one remembers that any more. It is an echo of a vanished life, the Cretan truth stamped out by the Greek; the rightful kings reduced in the stories to monsters worthy only of slaughter. He has fallen from his starry sky and has no light left. He languishes in his dark labyrinthine prison, picking the bones of youths, awaiting the death from which he will not return. The gods and kings of Crete are defeated, crushed under the heel of the victor.

Yet before the Chartres labyrinth, before horns and cloven hooves were synonyms for evil, before Theseus swept Ariadne off her feet only to abandon her, before Pasiphaë was cursed to love the god's white bull, and long before the sun priest and moon priestess of Crete ritually coupled on the plain of Gortyn, the Paleolithic minotaur was dancing on the walls of caves. We will be peeling back the layers of culture and myth to expose the bedrock of this archetype. For this we must make a journey back to the beginning of modern humans in Europe.

Placed in context in the primeval world of the Stone Age, our fearsome vision of this monster reveals a complex nature we no

longer remember, but we have whiffs of bestial behavior and it excites our fear. It's far too easy to condemn him to a sulfurous existence. When seen through the filter of the Paleolithic he becomes an epiphanic channel. He is still a fearsome beast, but the potency of this ancient minotaur is not savagery. Rather, he is an agent, similar to Picasso's ultimate depiction of him, nourishing the fertile, opening the arterial route to the heart of life. This life affirmation assumes an intimate knowledge of death, the ultimate transformation. Unlike his modern trapped descendant, the ancient minotaur has dedicated his life to being in this place of transformative power, passing wilfully from life to death and back again, and from animal to human and back. He is fluid, slipping between the worlds, in a state of controlled ecstasy.

The Paleolithic minotaur is an aspect of humanity set only slightly apart from the spirit-animal life among which he moves as liaison. Like shamans in hunter-gatherer tribes the world over, he seeks out his spirit helpers to learn the ways of healing. Deep in the chambers of caves, he emerges through the epiphanic veil, appearing on the stone walls, trance-dancing at the heart of the labyrinth, facing down death and focusing his shamanic powers of life through the spiritual lens of the firelit labyrinthine underworld, far below the frigid snows of the Ice Age. Imagine a very different world, where survival relied on weaponry fashioned from the stones and bones of nature, the strategy of the hunt, the artistry of protean adaptation, enfolded in an intimate community of people telling and retelling the mythic tales. And the wellbeing of your people was in the hands of the shamanic minotaur.

DEEP COLD

Unlike the sunny, poppy-strewn fields of Crete, the Paleolithic world might well have been another planet; a frigid world roaming with gigantic beasts, where human survival required a completely different set of cultural tools, some discovered for the first time. Here is the birthplace of the labyrinth in human consciousness, the sacred enclosure of the shaman/minotaur; the winding depths of almost 300 caves where artists labored to commune with spirits.

Global cooling had, for about two million years, caused the periodic expansion of the polar ice caps. Accompanying shifts in temperature swung the weather pendulum from temperate to frozen and back again over the millennia. 25,000 to 18,000 years ago, the last and most ferocious glacial period, the Last Glacial Maximum,

54

was at its peak, burying continents in ice across the northern top of the globe from Seattle to southern Britain to Mongolia. Dry, treeless, frozen steppe land reached across the Bering Strait to the glaciers that covered North America and Greenland. The weather in the planet's north was savage, making human habitation there impossible.

So much water was frozen into ice that thousands of miles of coastline were exposed that are today drowned by the sea. The oceans were at times 350 feet lower than they are today. Beringia, as wide as India, stretched between Alaska and Siberia. It was possible to walk from France to England and on to Ireland. The Adriatic Sea was a dry valley. Colossal glaciers scoured out canyons, shoving monstrous polished boulders down the mountainsides then retreated, marooning these 'erratics', these lost megaliths, in placid valleys.

Where the ice ended and the tundra and steppe began, well-watered grasslands stretched for thousands of miles. Even further from the ice, dark swathes of coniferous forests covered the land. In drier areas deciduous cold-temperate trees dotted the grassy landscape. Over the millennia, as the ice sheets contracted and expanded with the changing climate, forests shrank, became woodland or tundra and rivers shifted in their beds, carving canyons through the mountains. The lowlands were cold, dry steppe lands or alpine meadows with patches of woodlands.

Dates vary, but this era, known as the Last Glacial Maximum or LGM, lasted from around 21000 BP to 17,000 and was the coldest period of the Paleolithic. In southern Europe temperatures were significantly colder than today, estimated to be about 40 degrees Fahrenheit lower than modern temperatures. Freezing winters lasted up to nine long months and bitterly cold winds relentlessly swept the mountains. Blizzards of dust howled across the dry, cold land, depositing soil that would one day enrich the lands and pockets of French winemakers. Glaciers crept close to the frozen valley floor of the Pyrenees, home to some Paleolithic cave artists. A little farther north, the deep winters would keep small family groups close to home-fires made in the rock shelters of steep limestone cliffs. These homes, generally selected for the south, and west-facing facades, the better to absorb and hold the warmth of the sun, were shielded from the chilling winds by hide-covered scaffolding. They overlooked rivers draining what would become the Dordogne area of southern France. Living off stored food and what meat they could hunt nearby, they waited out the vicious cold. Creatures

undeterred by the frigid conditions roamed the deep snows; small, sturdy horses in heavy winter coats, wooly mammoths digging for grass with their curved ivory tusks as long as seven feet, and black bison mantled with snow, their breath steaming in the frostbitten air.

In spring, as the icy grip of winter loosened, grasses sprouted and passages opened through the narrow valleys, streaming with glacial melt water. Small groups of families gathered from their winter retreats into large outdoor encampments to share stories, arrange marriages, introduce new children and trade goods, and to participate in the seasonal miracle. In stark contrast to the deprivations of winter, what must have been a blessed orgy of abundance flooded into their lives, a gift of the gods. Huge herds of reindeer appeared from the more temperate southern plains and plunged through the river fords, migrating to the endless open summer grasslands of northern Europe. Behind them followed the predators; the lions, the hyenas and wolves. Salmon crowded up the ice-free rivers and creeks and slack, hungry bears, emerging from winter hibernation, waded in to feed. The human predators took their place alongside the other hunters, dining on this seasonal feast. Later, in the fall, the herds would return, sleek and fat from their summer feast of lush northern grass, en route to the warmer south. Many would fall to the razor-sharp stone weapons of the gathered tribes. The bones piled up. They killed and butchered as fast as possible, drying rack upon rack of flesh to store for the difficult winter they knew would come.

THE ANIMALS

This was a world of primal behemoths, grazing and hunting in the chilly shadow of the glaciers, whose slow-moving blue walls could stretch up to two miles high. Gigantic animals, unbelievable in our time of civilized diminution, vastly outnumbered the humans; the mammoths were 13 feet high at the shoulder with long, curving tusks and would easily fill a modern living room. Primeval oxen, called aurochs, were the size of SUVs, the powerful bulls standing over six feet high, 11 feet in length, and loaded with attitude. The Megaceros, a type of elk, sported a barbed 12-foot span of antlers that they sprouted anew every season, growing like small trees from their heads and supported by massive necks and shoulders. Cave bears weighed half a ton and could stand almost 12 feet high, 14 when they stretched their arms up, as they did to slash at the cave walls. Shaggy bison, wooly rhinoceros, horses and huge herds of

reindeer roamed this wild world. Predators such as leopards, hyenas, wolves and slinking prides of cave lions, bound by the bloody imperatives of survival, prowled the edges of the herds to bring down the old, infirm and easy targets.

Rediscovering through science what hunter-gatherers have always known, animal behaviorists have revealed the societies of modern wild animals to be intricately complicated. The hierarchy of the wolf pack, the maternal focus of the elephant family, the elk's battle for mates, and the stallion's passionate defense of his herd, give us a glimpse of the larger 'cultures' of animals among which our ancestors lived. The small society of humankind, so vastly outnumbered by these teeming tribes of creatures, had to be scrupulously observant, resourceful and determined to survive.

The animals were their mobile one-stop-shopping center for food, materials and clothing. The people intimately knew the herds on which they depended; their behavior, their territory, their migratory patterns, and the other predators that also fed at this moving trough, all vital information for a successful hunt. The herds were a fountain of life, and yet the threat of death was ever-present.

METAPHOR AND SPIRIT

The relationship these first people had with the animal world was a symbiotic blending of their identities as fellow creatures. This alliance extended beyond the mere feeding and clothing of the body to the integrity of the spirit, a seamless integration of survival in the physical world with the nourishment of their spiritual landscape. All hunter-gatherer peoples have a cherished relationship with animals they hunt, and with the animals that hunt them as well. The practicalities and dangers of providing life-sustaining food and materials during the Paleolithic would have been intricately interwoven with a world of metaphor that was consistent and universally sacred. However, what we term 'metaphor' was to hunter-gatherers literal; a multidimensional integration of complex relationships. This assumed that the animating, life-giving principle was the same for humans and nature. There was no distinction made between them. By shifting this focus away from humans as separate from the rest of nature, almost impossible today, we can begin to approach how ancient people perceived their universe. Their nature-centered relational web of spirit illuminated questions of right living, contacts with the spiritual realm, the origins of things and people, and the meaning of their deaths. Their worldview was

categorized into what was an intricate encyclopedia of knowledge and belief, a cultural map. As we will see, at its center is a route through the labyrinth, where the dancing shamanic minotaur presided.

Although it can be precarious to extrapolate too freely backward from modern hunter-gatherer societies to the people of the Paleolithic, the similarities of lifestyle, supported by myth and archaeology, can help us appreciate and interpret a way of thinking very different from our own. Consider one abbreviated example that demonstrates the complex level of integration of metaphor with the natural/spiritual world. In his study of the world view of the Oglala Sioux, Joseph Epes Brown gives us a glimpse into this beautiful interweaving of ideas, spinning off from the central idea of wind.

Wind is especially powerful and mysterious because it is invisible and can only be detected by its effects. The cocoon is considered to be a mysterious bundle from which the Whirlwind emanates, and so the moth and the butterfly, which emerge from cocoons and whose fluttering wings create wind, are part of the complex. The Whirlwind power enwrapped in a cocoon was important for warriors to tap so they could also become invisible, powerful as the wind and as difficult to hit as a butterfly. Photographs of Plains Indian warriors from the 1800s show cocoons dangling from their war bonnets. Just as the Whirlwind spins and twists and kicks up dust, the excellent warrior engulfs his enemy with confusion.

The bison is part of this wind and power complex because the Oglala say the cow blows a red film over her calf just after its birth to protect it, as the cocoon protects the moth until it matures. The bull bison is observed to scoop dirt carefully with his hoof and direct it purposefully into the breeze as a prayer to the Whirlwind.

The spider provides another direction of logic as its newly hatched children spin webs that are caught in the wind to carry them away. The spider's web has an aspect of invisibility and invincibility; bullets or arrows cannot destroy it, as they pass right through without harm. Spiders too build webs on the ground by anchoring four points, one for each of the cardinal directions, or quarters of the universe, that define sacred space in the Sioux tradition. Finally, the bull elk is a member of the Whirlwind complex for his mysterious ability to attract mates by whistling, and so controlling the power of the wind and transforming it into the song of life-generating fertility.

The overarching concept is wakan, or sacredness. The Four

Winds and four cardinal directions are likewise associated with specific colors, animals and birds as follows (although there are variations among different tribal groups);

West	North	East	South
Fall	Winter	Spring	Summer
Black	Red	Yellow	White
Blacktail Deer	Buffalo	Whitetail Deer	Elk
Swallow	Magpie	Crow	Meadowlark

Each of these sets represents a paradigm of symbolic language so that mention of any one member of a set refers to all other members of the same set and infers relationship with the other three sets. A song that includes the color yellow and a crow, by this logic is also a song about the east and spring. A shaman who sings of a swallow, a buffalo, the color yellow and an elk has symbolically invoked aspects of the four directions and so, each of the four quarters of the universe combined in some way. The division of the universe into static quadrants, often represented by a cross pattern, gains the movement of life from birth to old age and from season to season when the static cross becomes the symbol of the swastika. The bend at the end of each arm implies a segment of a circle and the movement inherent in the four arms both causes and is caused by wind, the breath of life.

The Four Winds of the sacred cardinal directions are four beings, four brothers in Sioux myth, united into one being, an immaterial god whose substance is never visible and cannot be comprehended by man. This is Wakan-Tanka, the "Great Spirit", the animating principle of the universe. Prayer and song, channels through which human spirit reaches the divine, are products of wind, of breath, and breath is life. This elegant logic that weaves together ideas of protection, invulnerability and invisibility with creatures, to us, as diverse as butterflies and bison, into a magnificent web of divinity is the poetry of a hunter-gatherer lifestyle. There is no reason to believe that the Paleolithic hunters were any less poetic at ordering their universe.

The animals that the Paleolithic people chose to paint on the walls of their caves were selected for very specific reasons, reflecting the metaphors they embodied and the artist's relationship to them. The Whirlwind complex presents us with a hunter-gatherer logic that makes ethnographic analogy a useful tool to shed light on these paintings. By comparing the Oglala nature-centric cosmovision with evidence from the Paleolithic, we can begin to

appreciate both from a new perspective. Overlaying these yet again with the sacred space of a cathedral and the centuries melt away to reveal an essential humanity touching spirit. The labyrinth in the center of Chartres, for the awe and mystery it induces, may as well be in the deep, painted chamber of an ancient cave.

Understanding just the bones of the Whirlwind Complex, let alone fleshing out the subtleties, also suggests an appreciation of the difficulty of interpretation as we grapple with stretching our domesticated minds to see the world through Ice Age eyes. The metaphoric possibilities we can bring to an imagined interpretation are endless. Animals can be dangerous and unpredictable, swift, wise and foolish, humorous and crafty. They can be vicious or timorous, resourceful and belligerent, escape into impossibly tight spaces or soar to the sun. There are isolates that meet others of their kind only to mate, or herd animals raising their young among an extended family. There are stealthy predators or scavengers that pick the bones of another's kill. They live in water, dwell in holes in the ground or roam the icy plains oblivious to the numbing cold. They build webs, nests, lay eggs or birth their young directly on to the windswept plain. Ultimately, we will never know the Paleolithics' even most obvious conceptual categories of the animals they painted, let alone the subtleties implied above by the Oglala Whirlwind complex. But ethnographic information gleaned from living hunter-gatherer societies casts a light backward over the darkened millennia, revealing shadows and highlights of the mysterious Paleolithic.

CHTHONIAN CATHEDRALS

The painted limestone caverns created in Ice Age Europe are often referred to as "cathedrals", an apt analogy. It conjures up a sacred space wreathed in incense and candlelight, where music praising God soars on uplifted hearts to the vaulted ceilings and echoes from stone walls, where images of saints radiate blessings on to the congregation from their respective niches, and the glory of the spirit is channeled in the multicolored beams of lights from roseate windows. It is an involved chamber of holiness designed to open a conduit between the human and the divine. At the center of many great cathedrals of Europe lie labyrinths, stone inlaid paths worn by centuries of pilgrims. Many parallels can be drawn between the painted caves and cathedrals, and although the awe-inspiring personal experience of the divine is unchanged, the Paleolithic path

is decidedly different. They were discovering and giving form to the earliest metaphoric journeys to the Center.

Put yourself there, on the lip of a sacred cave when humankind was new to the world. Imagine a stone mouth and the mist that unfurls and evaporates in the warm sunshine. Imagine walking into the yawning darkness with your guttering pine torch, entering the original, physical labyrinth of human experience. The birdcalls, the humming of insects, the sounds of life in the upper air fade as you enter. The daylight that reaches into the opening is quickly swallowed up.

The temperature is chilly but constant and it is utterly still, a marked change from the buffeting winds outside. In the diminishing light the signs that others have been here before are evident. The long-cold ashes of a small fire against one wall are there not from having cooked a meal, but rather from making charcoal for the artist's palette. The dark interior is not a place for family gatherings. They did not live in the caves, but did sometimes shelter in the daylit entrances. Here is a dangerous, sacred enclosure that winds into the very womb of the dark earth. The painted head of an ibex looms in the uncertain light from the suggestive folds of stalagmites, the stony drips reinterpreted as trailing fur. A pattern of red dots lines a section of ceiling. Up ahead, a rhino marks the entrance to a side chamber. Turning a corner, the floor drops downward and the passageway narrows. In places it's necessary to squeeze through holes in the rock that a cat might find challenging. Breathing slowly to keep your body from swelling with panic, you push through. The floor is damp clay, slippery, and smells of clean earth.

You emerge into a vast, enchanted space, a world utterly different from the upper air. The torchlight barely touches the distance. Whiskered with crystals, the walls glitter and sparkle in the flickering light. This fairy landscape is solid, as a steadying hand on the wall proves, and yet it wavers, melts and leaps back as the torch approaches. The ceiling is dry, yet drips and runs like wax. Giant pillars of stone loom out of the darkness and stalagmites bristle up from the ground, casting shadows that grow and shrink with the wavering light. Wings of sparkling stone lift and stretch as if a creature is materializing out of the rock, its calcite body gathering stony feathers to its breast. Shadows leap and shift. Beyond the reach of the firelight, the darkness is a presence unto itself, a shadow being intruded upon in its lair and held at bay for a time by

the glimmering light.

This is a living world molded from stone and water, one working eternally against the other to create slow, constant change. There is dynamic power charging quietly beneath the stones. The paradoxical enchantment of a world both solid and fluid conspires to turn thoughts from their normal pathways of terra firma to wander in a terra incognita of possibilities. It is impossible to stay in here for long and not feel yourself moving among spirits.

Cave bears have slept here for centuries. The huge footprints are everywhere. The walls are polished where they rubbed their heavy bodies, following their scent to find their way in the dark. Higher than a man can reach, the walls are slashed where they have stood on their hind legs to stretch and claw as if reaching for something within the rock. In the dry places untouched by the flow of winter water they have dug wallows in the floor to sleep off the cold season in utter darkness and give birth to their young. Some too long in tooth to face another spring have died. Their bones litter the floor, scattered by wolves. Some of the teeth have been removed by a previous human visitor to be made into a necklace, but two have been carefully tucked into natural holes in the rock, like boney seeds, set to regenerate a new bear. There are few paintings here, as if this room, so dominated with the spirits of bears, has left no space for any other animal. Only at the far end of the chamber does a spotted panther painted in red share a wall with a bear. Beneath the panther, a bear's muddy paw print reaches toward the cat's belly.

A path appears at the far side and you make your way around a shifting rock pile that, in some distant era let go from the ceiling. Climbing up a jagged path, the torchlight touches folds of pink stone that hang like loose flesh from the ceiling. Here and there on the pendant stalactites are images of aurochs, rhinos, horses and mammoths drawn with a finger through the soft white clay. Farther along, a smooth rock face looms out of the darkness and is covered in round spots of red paint. Someone with a small hand, a woman perhaps, or a young person, dipped a palm into a palette of paint then pressed it purposefully against the wall over and over again. The faint traces of fingers, red with paint, reveal the position of the hand as the artist created a pointillist bison from palm prints.

At the end of a corridor of fluted limestone splashing water tumbles down the wall. Ahead, a fantastic grotto materializes out of the darkness. A cleft in the flesh of the wall is draped with glittering folds in tones of dark reds and browns. It is a vulva of stone tucked

here into this secret place of the earth. Water from deep inside slides down the folds and pools in a calcite basin. Sentries of short white stalagmites stand like a cluster of unlit ceremonial candles at its rim. Ibex are engraved on the lip of the niche facing in, and, around the rim on the flank of the stone, is a panel of horses and aurochs floating towards the grotto in their otherworldly way to drink deeply of the waters of the earth. Nearby, nested into the flesh-like folds, a lioness sits showing her teeth in a warning snarl, while a male stalks her, awaiting an invitation to mate. Someone, possibly in blessing or recognition, has dipped a finger into the blood-red mud of the cleft and drawn streaks on the throat of the male.

There are more pictures now, deeper down the tunnels that open into dream chambers. The ancient artists who journeyed into this cave used engravings and red paint in the front rooms of the cave. But here, in what appears to be a transitional space, the art is primarily engraved, there is little in the way of color and paint. Beyond, in the deepest reaches, the paintings are almost exclusively black. Centuries of raindrops have percolated through miles of limestone and arrived at this place, running along an edge of stone and clinging to the ceiling long enough to leave behind tiny encrustations of crystal. The droplets' patient ministry of magic, each leaving a deposit of chemicals, has allowed stone blades to grow very slowly from the ceiling.

One hangs like a signboard at the entrance to the deepest gallery. Below it, the ground has fallen away as a subterranean cavity collapsed into a void. But while the floor was still in place, an ancient hand traced an owl here with a finger, the buildup of material still fresh on the edge of the lines, as if you could turn and find the artist wiping his hands. The owl is a rare subject in cave art and this one especially so. For although the face of this night creature is clearly watching you enter, his body is turned backwards, as only an owl can do. Below his pointed beak, the feathers of his back fold together, composed and still. He is poised at the entry to the deeper caverns. Like the Roman Janus figure found at doorways or the turn of the new year who has two faces looking in opposite directions, this observant and paradoxical owl looks both forward and backward, both into and out of the labyrinthine darkness. Posted here at the entrance to the deep secrets of the cavern, he is both guide and guard, a nocturnal creature of flight set in stone and gazing back towards the light.

Beyond, a large block of stone has fallen from the ceiling. It is the

only one of its size in the room and its unusual squared facets make it appear alien to the rest of the melted architecture. A fire may have been lit upon it once long ago. A scattering of cold charcoal lies here, beneath an intact bear's skull. In ancient times, a hand carefully placed it upon the stone; not in the center, but on the edge so that its canines curve over the rock and the hollow eye sockets observe the room. There is a purposeful mystery here.

A branching narrow tunnel meanders deeper into the earth. Along the way, herds of gigantic primeval deer, horses and bison prance upon the walls. Here are black-banded rhinos and finger drawings of vulvas. The tunnel narrows and the floor drops down, terraced by water formations, before opening out into one final, enormous room. The labyrinthine corridors have led you to the deepest chamber in the cave, the farthest from the light of the sun and the busy energies of life it feeds. Here, there is an unlit world building its dark secrets infinitesimally drop by drop over untold millennia. Here there is magic and sacred power in the womb of the earth. Here is the center of the labyrinth. And here, as the legends tell us, is the lair of the Minotaur.

THE MINOTAUR

In the deepest room of the cavern of Chauvet is a place named the End Chamber. The walls teem with animals. One grouping of attentive lions faces another pair across an expanse of wall scored by bear claws. Unlike the other couple encountered earlier in the passionate throes of the mating dance, these two lions are affectionate, the female rubbing against her mate. A lone chubby rhinoceros in the center seems to be their prey. One of the lions is decorated with a semi-circle of 10 red dots on its flank daubed on by a finger.

The panel of prowling lions is followed by a herd of rhinoceros. One is drawn with its horn and back line repeated over and over so it has a quivering vibrancy of animation, or may suggest a herd lined up, one behind another, along an imagined landscape. Bison and mammoths making their way across the folds of the rock are pursued by another pride of lions that seems to issue from a hole in the wall. They stretch their faces forward as if to smell the animals they hunt.

On the other side of the recess a bison emanates, just the line of his back and foreleg flowing from inside a cavity like a wisp of smoke, but his muzzle accumulates form and appears detailed, face-

on and three-dimensional on the corner surface of the chamber wall. The body, represented by only a couple of lines, is implied, behind the full face and inside the cavity. His hoof rests on the nose of another lion. Above, a rhino is drawn in black. Its horn is red and its muzzle appears to spout blood, one of the few red things among all the black animals in this room. The rhino turns his bloody face into the recess, the hole from which the animals appear to stream, almost all facing one way; towards the upper air.

The recess in the wall deepens and narrows at its center to a dark hole. There are a few other vagrant animals further along, lions tucked into a stalagmite, a horse framed in a shadowed panel of stone, a bison and the suggestion of a rhino. Yet the artists realized the focus of this flood of animals as issuing from this womb of stone, spilling forth life forms. Just opposite this well of life a pendant rock hangs from the ceiling, its muscular limestone bulk tapering to a point. Were it flesh, it could lift up and enter this womb in the wall.

And here, on the tip of this phallic stone, a reverse lingam, is a Minotaur. We see him from behind. His shaggy bison head is carefully drawn, the horns curving up and forward, the animal eye wide and expressive and looking back over his shoulder at whomever has entered his sanctum sanctorum. His shoulder/hump is strong and hunched, described by a single line beginning at the neck, inscribing the shoulder and continuing down the stone to become a vague human hand resting on his human left leg. The knee is bent slightly up and there is a sense of forward movement. The suggestion of a second leg that bears his weight completes the figure. There are no feet or hooves. There is intense power in the upper body, poised but pressing forward, shoulders twisted to the right, weight on the right foot, ready to lunge.

Directly in front of the Minotaur on the pendant stone, nestled at his chest level, is a large pubic triangle, the pubis deeply engraved to reveal the underlying white stone against the black charcoal that forms it. The female right leg is bent, her knee almost touching his, and the shading gives her thigh and calf depth and contour. Lines forming the buttocks were obliterated to permit the superimposition of the Minotaur, an artistic creative act of elemental potency. With brilliant insight the artist has melded the two figures into one by inferring that the one single line forming the Minotaur's bent left leg facing the vulva is also the outward-facing vulva's left leg bending inward. With a simple stroke, a potent union has taken place linking them eternally as parts of one another. This portrayal is an evocation of spirits, an essence of sacred procreative power. The sexual tension between the forward-pressing Minotaur and the vulva is undeniable. Its positioning on the prominent pendant stone opposite the womb flowing with animal life is primal and eloquent. Profound secrets of the power and source of life were called into being in the deepest chamber of this labyrinthine cavern. Here is the primal mythic ancestry of the ritual coupling between the Cretan Moon Goddess and the Sky Bull on the plains of Gortyn.

Elsewhere in the cavern, pubic triangles occupy significant locations, facing each other across galleries, at the entrances of side passages and directly above openings into deeper chambers. Their positioning is not at all by chance, but rather declares their commanding importance at strategic locations of transition, their implication of sexual fertility undeniable. Certainly this one, conjoined with the bison-man on this tip of stone, is emblematic.

The Minotaur has, through the ages of man, been a catalyst inspiring awe and revulsion, yet is always fascinating. Whether cannibalistic creature requiring a 'civilizing' execution, a sexual predator, a being of bestial power and potency, or an ancient shaman trance-dancing in the labyrinthine vortex, we cannot look away. The combined elements of a bull's head and a man's body are evocative of the raw strength of both creatures bound together into one vibrant being. The recognition of his dominion over the center of the labyrinth and its secrets began with the earliest humans and continues to this day. There is no essential difference between this primal image created by a Paleolithic artist 32,000 years ago and minotaurs drawn by Picasso, only layers of interpretation; humans touching spirit. The well of myth so resonant in our lives today originates in the deep springs of these black, dripping caverns.

This creature, half man and half animal, is by no means the only one of his kind in Paleolithic art. There is another minotaur, or 'sorcerer', as others have named him. This bison/man is seen dancing across the wall of the sanctuary in the cave of Les Trois Fréres. His left leg is lifted, while the right is firmly planted and his long bull's tail swings around his ankles. His arms end in hooves. He holds them out in front of himself, the left higher than the right. Another creature in Trois Fréres is even more famous and a composite of human and animal parts. His body is human as are his hands and feet, and he too appears to be dancing. His body in profile, he's leaning forward, left foot lifted just a bit to move him

forward in a prancing crouch, hands held out limp, as if in the process of transforming into paws. A luxuriant tail hangs down behind. Elegant antlers adorn a head seen face-on, decidedly not human, with the piercing round eyes of an owl. He has been called the 'Horned God' and 'the sorcerer of Trois Fréres'.

There are more examples of minotaurs throughout the catalogue of Paleolithic art and all appear to be dancing. Where does this image come from, this mythic mixture of potent beast and dancing man? Why does he re-emerge 300 centuries later in the black heart of the Cretan labyrinth, with the odor of bestial lust clinging to him? He is both man and god, a liminal being emerging through the veil of epiphany between our world and the next. He is the shaman who embodies the mercurial ability to move between realities in a mythic landscape, at once the bearer and focus of legend, the channel of healing and procreative power who dances at the center of creation with his goddess/consort while all around, in the winding subterranean tunnels, a flood of spirit life is released to the upper air.

CHAPTER 4

ARTISTIC INSPIRATION

"To man as a hunter, the divine became transparent
Above all in the animals."
Ivar Paulson

"We are faced with a harmonized collectivity of consciousnesses
equivalent to a sort of super-consciousness. The idea is that of the
earth not only becoming covered by myriads of grains of thought,
but becoming enclosed in a single thinking envelope ... and
reinforcing one another in the act of a single unanimous reflection."
Pierre Teilhard de Chardin

PIECING TOGETHER

To better understand what transpired in the labyrinthine caverns of the earth, we need to first have a sense of the lives early humans lived in the upper air, for each informs the other, each reveals different facets of what was becoming the rough jewel of human consciousness. It was the sparking of that prismatic intelligence that first shed light on the labyrinth.

The compelling path of the labyrinth can lead us to the center of ourselves, not only as individuals on a particular life journey, but also to our spiritual center as a species. To discover its power source we must explore the elements that make us humans; our evolutionary biology that made us distinct from other creatures and our cultural dynamism, which together brought about a convergence of evolution and spiritual desire. Given biological imperatives for survival, how did we fashion cultural forms to both address those biological imperatives and also to accommodate and revere the labyrinth? This, and the next few chapters, will probe the development of art, speech and brain functioning, the gifts that allow us to perceive the labyrinth and to give it expression.

It is simplistic to assume that all Paleolithic cave art is religiously

significant, arising solely from a shamanic impulse. The vast stretch of time and distance across prehistoric Europe, the unique geological character of each cave and the cultures that made use of them, the social and climatic variations over millennia, all exert varying pressures and conditions by which the creation of representational imagery was affected. Some are simplistic line drawings dashed off in the daylight openings of living sites, while others were planned in great detail, involved many people and were executed carefully over longer periods of time. Still others were produced in very remote pockets, large enough for only a single person and may have only been seen by a small handful of people until modern discovery. Paleolithic art is a huge and highly complicated subject that has given rise to many theories over the last century and it is beyond the scope of this book to explore all the options. It is a mistake to assume one overarching theory to explain it all. By doing so we perform a disservice to all the countless ancient people who lived in many complex cultures and whose imaginations were excited to create images in different ways for many reasons. Still, there are many sacred images in the caves that evoke the mystical and we will be exploring some of them.

What inspired ancient humans to produce art at all, let alone venture into dark and dangerous places, some of them miles underground to paint images in startlingly beautiful ways? The impulse to do so arises from a passion born worlds away from interior decoration. This was not art for art's sake, and certainly not a casual undertaking. Art was a necessary tool of survival.

The age of the prehistoric hunter-gatherers comprises a much greater expanse of human culture than the historical era. From our earliest origins over two million years ago to the beginnings of agriculture we have spent over 99.5 per cent of our existence without a trace of domestication. The 10,000 years since the introduction of agriculture is a mere instant compared to the previous millennia when people lived inseparably with the life-rhythms of the earth. Our existence in the farming and industrialized world has been compared to the final 12 inches from the goal line of a football field, while the other 288 feet represent human life before the domestication of plants and animals. It is breathtaking how out of touch with nature we have become in such a relatively short time. Yet, the evolution that took place over those tens of thousands of years has not been banished by our thin wash of civility. The emotional wellspring of the hunter-gatherer, shamanic religion runs both deep in humanity and close to the surface. The Stone Age hunter lurks just beneath the veneer of modernity.

This excellent hunter has brought with him over the centuries a mental and emotional tool kit that still links him to his primeval tribe, his physical world and the world of spirit. Art, one of these essential tools, still communicates its potent essence with an undeniable impact. Viewers are still brought to a state of hushed amazement by the tableau of horses in the cave of Peche-Merle and the deep chamber of the Salon Noir of Niaux, both over 17,000 years old.

Evidence allowing us to delve deeper into the lives of Ice Age people is rapidly accumulating. The avalanche of information amassed from research over the last century, and the increasing sophistication with which it has been retrieved, provides us with much more material to compare and contrast and new theoretical perspectives with which to evaluate and interpret it. New scientific tools make it possible to examine and date many of the artifacts, materials and microorganisms found in cave sites. The discovery of new archaeological sites in recent years has revealed many more pieces of the human puzzle. Post-Cold War Europe is open to Western scientists, allowing shared evidence to be reviewed across the continent as a contiguous whole, revealing cultural differences across the Eurasian landmass. Sophisticated computer models enable the compilation and analysis of information in ways never possible before.

A crucial element to deciphering the clues of Paleolithic life, however, has been the comparative study of ethnographies, the anthropological studies of living hunter-gatherer societies. From the time early European explorers began writing what seemed back home to be bizarre log entries reporting on the lifeways of exotic peoples, information has been compiling and interpretations increasing in sophistication. Cultural anthropology has endeavored to peel away our obscuring layers of bias to reveal the people themselves, unencumbered by critical comment or religious judgment. The resulting cross-cultural comparisons made between peoples as diverse as the Inuit of the frozen north, the cattle herders of Africa, the headhunters of the Amazon rainforest and the buffalo hunters of the American West present an intricately woven fabric of human life, the infinite elaboration of the human mind, body and spirit within every ecosystem. Yet, for every anthropological rule there is a creative human exception.

And within this panoply of diversity there are similarities as well that speak to our commonalities. The comparisons made between hunter-gatherer societies living in circumstances similar to those of the Paleolithics allow us to extrapolate on the more ephemeral aspects of their lives based on the hard scientific evidence of archaeology and ethnography. These allow us to make educated leaps of imagination that lend flesh and blood to the remote lives of Ice Age people.

RECONSTRUCTING LIFE

Twelve thousand years ago a little group of people returned to a hunting camp, as they had done for many seasons, near the confluence of two gently flowing rivers. They repaired their slab-lined hearths, dug trash pits, and rebuilt their round, hide-covered homes. They caught fish in the rivers, stole eggs from the birds and harvested whatever wild foods grew in the lush river valley from early summer to the late fall, when the snows came and it was time to move to the winter camp. During the easier summer days, successful hunters returned to the camp with the carcasses of reindeer. The meat was divided among the people, each cooking a share at their fireplaces. Circular pits near each hearth held containers where water could be boiled and food cooked by dropping hot rocks into it. After the meal, the bones were dumped in each family's trash pit and the camp tidied. With a full belly, a single person, sitting near the fire, set about replacing the lost or broken weapons. Taking up a large nodule of flint, he knocked off blanks, long, thin pieces of flint, and passed them around to others for finer working into blades and arrowheads. A season came when they did not return to their summer camp. The birds and reindeer were left to raise their young and live out their quiet summers unmolested. Season after season, gentle spring floods lifted the rivers over the abandoned camp, leaving behind layers of silt that slowly buried the bones of their dinners, the footprints of their tents and the tools left behind without disturbing them.

Hundreds of generations later, people mining for sand along the Seine and Oise rivers discovered the ancient camp. An archaeological team led by Professor André Leroi-Gourhan excavated the site, carefully exposing a large area and revealing where everything had been left in place long ago. The 'relaxed' site of Pincevent allowed the archaeologists to see the spatial relations of the undisturbed artifacts and bones in a way impossible to see in

the jumbled refuse of the confined space of a rock shelter. Painstakingly, the reindeer bones of Pincevent were retrofitted to determine how pieces of the animals were distributed. They determined that the whole group shared each animal the hunters provided. Imagine them returning with a reindeer, fat from grazing on the sweet summer grass, and the bustle of activity to prepare it for dinner, the division of the food, anticipation of the mouth-watering meal, the smell of roasting meat and preparation for drying what wasn't eaten to save for the long winter. And afterwards, the contentment that comes with going to sleep with a full belly.

Just north of Pincevent, the site of Etiolles had been a flint-knapper's paradise in 12,500 BCE. Enormous nodules of fine-quality flint were quarried and worked in such quantities that novices could practice on the large pieces, not only on the leavings of the experts. Sorting through 25 piles of flint refuse, as had been done with the reindeer bones, French archaeologist Nicole Pigeot reassembled the flint blades back together into the original nodules to chart the moment-to-moment decisions made by each toolmaker. Through a similar technique archaeologists have deduced the most talented flint knappers sat closest to the fire, because the rough stone chips of the less experienced lay on the periphery. Whether their location status brought the experts within reach of a hot meal, earned them more light, more warmth or some other luxury is unknown. After more than 100 years of increasingly exacting study we know quite a lot about people of the Ice Age. We can study the Paleolithics' flint-knapping techniques minutely, examine their skeletons and learn their ages, chart the impressions of long-decayed soft matter in the skull to determine potential thought capabilities, deduce their ailments and even whether or not ancient people were right-handed. We can chart the origin and flow of certain trade items like obsidian, flint and seashells and what they ate for dinner. We can tell from microscopic pollen grains which plants were buried with a body and in what season they died.

We can assume indications of the heart from finds in the soil; the gathering and sharing of food, the instruction of the young, the 'kitchen talk' of the women as they cooked. By comparing the hard evidence at Pincevent and Etiolles with modern hunter-gatherer activities, we have a snapshot of life around the campfire, 12,000 years ago. From there, it is an easier reach deeper into the Paleolithic. Yet, although ancient traders journeyed great distances, we know only that a body was laid to rest with treasures from the

sea. We can map the origin and ultimate destination of the shells of a necklace found in an inland burial. What happened between the sea and the grave is a mystery. Who first thought to pick the shells up off the beach and brush the sand away? Who drilled the holes in such a way that they would lay well on the throat? Who killed the stag and made the leather thong that bound the shells, after first carefully lining them up according to size? Or were they held together with woven grass rolled along a hide-covered hip by a work-hardened hand to twist them together? Was it a trophy, a gift, or a ceremonial emblem?

Science can microscopically examine physical evidence and discern obscure patterns to unlock marvels undreamed of not long ago. But mysteries will always remain. What ceremonies they celebrated at certain times of the year and what stories they told are entirely lost. What were the songs sung for the dead, to guarantee the health of a new baby or success of the hunt? What did they think of the celestial show they saw on sparkling nights? What rituals did the young women observe at first blood? These are life experiences that leave no trace. Their emotions travel the gulf of centuries as shadows only, by gifts left for the dead, patterned stains in the soil, tangible bits of life left behind for the centuries to cover and keep, and perhaps to be found again, miracles to be marveled over, washed from a riverbank or turned up in a garden. And most tantalizing, as the fossil symbols of art. Delicate carvings of a bison licking a flank, a sinuous salamander, a deer giving birth, paintings of snarling lions, stolid mastodons and wounded rhinos lend us precious moments of a vanished time. When and why did our ancestors come to make art? The exploration of this topic is a tantalizing balance between scientific fact, ethnographic information and interpretation, yoking leaps of imagination with the evidence.

ANCIENT ANCESTORS

The unfolding revelation of the story of the human family is an ongoing mystery. Yet to find our way to the labyrinth we must follow this path for, in the discovery of the first glimmerings of symbol making we find the defining lines of humanity. The identity and understanding of our ancestry hangs sometimes literally on fragments; a chunk of cranium, a single tooth, the chance survival of a bit of life. And what do they mean? Are cut marks on skeletons the result of cannibalism? Are scored marks on a bone from idle doodling, an accidental by-product of its having been used as a

cutting surface, or a primitive lunar calendar? When did the lights of consciousness flicker on? The arrangements of dry bones and their accessories entice, suggesting the twinkle of imagination, dreams and dance. This ponderous callipering of fragments from all over the world is gradually assembling, chip by chip, into a mosaic of primeval humans, artifacts and events.

The ancestral family tree has undergone significant alterations since Bishop Usher announced the world's creation in 4004 BC. New limbs have sprouted and others pruned as skeletons of unknown creatures yield themselves to the light of day and others are released from the cool darkness of storage sarcophagi for re-examination with new tools. Yet the spotty discovery of remains leaves puzzling gaps in the archaeological record.

We know Homo ergaster, ancestor of both European Neanderthals and modern humans, left Africa more than 1.5 million years ago. These archaic humans expanded relentlessly into different climates and ecologies, spreading as far as China and Java in the east and into the cold reaches of Germany and England. The restless Homo ergaster who ventured into Europe adapted to its increasingly colder northern home by accumulating a heavy body supported by a massive skeletal frame. This also became the signature of their descendants, the Neanderthals, people well adapted to the Ice Age. Meanwhile, those remaining behind in the warm equatorial environment of Africa transformed into Homo sapiens; us.

These two species of intelligent humans eventually collided. Some Neanderthals of Europe, in one wave of expansion, backtracked as far as the Middle East. Here, they encountered the African Homo sapiens making their way north. Archaeological sites in the Levant and Anatolia leave a confusing record, as there is evidence that both types of humans coexisted for upwards of 60,000 years, sometimes at the same site, perhaps together, perhaps not, leaving a tangle of archaeological information. The strata of living sites have become, or always were, jumbled so we don't have clear indications of which level is undeniably Neanderthal and which Homo sapien. Although skeletal remains are clearly identifiable, as are the tools each species used, just who engraved which shell, Neanderthal or Homo sapien, is not so easily discerned. Still, the volume of Neanderthal remains that can be construed as art, largely represented by perforated shells, teeth and incised bone, are paltry compared to the Paleolithic wealth of Europe.

Although our species evolved in Africa for over 100,000 years before moving into other parts of the world, they created little that can be considered symbolic in the archaeological record. They appear to have had the capability biologically and neurologically to make art, and very occasionally did, but seem to lack the cultural impetus to do so in any consistent way. Scientists have come down firmly on both sides of the issue; the art that has been found in Neanderthal sites are either the one-off creations of the occasional early genius or are proof that Neanderthals were sophisticated abstract thinkers whose talents have been ignored. In 2003 a natural stone, altered to create a face, was found at a Neanderthal campsite on the banks of the Loire River, continuing this debate. It is dated to about 35,000 years and has a bone splinter jammed through a hole in the rock so that the ends of the splinter look like eyes, and chips were knocked off of it to make it look more like a face.

Finds here and there don't indicate a cultural pattern. However, like the emergence of multi-colored flowers spreading over a primeval world cloaked only in green, an abundance of symbolic expression burst upon the world 40,000 years ago, leading some to suggest a neurological mutation had occurred among modern humans that would lead, eventually, to the symbolic expression of the labyrinth.

Ten thousand years later, migratory waves of these humans moving into Europe were inspired to create a blizzard of what we call 'representational art'. They painted on cave walls, engraved on rock, sculpted bas reliefs, modeled in clay, and carved portable objects of bone, stone and shell. They probably decorated hides and carved wood as well as making nets and basketry. Some female figurines appear coiffed in elaborate braids. Body decoration, a primary art form among tribal peoples, uses the skin as canvas and may have included body painting as well as scarification, tattoos and piercings. But nothing of these perishable arts remains, except arrangements of beads in the soil, suggesting garments.

The technical and cognitive capacity for symbolic art, the creation or incorporation of an object that has some significance beyond the merely practical, certainly existed in Africa and elsewhere. Evidence includes the presence of ocher and incised and perforated artifacts at various sites. Very ancient peoples may well have had rich traditions of song, story, dance and body painting, but these leave no trace. In Australia, 60,000-year-old meandering macaroni-like lines drawn with the fingertips represent their oldest artistic tradition, while pecked and engraved geometric forms and abstract suggestions of animal tracks are close behind. In Africa, beads from about 75,000 BP have been discovered in what may be the earliest fashioning of an ornament. But before 40,000 BP they do not incorporate representational or iconic images; depictions of something that exists in life and which functions as the symbol of a deeper message, a metaphor, as opposed to a pattern of lines, chevrons or dots.

Finds in Africa have led some to the conclusion that the "creative explosion" of art in Europe had a long incubation in Africa and the Near East. Others suggest the incubation took place in India where modern humans may have paused on their way to Europe. Somewhere along the trail of this African exodus, an aesthetic key turned in the early human mind, unlocking a treasure box. By the time fully modern humans pushed into Europe they had evolved an elaborate system of symbolic representation, an appetite for self-expression and representational art to display it. Unparalleled in its richness and diversity, this talent for creating metaphors would lead ultimately to the labyrinth.

The Western tradition gave birth to the study of art history and a cultural aesthetic determined the definition of what constituted 'art'. Until fairly recently art history texts opened with Egypt and Mesopotamia and drew a straight line from there to the Greeks and Europe, with a nod to Asia, largely ignoring the rest of the world. Implicit in this ethnocentric perspective was blindness to a wider human creative potential. Debates continue over what constitutes 'high' art and what is merely craft or 'folk' art, or if there is a distinction at all. Picasso's 'Les Demoiselles d'Avignon' (1907), which imposed African tribal masks on nubile French women in a brothel, rocked the art world by crossing that divide and birthing the Cubist movement. Art originated among tribal peoples, whatever the West may think of it, releasing the power evoked by visual symbols. But what was the impulse that compelled ancient humans to create art in the first place? Very simply, the recognition of metaphors to move the human spirit.

ART AS ECSTACY

Art is a route to ecstasy, opening access to the entire spectrum of human emotions. As Ellen Dissanayake explains in *Homo Aestheticus*, art 'makes special'; by creating or manipulating something artistically, one sets it apart from the mundane. As a

reciprocal process, both the creation of art and the participation in it evoke emotions. It captivates our attention, affects our senses and intensifies our emotions. Humans need to stimulate their body and fire their brain with play and surprise. They need to alter the normal flow of events and expectations, and to 'make believe'. Or taking it one more step, 'make belief', where imagination intersects with reality.

Life without art is boring, as acres of Stalinist architecture will attest. Art is as essential to our emotional lives as is food and sex to the physical. We have evolved a nature that resonates to the entertainment of sensory experience and, as we'll see, when deprived of that our brain and body invent their own entertainment. Transcendent music, the exhilaration of color and form, the dedication, sacrifice and luscious enjoyment of a ritual meal and the muscular poetry of dance are emotionally cathartic expressions. They make us laugh, cry, wonder and think, linking sensual stimulation with intellect, and help us to live well in the world. Nature has seen to it that those things we must do to guarantee our survival make us feel good and want to do them. As a biological and cultural imperative art helps us to flourish.

Our assumptions about art are culturally determined. In the Western tradition 'high' art is stereotypically seen as the result of individual geniuses who possess a unique vision. Yet people from non-industrial cultures need to be taught how to 'see' a photograph, just as we need to be taught how to 'see' an Australian Aboriginal Dreamtime painting as a sacred landscape and not simply an assemblage of colorful dots. Concepts of spatial arrangement and definitions of color vary widely around the world. Even in our tradition the agency that inspired the fashioning of icons in Christendom prior to 1400 was believed to be purely miraculous in origin. Many would argue today that the catalogue of great art is equally miraculously inspired. When attempting to enter into the mind of a Paleolithic artist we must be wary of interpretive traps set by our own cultural perceptions.

We express our world through language in unavoidably culture-laden words, and their origins reveal much. The standard dictionary definition of 'art' is a vast and vague category we define as 'human ingenuity, the conscious use of skill, taste, and creative imagination in the production of aesthetic objects'. Further definitions of 'skill', 'taste' and 'creative' are highly subjective. The Indo-European roots of the word are 'ar', meaning to fit together, and 'er', to set in

motion, to exist. Cognates include arm and root words for 'tool', and 'to arise' or 'appear'. In these words there are echoes of a primeval era when the resources of the natural world were first taken up and transformed into useful, inspirational and beautiful objects. It was a mutual creation; by bringing a piece of art into existence from nature, a communication was established between the human and the natural world, inseparable from the divine. To 'manifest' means hit by the hand (from the Indo-European word for 'hand'), and to thus become evident; to draw form out of formlessness, to capture an essence and make it available to the senses. The raw gift of nature, molded through the playful mind and transformed by hand into a valued object defines our lives more fully, helping us 'to exist' more completely in the world. The 'manifestation' of inspiration then becomes a sacred act of giving form to spirit. Art is the reciprocal expression through which an emotion becomes an artistic metaphor that in turn evokes a feeling. The Paleolithics excelled at this, turning elements of the natural world into art.

The dark flip side of this linguistic coin is manipulation, guile and trickery when the artist becomes artificer and ingenuity becomes expediency. 'Ingenuity' is related to 'engine'. In the eras preceding machinery, 'engine' implied both native talent and begetting, but also evil contrivance. Daedalus is known as the 'artificer' and occupies an equivocal niche in Greek mythology. Like other mythological smiths, Daedalus possessed gifts allowing him to create useful and beautiful, but also dangerous things. He made magical toys, but also designed the bull in which Pasiphae hid to mate with Poseidon's bull, built the labyrinth to hide the Minotaur resulting from that union, and fashioned wings so he and his son, Icarus, could escape King Minos' wrath. Daedalus, artist and artificer, agent of emotions, is everywhere in the myth, the fulcrum supporting the interplay of passions.

Artistic manipulation can slide across moral lines with ease, blurring the distinction between high purpose and scheming, resulting in suspicion of the artist's motives. Inspiration, intellect and desire merge in the 'manipulative' hand, to bring the immaterial dream into existence and involve (and possibly implicate) others who witness the creation. Positive and negative handprints in cave art, which will be discussed later, are particularly evocative in this light. Whether a signature or covenant, a handprint is an intimate and unique channel of expression. The power to create effectively

from a moral center, to control and direct emotion in others, demands a suspension of ego to prevent the dark plunge into sorcery. The union of human and divine expressed in art must be channeled through the good angels of higher being to avoid the taint of selfish manipulation. The conscious manipulation of emotions to achieve a 'good' end is a dangerous, slippery, moral slope.

Shamans, the healers of hunter-gatherer tribal groups, cultivate and communicate power in both spiritual and earthly realms through song, dance, ritual performance and the creation of ritual objects, so may be considered artists. They focus and redirect energies to correct imbalances and promote harmony, guiding damaged souls through the transitions of life and death. Those who make a Faustian pact with evil, using their gifts to harm instead of heal, become witches, feared and excluded from the company of others.

Exclusivity in modern art occurs when the artist's vision is obscure. Everyone can enjoy a Monet, the daubs of color that coalesce into a sunny French afternoon. But when the artist creates an unfamiliar or disturbing image that deviates from convention, difficulties arise. Some viewers struggle to see the point of Jackson Pollock's drippings or the raw cruelty revealed in a Goya. These unfamiliar or 'not-beautiful' creations reflect the artist's personal vision or angst, rather than what is popular or 'acceptable', and require a critic or art historian to interpret them. Demanding, and receiving, vast sums for a painted soup can label, is the height of pop art manipulation, and that's precisely the point. The apparent exclusivity of this type of art smacks of indulgent snobbery and expensive nonsense to those who don't 'get it'.

How does this dual nature of artistic ecstasy and manipulation help us to flourish? Is there an adaptive or evolutionary mechanism at work? At its most influential, art that taps into a deep current of shared human emotion and expresses the profound truth discovered there creates a cultural frisson of fascination and recognition, a symbolic representation of an unrealized kinship, whether for good or ill. The soaring beauty of the human spirit is made as equally apparent as its twisted evil. Michaelangelo's "Pieta" moves us to tears with its grace and tenderness. We are moved as well by a photograph of an Abu Graib prisoner wired to a box with a black hood over his head, but with shame and outrage. Once expressed, the emergence of emotional recognition generates a need to 'settle out' the disturbance of a revelation. They must be acted upon and codified into social behavior. Ecstasy is as likely to involve pain as

pleasure. The need to surprise, play, startle and adapt to dramatic change are fed and eased by art.

By making certain kinds of art exclusive, it is invested with social importance not shared by more common creations. When this type of art is revealed under special circumstances, its impact is considerably more effective. Painting and engraving images in caverns miles underground in dangerous terrain, some in impossibly tight spaces which allow entry to only one person, others requiring a community to carry and build scaffolding, images borne in the mind's eye and executed to perfection on the uneven natural surface below ground, an art almost exclusively of mysterious signs and animals chosen for their iconic importance then given a magical existence through the ministry of the human breath and hand – this is sacred art. It has lost none of its power over the eons.

SANCTIFIED ART

Art that is generally available becomes common to some degree as familiarity begins to equate with ordinary. Humans need novelty to excite deeper passions. Remove art from the reach of everyday life, sequester it away in a sacred space and it becomes sanctified; 'more special'. The paintings and sculptures of the Sistine Chapel, as narrative art, were originally reserved for the Pope and his select company exclusively, contributing to the mythos of his elite power. The kivas of the American Southwest, underground temples where rituals are performed and important meetings held, are similar sacred spaces. To consult the oracle at Delphi in the holy of holies was to request an audience with the god Apollo. Holy objects, books or ceremonial equipment kept in these places become charged with numinosity. Similarly, the emotional investment of ceremony involving candles, music, incense and chanting can transform a common space into an uncommonly sacred one.

The images chosen and created in the dark chambers of caves were in some ways different from those portrayed on the tools and mobilary art of everyday life. This is in part because of the interplay between the character of the cave and the creation. Some subjects appear on tools or as sculpture that never occur in the caves. Although the Paleolithics clearly were talented enough to paint a bison or horse in delicate realistic detail, showing musculature and a range of animal emotions, the very few human images that appear in caves are distorted, cartoonish and incomplete. Yet what amount to evocative portraits, indicating hairstyles, beards and the suggestion

81

of clothing, were engraved or carved and carried above ground, the 'goddess' images being the most well known. Humans, as they appeared in waking life, were not to be put on the walls of caves. Hands, vulvas, penises and torsos appear in many contexts, and the composite images of 'sorcerers' mentioned earlier dance across the walls. But to fix a fully realized human image on the cave surface was to place a person's likeness where it didn't belong. The sacredness of the deep caves was reserved for iconic animals, signs and only fragments of humans. We'll explore this and other choices made and techniques used more fully in later chapters. For now we'll look at why art is a vital survival element that set these humans on the path through the labyrinth.

What the industrial world separates out into categories of art, religion and craft are, in hunter-gatherer societies, aspects of the same dimension; a continuum of life, spirit and social inclusion rather than separation. If all of existence participates in the same animating principle, that spirit runs through everything in varying degrees, but some things are more sacred than others.

Among traditional peoples, communally validated experiences, rather than individual, make sense of the world. Participation in ceremonial dance, feasting and music create a shared emotional state that confirms one's identity and relationships. The individual is cultivated so as to be a better member of the group. Categories within the larger community, women or men, members of a warrior society, married or unmarried people, shamans, initiates and so on, have their status of exclusivity that define them in the context of the tribe as a whole. Their unique songs and dances and prescribed times and places in which they are performed solidify identity. As a culture increases in complexity and deeper social divisions appear, so do artistic badges of recognition and social stratification. Costuming, jewelry and ceremonial accessories that require rare or expensive materials, unique talents and intensive time commitments to make are reserved for elevated social positions and unique ceremonial occasions. Art advertises a person's status and everyone else's expectations fall into line accordingly.

Transitional experiences such as death, puberty, marriage and war were, and continue to be, eased through ceremony. The anxiety created by a transition settles out during a ritual to become crystallized in art, a tangible expression of disturbing emotions that can then be dealt with safely. Arts and ceremony developed together to interpret and transform reality and influence the outcome of the

life event. Creating a costume, receiving the inspiration of a song, building a shrine, learning a dance and making an offering were done in concert with spiritual powers and made use of symbolic materials and images that represented deeper truths. Transitions were eased, boundaries dissolved, acceptance and trust attained through the shared experience of art and ritual. A cultural matrix of rituals involving all the arts binds a tribe together and unites them with their spiritual world.

EGYPTIAN EXAMPLE

Since the prehistoric Paleolithics left us no guidebooks, let's look at a ritual of one of the earliest civilizations that did, Egypt, to show how art and ceremony ease transitions. This particular ancient Egyptian pageant incorporated the archetype of the labyrinth. The Egyptians were the most religious people in the world, according to the Greek writer Herodotus, who was dazzled by their involved and time-consuming rituals. Their elaborate ceremonies were built on an ancient shamanic religion in which the journey from death to resurrected life is framed and focused within a labyrinthine structure representing the interface between life and death. Dead pharaohs were reborn in the afterlife through involved mystical ceremonies and mummification. Central to the rituals was the passage of the mummified body through a dangerous labyrinthine underworld, culminating in the safe arrival of the pharaoh in the realm of the sun god where he would be reborn into the prime of life for all eternity. Eventually this privilege was extended to ordinary citizens as the guiding myth of the death and resurrection of the god Osiris was popularly embraced.

The transition between the old year and the new, a hinge in time when past and future collide, can be a spiritually precarious time when energies must be focused appropriately. New Year observances involve a retelling of the creation of the world or the founding mythic event that defines a people, and its re-enactment revitalizes their culture. The Egyptian New Year celebrations were monumental. Forces were brought into balance and the world was made new again. In this eight-day pageant, art in all its forms dovetailed with the ritual of renewing the world; costumes, poetry, music and temple architecture combined to carry the celebrants together into the future.

The Egyptian New Year marked the annual rising of the Nile. Fed by seasonal monsoons in distant Ethiopia, floodwaters appeared as

if by miracle in the rain-free Nile Valley and replenished the land, covering it with black silt. The inundation linked the seasonal rising of the star Sirius with the 'rising' of both the Nile River and Osiris.

In an extravagant passion play, costumed priests re-enacted the mythic murder and dismemberment of Osiris by Set, symbolic of the death-dealing desert, and his reassembly and revitalization by Isis. This took place in an island temple representing the first land to emerge following a watery Creation. The interior chamber was reached by descending a labyrinthine winding stair symbolizing the journey of the dead through the Underworld. Although Osiris was incapable of returning to the land of the living, his son Horus acted as intermediary. Significantly, the ritual's key moment, the transfer of life-generating power from the Underworld of Osiris to the living world of Horus, took place at the center of the labyrinth inside the temple. Too sacred to be witnessed by any but the select priesthood, it was particularly potent as a result.

The crowds, after days of incense-wreathed rituals, singing, chanting and parading of extravagantly costumed participants, waited anxiously outside, anticipating the ritual 'calling out', or recognition, of Osiris's return from the dead by Horus. This grand finale represented passage of the power of life from the underworld throne of Osiris, by way of the labyrinthine stair, to his son in the middle world, carrying the promise of resurrection to all who participated. The stars had quite literally aligned, links between Egyptian identity and the land were reestablished, fecundity was guaranteed, the world was made new, and an intense emotional catharsis was experienced by all participants. As we'll see in subsequent chapters, this passage of the power of life and death by way of the labyrinth is an echo of events in the deep caves of Europe.

SECRET ART

Even in the most egalitarian cultures some art remains hidden except under very strict circumstances. To circumvent or defy the ceremonial process of the art's proper revelation was to court disaster. These are the magical works and rituals, such as the 'calling out' of Osiris, that open channels to intense potency and are not to be toyed with nor diluted in any way. Ritual objects such as Aboriginal churingas, Native American ceremonial pipes or holy books are not to be handled by the uninitiated or the unclean, nor exposed to the dilution of general view. Sacred statuary is paraded

through Latin American streets only on particular religious holidays following extensive ceremonial preparation. Specific locations are designated as ceremonial sites for male and female puberty rites, common among Australian Aboriginals and Native Americans. Potent shamanic rock art images are created and revealed to initiates under ceremonial conditions for maximum impact. Certain Australian sacred sites are guarded by images depicting broken and mutilated bodies, curses to befall anyone who transgresses the clearly marked boundaries.

Imagine the effect of a stunning revelation of magical images in the dripping gallery of a deep cave. Like the Egyptians, an Ice Age celebrant prepared by extensive ritual to anticipate a manifestation of the sacred, waited in the utter black silence of a cave. Exhausted from dancing and dizzy from fasting, the young initiate was perhaps led to this black chamber by costumed family members transformed into the embodiment of spirits, similar to Kachinas of the American Southwest. Suddenly, torches blaze and the initiate is temporarily blinded by their brilliance. He is lifted out of himself by voices and thunderous drumming echoing down the subterranean caverns while all around him spirit animals are tumbling, falling, leaping and spinning, just as he has been told in the stories and songs. They exist here, their spirits fixed on these walls where they can be summoned to share their power. Or, perhaps alone, a woman seeks a sacramental connection with the divine and finds her way to a remote pocket of a cave to paint a vision. A parent seeks a blessing for a child and carries her far into the cave to spray magical pigment around her small hand, leaving traces of his own as he holds hers in place on the wall. Trance-induced vision quests are still conducted in remote, spiritually charged places around the world that become galleries of spiritual revelations engraved and painted on rocks or marked with a handprint.

This art was not the sole inspiration and decision of the artist, but resulted from conversations with the natural and spiritual world. The artist did not consciously decide to paint a bison. Just the opposite; normal consciousness was actively altered. The bison 'painted through' the artist, whose hand then becomes the 'manipulated' tool of the gods, a mediumistic organ of spiritual revelation. While in a trance state, hallucinations pour into the spirit traveler through every sensory receptacle. Accompanied by the auditory hallucination of song, the words and tune well up from the spirit world as a message of healing and allow the vision and song to entwine, becoming a

transformative medicine. The painting of the image then assumes the song. It has been recently discovered that cave locations which produce an echo have a higher percentage of art than those that do not. The Paleolithics heard the gods speak to them in the magical language of spirit and reproduced it, incorporating the message into a catalogue of transcendent experience. Dances of power are likewise granted to supplicants whose bodies are taught by spirit powers. What evolved into the Greek Muses, the nine sister goddesses who inspire the arts and sciences, began among ancient people as a guiding inspiration channeled directly from the spirit world. Agency was not the conscious decision of the artist, but rather the artist being 'taken' by the power of spirit.

This experience is only at a slight remove from Jackson Pollock after all. He laid his gigantic canvases on the floor so he could enter into the paintings from all sides. He felt nearer the paintings this way, actually 'inside' them, tapping into what the Surrealists called a "psychic automatism"; the revelation of the artist's unconscious moods. During the creation of the work "Lavender Mist 3" Pollock dipped his hands in paint and made handprints in the upper right corner, as did the cave painters of the Paleolithic, perhaps as a signature or a covenant, perhaps both.

The sudden, prolific creation of mobile, ornamental and painted art that blossomed during the Upper Paleolithic represents a major human cultural shift. This 25,000-year span is distinguished by several uniquely identifiable technologies indicating different cultural traditions; and yet the symbolic content of the cave art retained an amazing consistency. This era represents a watershed moment in the spectrum of consciousness, an evolutionary leap described by Christian mystic and scientist Teilhard de Chardin, as a shift in the "noosphere" ('noo', Greek for 'mind'), an interconnection of grains of human consciousness, a thinking layer of the biosphere. Nothing endures in culture unless it has some selective advantage. Art plays a vital role in the success and social cohesion of human society. To convey profound social and spiritual information through the representation of artistic metaphors is key.

Artistic creation is a deep psychic river rolling through human experience and having its Western headwaters in the era of the Paleolithic. Geneticists studying information gleaned from the human genome project have proposed that human evolution has accelerated enormously, beginning about 40,000 years ago due to increasing population and adaptation to new climates and microbes.

There was a correlate cultural surge as well. The desire to play, startle, provoke and transcend through the medium of art is universal; from body-painting in the Australian Outback, Islamic architecture, Tibetan tankas, African masks, the Louvre's miles of Italian Renaissance oils and Andy Warhol's soup cans. Humans need to make art to thrive.

At some point along the evolutionary journey of humanity, a unique juncture of the suspended particles of spiritual awareness, cognitive capability, technical invention and social necessity passed through the lens of the labyrinth, as did the life-essence of Osiris to Horus, and precipitated out into art at the same time Homo sapiens pushed into Europe and the land of the ancient Neanderthal. And then there truly was an explosion of art not only in what is now Europe, but also all over the planet. Where social change had been moving like the glacial landscape, it now burst open like a piñata of innovation. The noosphere reverberated.

CHAPTER 5

THE OTHER HUMANS

*"The original spring, primordial water, sacred water holes, caves ...
are eternal symbols of transformation. Water is an agent of
purification, healing, and rebirth, a means for the repolarization of
profane into sacred reality. It is not surprising that shamanic
initiations and the call to healing often occur or are experienced in
a cave, a grotto with a spring, or at a water hole...Caves, after all,
are places of ... Mystery, in fact, an expression of the self..."*
Holger Kalweit **Dreamtime and Inner Space;
The World of the Shaman**

FIRST ENCOUNTER

The small hunting band was making its way along the flank of a
grassy hill, facing into the wind to avoid being detected by the
reindeer up ahead. They were new to this land. They had brought
their families to this well-watered valley after splitting off from the
larger clan in search of peace and better hunting. It was difficult to
leave them, but the land here was good, the animals plentiful, and
putting space between the older brothers was necessary now. Last
winter had been harshly confining and tempers were raw. And they
would see them again at the Waterfall Meeting after the snows.

Bending low, they crested the hill, spears cocked. Hearing the
animals up ahead, they signaled to spread out then stood slowly to
sight in on their quarry. Arms froze in place as they saw not only the
deer, but also another group of animals that now had seen them.
They too hunted the deer, but the hunt was forgotten in the moment
of shock. They appeared to be people; very strong, very white-
faced people dressed in rough skins. Some had hair like fire and
their eyes were wide with astonishment. The newcomers spoke
softly together and agreed to approach warily but respectfully, for
these white creatures may be ghosts, spirits of the land or perhaps
ancestors. They were surely powerful. As the distance closed

between them, one of the newcomers pulled a thong from around his neck, startling the Old Ones. Suspended from it was an ivory carving of a full-figured woman without head or feet, but enormous breasts and deeply engraved vulva. If they were spirits or Old Ones, it was best to offer a valuable gift. The Old Ones hung back, talking in a strange, nasally language that hummed and rolled from one to another, their hands chopping and swimming in the air to complete their thoughts. One who wore a bear pelt stepped forward to cautiously accept the gift of the woman. In his enormous, rough hand it looked like a toy. He dangled it by the thong and stared at it in stunned amazement, turning it back and forward as if he expected it to move. Never before in his life had he seen such a thing. He held it to his broad nose, smelling it, examining it carefully with intelligent, curious eyes that peered out from under heavy brows and ran his calloused thumb over the surface. Carefully, he clenched it between his teeth to test its hardness and tasted the cold bone and the sweat of the wearer. Then he gazed long and thoroughly at the newcomer, his considering eyes traveling the distance from head to feet and back again.

His fist closed over the necklace with the finality of a decision having been made and, with the other hand, he reached into a pouch and brought out a tool, a heavy hand axe, and held it out on his open palm. The newcomers whispered that this was a good sign, but why would gods have such primitive tools? Perhaps they had special powers. They had seen them before at old campsites, but had no idea where they came from. They would take it to the shaman and ask him to inquire of the axe. They would ask the shaman to give them a word for these beings that would place them in the world.

The axe was accepted and the newcomer reached out his empty hand, also palm up, as a gesture of friendship. The Old One stared at the empty hand for a moment, unsure what was to be done for there was nothing in the hand. Then it seemed he knew, although it was strange to him. He placed his hand on the newcomer's dark palm and it felt quite small. Drawing his hand away he looked at it, sure that some of the dark color would have rubbed off and amazed that it had not. He looked into the clever dark eyes in the narrow face of this new creature, framed in black hair braided with bits of hide and feathers, took in the slender build, the carefully made clothes and tentatively touched the beads that hung from his hair. The Old One's eyes were tender, as if seeing a vision of a wonderful child. They could use the axe. It seemed their tools were all small just as they

were and could not be very effective.

ART SAVES LIVES

Venturing back in time along the pathways of our human history we inevitably run into others who were very much like us; the Neanderthals. The more we learn about them, the further we banish the unfortunate image of a dumb brute. These were ancient, sensitive, capable people, yet they washed away into the landscape before the tidal surge of the immigrant Homo sapiens. Modern humans like us overwhelmed the local competition in Ice Age Europe to become the predominant species on the planet. Although the reasons for the success of modern humans and the extinction of Neanderthals are varied, complex and still debatable, the melding of some essential ingredients significantly impacted this change; our ability to comprehend profound metaphors such as the labyrinth, to communicate the cultural subtleties of these metaphors, and to represent them artistically. Since we are headed deep into the cultural landscape of Paleolithic Europe, the 'problem' of the Neanderthal–Homo sapien co-existence needs to be explored as part of the context for the emergence of the labyrinth.

Homo Neanderthalis developed in Europe 300,000 years ago and their ancestors preceded them by another 200,000. Neanderthals traveled as far south as the Middle East and into Southwest Asia during the Middle Paleolithic, roughly 300,000 to 40,000 years ago. Theirs was an astonishing run of time. During this long period they manufactured distinctive stone tools with little variation called Mousterian, after the site of Le Moustier in France where they were first discovered in 1909. Found together with Neanderthal skeletal remains, they proved conclusively what was then a startling connection between the two; ancient humans who made tools.

During all this expanse of millennia, the Neanderthals managed to survive quite well without art. Only near the end of their existence did they produce a few decorative items, probably the result of interaction with the new neighbors, since they do not appear at any other time in the archaeological record. They may have imagined and created these items on their own. They may have traded for them. But they may also have been the Paleolithic equivalent of a kid copying off another student's work or just outright stealing it. Proof that they wore ornaments has been found at only two sites. At Quincay they found six perforated teeth and, at Grotte du Renne, Neanderthals apparently wore necklaces. Their

remains were discovered together with perforated teeth and bones, ivory beads and finger rings and fossils carried many miles inland from the sea.

Evidence of illness and injuries among Neanderthal skeletal remains testifies that life in the Stone Age was no picnic. Their robust bodies required significantly more calories than moderns to survive, and so they hunted predominantly large, solitary animals like wooly rhinoceros. The mileage on an Ice Age hunter racked up fast. In fact, Neanderthal injuries and evidence of trauma compare with those suffered by modern rodeo cowboys, another group that interacts with large, dangerous animals. Rarely Neanderthals reached the age of 40, with life expectancy probably well under 30. Examination of bones of the 206 individuals found gives us only a limited range of statistical information, however, and compared to the millions of Neanderthals who ever lived this is a thin board on which to stand.

Infant mortality was high, as it is today among people who lack sufficient food and medical attention. Factor in the desperately cold climate and gigantic predators and the odds of survival are even lower. We have few remains of elderly Neanderthals, that is, past the age of 35, but severe arthritis appears to have been common among them. The skeleton buried with flowering plants in the famous grave of Shanidar, Iraq is a poster child for the rigors of Neanderthal life. He had lost his left eye from a blow to the head, had his right arm amputated above the elbow, and suffered additional injuries to his ankle, hip and foot. The Old Man of Chappel-aux-Saints, who may have been about 50, endured painful arthritis and had lost most of his teeth. These men were obviously unable to hunt, not very mobile, and had to have been cared for by their people. This simple fact gives us a tantalizing glimpse into Neanderthal society. These 'old men' were valued sufficiently to maintain their lives at some cost of mobility and convenience to a band of traveling hunter-gatherers. The Neanderthals were compassionate people who nurtured their disabled.

Although Neanderthals lived at the mouths of some caves, their primary dwelling place was in the open air where remains more delicate than bone and stone have not survived the eons of exposure. However, even in cave sites that have been excavated, there is no significant accumulation of what could be called 'art'. We have very few intentional burials from which to glean information, a repository for valued items in any human culture, and these were

sheltered in caves. They may well have left their dead in trees, as did the Plains Indians, or in the open to be devoured by animals or carried off by birds, as has been done in Mongolia. Those who were about to die may have just stayed behind while the rest of the tribe moved on, as among Inuit and Middle Eastern pastoralists who make hazardous seasonal journeys. Burial was not a common practice and the few that have been found are from a comparatively recent period.

The Neanderthals' limited communication skills, immense physical strength and endurance, adaptation to the frigid climate of the Ice Age, successful hunting and foraging techniques and a detailed familiarity with the ecosystems in which they lived served them well for a very long time. There were a few modifications over the millennia that occurred in the stone tools they knapped, but little technological advancement until near the end of their existence. The Chatelperronian is a tool kit that appears at the time Neanderthals and modern humans shared Europe. This was undoubtedly the Neanderthal response to the breaking wave of Homo sapiens entering their territory. Multiple factors probably led to their undoing, but the stagnation of their culture, or their inability to adapt under pressure from the new arrivals was significant.

SYMBOLIC BEHAVIOR

Around 50,000 BP Neanderthals began to enter the black depths of caves. Long before Homo sapiens entered Europe, Neanderthals were making their way down torturous passages to pursue what could only be ritual activities. The recently discovered French cave of Bruniquel had been sealed by rock falls and lay undisturbed from Neanderthal times. There is no indication that Homo sapiens were ever in Bruniquel. One day in the distant past, a group of these early humans answered an inner call and made its way into a chamber in the earth. Here, they arranged broken stalagmites into two circles, one 13 by 16 feet and the other much smaller. Nearby they built a hearth and lit a fire. Although the floor has not yet been excavated there are no obvious indications of tools at the site. A burned bear bone in the firepit suggests a meal or offering. Neanderthals were apparently venturing far into the caves to experience the mysterious atmosphere.

They had to have had a unanimous plan to create this crystalline circle of stone. But even more important, they had to have had a common belief that brought them into this deep darkness to arrange

stalactites into some sort of magical enclosure. When communing with the spirits, people create a sacred space through which mortal and divine can touch without danger. The Neanderthals who visited Bruniquel had a vision of what was required of them; to build a structure designed to carry them to a non-ordinary reality or protect them on their journey there. Just where that portal took the Neanderthals will forever remain a mystery. It is our earliest evidence of people pursuing ritualized ecstatic experiences. Yet, despite suitable cave walls in Bruniquel, and the evidence of ceremony, they made no art.

Symbolic behavior among Neanderthals is evident elsewhere as well. Loved ones were buried with obvious affection and attention to a deeper mystery. Burials often included ocher, a soft iron oxide with a color range from light yellow to blood red that was prized worldwide in hunter-gather societies from Africa to the Americas. It was used as a paint and powder in both decorative and ceremonial capacities for hundreds of thousands of years. Beyond its use as a coloring agent, ocher has practical uses as a preservative, anti-bacterial agent and metallic abrasive. It first began to appear at campsites in South Africa 900,000 years ago and was a primary medium in the painted caves of the Paleolithic. Large collections of ocher have been found in South African deposits dated to at least 125,000 years ago, some described as 'pencils'. Others had been scraped to remove powder. Since the beginning, people have colored their tools, clothing and themselves with ocher as part of ritual behavior, or simply to set them apart from the ordinary.

The presence of ocher in Neanderthal graves has been interpreted as an indication of ritual behavior. They possibly painted their body in life as well as death, and may have left the red-colored stone or powder as grave goods. That the deep reddish color resembles blood, a symbol of life, suggests a belief in the continuation of a life force after death. Biologically, the color red stimulates the human heart rate and excites the brain. Culturally, its interpretation is ambiguous. It holds a prominent place in the color scheme of all human societies and is the first color most babies learn to name. Psychotropic amanita muscaria mushrooms, the fairy tale red mushrooms with white spots, are highly toxic, yet ingested in Siberia as sacred hallucinogenic plants. The tomato struggled for acceptance after its introduction into Europe from the New World, having to overcome rumors of its alleged poisonous nature. Its nickname, 'love apple', and its assumed properties as an aphrodisiac

no doubt helped dispel prejudice. Blushing red cheeks can be the charming indication of virginal embarrassment or the warning flag of anger, or both. Red blood accompanies birth, but can also signal death. The color red has been a stop sign along the human highway for a very long time, exciting our attention before we proceed with caution. The use of blood-colored ocher is a provocative suggestion of early symbolic thinking.

A boar's jaw placed in the hands of an adult, antlers left in the grave of a boy, mountain goat horns arranged around another and a fourth sent on his way with a stone sculpted with cup marks and placed over his heart reveal a recognition of death as a significant departure. Yet these occasions were rare. These symbolic and tender acts telegraphed over the millennia tell us the Neanderthals may have imagined their dead to continue on in another world, in another form.

For 200,000 years small tribal groups of Neanderthals went about their lives with persistence and consistency. There were only tiny deviations off the well-trod Neanderthal path, like the stalactite circle at Bruniquel. That was all about to change. Competition arrived in a big way with the new kids in town, anatomically modern humans who entered Europe about 40,000 BP. Manipulating the environment, and responding adroitly to dramatic changes in climate, became high art, and adaptation the order of the day.

NEW KIDS ON THE BLOCK

The remains of Homo sapiens, four adults and a fetus, were first discovered in 1868 in the rock shelter of Cro-Magnon in Les Eyzies de Tayac, France, along with stone tools, engraved bones, personal ornaments and the remains of extinct animals that undeniably established their antiquity. There was little to compare to this find and the ancient people were named after the rock shelter owned by Mr Magnon where they were found. After more than a century of discovery and analysis we now have a cultural time-line built painstakingly on the excavation of numerous sites and museums full of artifacts, which allow us to distinguish one cultural horizon from another. Generally, the anatomically modern humans who populated France during the Upper Paleolithic are referred to as Cro-Magnon, but there are separate cultural distinctions ranging across the Paleolithic based on different types of tool assemblages under that umbrella term.

The earliest of the Cro-Magnon cultures, named the Aurignacians

for the tool industry first found at the site of Aurignac, rolled into Neanderthal territory like a tornado of creation that must have been baffling to the very different brain of the Neanderthal. Imagine the jaw-dropping arrival of these lithe humans with narrow faces, chins, big eyes, quick wits and amazing tools. To the Neanderthals, they would have resembled their own children, who did not develop the distinctive heavy brow ridge and wide nose until adulthood. They may have made the mistake of thinking the Aurignacians were childlike, eliciting a protective response that was tragically off the mark.

Language flowed from the newcomers like bird song, sounds the Neanderthals had never heard and couldn't duplicate. It is a likely possibility that the Neanderthals of the icy north would have been quite pale and DNA samples have shown that at least some were redheads. The Aurignacians, however, were probably dark-skinned, having adapted to the African sun. And they were snazzy. These exotic, nimble people were dressed to the nines in jewelry and ornamentation. They rattled with necklaces, beads, bracelets, armbands made of shell, fox teeth and ivory and had sewn carved images into their clothing. They may well have worn feathers and fringe and painted their bodies. They carried elegantly decorated tools and weapons, carved images of animals and chubby female figurines. Consider the impact of Jimmy Hendrix and a tide of hippies in full-feathered regalia backed by a psychedelic soundtrack rolling into a white neighborhood blue-collar bar in 1967. These newcomers were people to be reckoned with.

Imagine the first face-to-face encounter. What must the Aurignacians have thought of the Neanderthals? In a world populated by a diversity of animal life not seen since, here were powerful, pale-skinned-people-like creatures, so much like themselves yet so different. These human creatures would have certainly stood apart from rest of the animals, but to what category would they have been first consigned? Ghosts requiring caution, ancestors worthy of respect or beings wise in the ways of the land from which the newcomers could learn? And, once the newness wore off, were the Neanderthals mere competitors for territory and resources? Communication would have likely been limited and fraught in a clash of such different humans. Yet as a part of the natural world of these modern hunter-gatherers in which all things were integrated into a cohesive web of life, the Neanderthals would have commanded some level of reverence and respect, as did all other animals. This does not mean that a love-fest between the two species ensued and, ultimately, they competed for the same resources. Once the Aurignacians had incorporated these strange humans into their cultural lexicon, a full range of responses may have resulted; they may well have married them, hunted them down or starved them out. By comparison, when Native Americans first encountered Europeans, they met them with wary respect. After the acquaintance had soured beyond redemption, slaughter on both sides was a justifiable solution. The Aztecs, having determined that the Spaniards, their horses and attack dogs were clearly not on a mission of friendship, rejoiced in dismembering their European captives and tossing the body parts back inside their stockade walls.

All we know for certain is that once these fully modern humans appeared about 40,000 years ago, the Neanderthals, who were probably always thinly spread on the land, began to disappear. The two co-existed in Europe for about a 15,000-year transitional period until the dwindling Neanderthals were eventually pushed to the far reaches of the Iberian Peninsula. Here they clung to life in small pockets until about 28,000 years ago, then vanished from the fossil record as it now stands. There is the possibility they may have survived longer based on new finds in Gorham's Cave, Gibraltar but, at this writing, the Gorham Cave discovery is still controversial.

The nature of the relationship between these two types of humans is the subject of much conjecture, but the Aurignacians were vastly more successful. To move from Africa into the frozen tundra of the north and not only survive but displace a population that had lived there successfully for over 300,000 years demonstrates evolutionary development and adaptive skills of startling magnitude.

In *Scientific American* (August 2009), Kate Wong points to a variety of conditions and predispositions that contributed to the Neanderthals' disappearance. Their populations were probably always small and mitochondrial DNA research proves they were fragmented into three subgroups living in western Europe, southern Europe and western Asia. They were hunters of large animals and evidence that they took advantage of other foodstuffs such as grains, marine animals and birds is minimal. Their women and children may have been involved in the hunt as beaters, which could have put them in harm's way. Although it may seem like a small item that they never developed needles indicates that their clothing and tents, made of hides, were not as efficient against the cold as they would have been if they were sewn. Combine these limitations against the

dual onslaught of the Last Glacial Maximum and encroaching modern humans and the tipping point for Neanderthal survival is reached.

Modern humans exploited everything edible in their environment and their smaller bodies made much more efficient use of the calories. Their varied diet implies a more reliable food supply and a division of labor, with women and children hunting small animals and collecting plant foods while the men hunted big game. Keeping women and children largely away from dangerous hunting helped insure their wellbeing. Although the Neanderthals had endured arctic conditions before and survived, during the Last Glacial Maximum the temperature was not only extremely frigid but erratic. Wild swings in temperature would, in the span of a lifetime, seesaw from temperate to tundra, dramatically affecting the animal populations and vegetation. Migrations changed, water sources froze, dried up or became raging torrents. Neanderthal hunting practices, relying on tree cover, was ineffective as grasslands replaced trees. Nothing was dependable for very long and the ancient, unchanging way of life of the Neanderthal could not adapt in time. Modern humans, around 30,000 years ago on the other hand, for reasons not yet understood, suddenly began to live long enough to become grandparents. This means their reproductive years were increased so populations could expand. Additionally, within the span of a longer lifetime, more specialized knowledge could be gained and, particularly for our purposes of exploring the labyrinth, passed on to the next generation. Increased longevity expanded social networks and established deeper ties and greater knowledge over time.

What role did art play in the ability of the Homo sapiens to flourish as they did? What was it about the Aurignacians that made the creation of art possible and necessary? It is a chicken-and-egg argument upon which scholars have yet to agree. The biological need to create art spurred cultural growth. In turn, the symbol systems defined by art stimulated and reified cultural refinements that extended over at least three contemporary generations; time enough to establish abiding traditions. One of the most significant symbolic constructs expressed by Homo sapiens was the idea of the labyrinth as a spiritual journey to other worlds. The Aurignacians were inspired to create a proto-labyrinthine narrative that fulfilled a multitude of cultural needs. This codifying of the experience of deep trance as journey provided a structure within which the perils of

Paleolithic life could be ritually framed. Where the Neanderthals may have been cognizant of the labyrinthine experience, as we will see, the Homo sapiens developed it, artistically represented it, and took it to the cultural bank, while the Neanderthals dwindled away.

HOME VS. AWAY TEAM

A significant distinction between the two species was language. Neanderthals were intelligent humans with remarkable skills and longevity as a species. There has been much speculation as to whether the Neanderthals had a language and it is widely assumed that they could speak. However, anatomical evidence, combined with the rarity of symbolic expression, suggests that the Neanderthals had a literally and figuratively limited vocabulary. As the clever Aurignacians moved into their sphere of unwavering routine, the Neanderthals proved incapable of the same facile adaptation to change.

Professor Steven Mithen makes a case for the evolutionary development of singing and dancing as vital communication techniques among very early humans. The evolutionary change to bipedalism not only freed the hands, but also changed the pelvis, restructured the spine to locate the brain stem at the base of the skull, altered the throat and mouth structure, and expanded the vocal abilities. Rhythmic movement and entrainment, the involuntary swaying of the body to the sounds of music, were increasingly perfected as humans became more gracile. Mithen points to early human abilities to demonstrate emotions through body language and vocal musical expression employing pitch, range and volume as valuable during hunts, to impress potential mates, to create comforting communal humming at nightfall, and possibly fulfilling the vital human need for play as pure entertainment.

Add to these abilities a vocal dimension that allows for teaching children, calming babies and communicating important messages to other members of the group, and the neural network is in place to enter into the world and feelings of others; the primary foundation for complex social interactions. The awareness and appreciation of another's desires and beliefs as being different from one's own requires what Mithen describes as a 'mind reading' capability; we observe the outward signs of body language, expression and verbal accompaniment, determine that the thought behind them is different from ours and act accordingly. This awareness is the foundation of consciousness. Where a cat twitching its tail gives the body-

language signal that she is about to pounce on her playmate, the human combination of verbal teasing, fast and complex physical moves and the history of relationship among the participants makes a basketball game in the park a complicated social interaction with many potential social reverberations. The creative use of insults alone can determine whether the 'game' remains in the realm of harmless fun or tips into a more serious feud.

Mithen describes the language capabilities of archaic humans as "Hmmmm; holistic, manipulative, multi-modal, and musical", the precursor to language. Although earlier hominids had this communicative capability, Neanderthals elevated it to a high degree. He adds another 'm' for 'mimetic', the ability to imitate the calls of animals and to use vocal gestures representing their physical characteristics. "Hmmmmm" is described as a collection of holistic expressions, each communicating a complete message, rather than individual words and grammar that can be recombined endlessly to express a much wider range of thoughts. These holistic expressions would have been the equivalent of our 'stock phrases' that act as a shorthand to describe something obvious and familiar. Where they may have had a combination of vocalizations and body language that was understood as 'come with me to hunt deer over there', we have elevated 'at the end of the day' to the status of a national colloquialism, usually said with a hand held out, palm up and perhaps a shoulder shrug to express that all is apparent. We all know what is meant by this phrase and don't need to define it further, saving us the time and energy of expressing ourselves in 'longhand' terminology. In addition, a camaraderie is implied; 'we are all on the same page', so to speak. Someone from outside this linguistic fraternity may need to have it explained. Even if the outsider understands the basics of English, they may mistake the significance of 'at the end of the day' to be a temporal one, rather than metaphoric.

The Neanderthal brain, although sufficient for successful survival in the bitter climate of Ice Age Europe for a very long time, was neurologically incapable of making the kinds of linguistic and creative connections that the Aurignacian brain could. Still, Homo sapiens populated Africa for 100,000 years and produced comparatively little in the way of art that survives in the archaeological record. Song, myth, dance, costuming and body painting probably existed, but these art forms leave no trace. What was different about Paleolithic Europe?

Anyone who has raised a toddler, for whom the whole world is new, is well aware of the burst of language development that accompanies a new adventure. This often includes colorful words and word combinations that don't exist in the accepted lexicon, but have their own logic, becoming the pet terms of the family and following that child through her lifetime whether she likes it or not. My daughter, for example, invented the graphic and apt idea of having an 'egg-knot' to describe her upset stomach, incorporating ideas of both potential and constriction.

Now imagine the stratospheric growth of language required to describe and live in the new world opening before the Aurignacians. Granted, it took them thousands of years to migrate from Africa to Europe, but the inexorable move northward would have exposed them, over those centuries, to topography, climate, flora and fauna they had never experienced. Unlike the Neanderthals, whose culture made no significant changes over the 300,000 years they camped around Europe, despite swings in climate change, the Aurignacians' brain wiring and capacity for storing, rearranging and communicating memories would have allowed for an accumulation of unique and continually transforming knowledge to be passed down the generations. One of the most significant challenges would have required dealing with the well-entrenched residents. It is fascinating to speculate how the two types of humans may have influenced one another culturally. As descendants of the successful Aurignacians it is easy and simplistic to assume biological and cultural superiority. But how might the presence of these intelligent, capable people who were so similar yet so profoundly different, and who had lived successfully in this land for hundreds of thousands of years, been catalytic to the adaptability of the Aurignacians? Nowhere else on the planet did Homo sapiens encounter Neanderthals than on the route to Europe. Although there is no way to know, there may have been a highly unique spark, whether communal or combative, between the two peoples that pushed the Aurignacians to levels of creation not achieved elsewhere.

Mithen has compared the Neanderthal brain to a Swiss army knife, that is, a set of tools each designed to perform a particular function but with no crossover of adaptability from the corkscrew tool to the scissors tool. Each tool in the knife performed its function, and then was folded away to make room for the next. Aurignacians, by comparison, had brains that functioned on a 'cathedral' model, a metaphorical central nave (the aisle in a church

that runs from the front door to the altar) representing general intelligence with four surrounding chapels, each connecting to the nave; technical intelligence, linguistic intelligence, social intelligence and natural history intelligence. Other experts, however, dispute this model, believing Mithen's categories to be an example of cultural bias. Although the Neanderthals possessed the capabilities of these modules in their Swiss army toolkit, and may be said to have had a version of the cathedral intelligence model, the walls separating the nave of general intelligence from the chapels, and the chapels from each other, were solid. No doorways allowed for the free flow of information learned in one chapel to be applied to another.

Somewhere along the evolutionary road map, according to Mithen, vandals broke into the ancestral Aurignacian nave of general intelligence and kicked down the walls between the chapels. They were able to access thought processes from one module and apply it to another. Where Neanderthals understood animal behavior from the standpoint of natural history intelligence sufficiently to hunt effectively, for example, that knowledge was not extrapolated into their social sphere. But the more facile brain of the Aurignacians was able to translate the knowledge of animal behavior into a metaphor for human social interaction. Coupled with their agile language ability this new imagination allowed them to create and adapt complex stories. People could be understood to be 'like' a bison or a horse or a herd of reindeer in a variety of ways, and vice versa, which adds levels of complexity to thought in both the natural history chapel and the social intelligence chapel. The interflow of concepts and categories accelerated so that technical innovation, for example, complemented increased awareness of the environment and innovative use of resources. Better hunting capabilities and effective social interaction made for more efficient use of time, advance planning, preservation of food and more complicated patterns of food distribution, in turn prompting changes in the social network and encouraging population growth; all things Neanderthals would have certainly benefited from had they the capability. And, beyond being rational problem-solvers, the Aurignacians were artists.

The language capability and cognitive fluidity of the Aurignacians was the rising tide that floated all these boats. The metaphoric application of one kind of intelligence to another across the ever-widening general intelligence corridor by way of language

made possible the assigning of metaphoric meaning to an image that could be communicated to others. Representational art became a social force. A carving was not just a pudgy female figure. It was a symbol with much deeper significance, perhaps connecting to ideas of fertility, pregnancy, women in general and sexual potency. And where language could intellectually explain these ideas, representational art resonated emotionally. The need, desire and inspiration to carve the statuette in the first place have their origins in the flow of human emotions that channel tidally to and from the spirit world. Just as snakes specialized in crawling and fish in swimming, these modern humans specialized in imaginative and metaphorical creativity.

If Mithen's idea is correct that Neanderthals had a 'Hmmmmm' language, based on a series of holistic sets of thoughts, musical expressions and prescribed mimetic accompaniments, it is logical that their lifestyle would not have changed and could not adapt to the arrival of the Aurignacians. Language is a fluid, dynamic engine, constantly transforming itself and the definition of the world it describes. The flexibility of word coinage, word usage and grammatical building blocks make language continually adaptable. The Neanderthals lived in small familial groups, cooperating with other Neanderthals when necessary, changing little or not at all, and able to communicate enough to maintain their numbers for a very long time. Indeed, their inflexible culture, according to Mithen, would not have required that they say anything that they hadn't already said for tens of thousands of years. That is, until the Aurignacians showed up and then they were tongue-tied. This rigid cultural continuity is apparent in their Mousterian tool assemblage, which remained unchanged for almost half a million years. One generation learned to copy the techniques of the previous one and taught it to the next with little or no variation. The inability to think in novel combinations or to communicate complex metaphors, explains their parallel inability to imagine and create symbolic art.

Once the dark-skinned strangers blew into town, chirping and singing like a flock of birds and rattling their jewelry, the Neanderthals were done for. Attempting to talk to strangers who were unaware of their holistic phrases and the ancient, unchanging contexts in which they were couched, and unable to fully imitate or understand the quick-witted newcomers' words, or even the concept of words, the epic run of the Neanderthal was over. The people of the labyrinth had arrived.

the Indian gamelan, the Nez Perce drum and the Australian didgeridoo.

It is Mithen's contention that musicality was a fundamental part of Neanderthal speech and living, expressing subtleties of experience and emotion not available to them in vocabulary and diction. Imagine a Neanderthal version of whale songs. Pitch, rhythm and tone go a long way towards expressing a complete range of emotive content. Gently humming to calm a fussy baby is the antithesis of a rousing, brassy Souza march, but they are both music and both are intended to evoke a desired response in the listener. Music, like other forms of art, is manipulative.

There are songs to fit every emotional occasion; syrupy love songs, the soaring glory of "Nessun Dorma", the blood pumping "Marseillaise", and, guaranteed to bring Irishmen everywhere to tears, "Danny Boy". Country-western ballads allow us to commiserate about life gone bad over a bottle of whiskey, blues and jazz tunes take us together down sad and lonely roads strewn with lost dreams and broken hearts, and rock anthems bring 30,000 whooping people instantly to their feet with lighters (or cell phones) flaming. And that is just Western culture. Music is the 'universal language' not only between cultures, but stretching back to the dawn of humankind. Making music together is a primal bonding event, inviting people to participate in an emotional experience.

Sound is vibrating air entering the ear and jostling the tiny bones inside, which in turn prickles minute hairs that transfer information to fluid in the eardrum. This is converted into electrical impulses in the brain, what one scientist referred to as "touch at a distance". If the tones are tuneful, regular and pleasing, we feel good. But if the electrical impulses are irregular, dissonant and unfamiliar the tones we hear can make us anxious, fearful or even angry. The premiere of Stravinsky's "Rite of Spring" with the Russian Ballet is a case in point. The choreography appeared barbarous and the music sounded cacophonous to the well-heeled audience. Arguments about the aesthetics of the performance escalated, fistfights broke out and a riot ensued. The brain chemistry of the audience was literally altered by the unrelenting dissonance. Neurons in the auditory cortex were unable to find a pattern in the sounds, which elicited wild fluctuations in the audience's brains, releasing an overdosing flood of dopamine and causing a form of temporary mass schizophrenia. Yet, within a year the culture had learned to find the patterns in the music, and after repeat performances Stravinsky was lauded as a

genius. Twenty-five years later the culture had become so acclimated to the unusual sounds that "Rite of Spring" was part of the soundtrack of Disney's "Fantasia". Humans are patterns-seekers. The culture had learned to find the deep structure beneath the dissonance. Our brains work overtime to organize the unfamiliar into recognizable categories. Culture had come to terms with what biology had initially deemed chaotic. We will encounter this organizational trait again later in this chapter when we discuss the importance of hallucinations.

Musical preference validates one's identity as part of a pattern and can be waved like a flag. Examples from popular culture are endless. Elvis's sexy performances of 'race music' had white parents of the '50s in a tizzy over the breakdown of racial and sexual bastions, and their girls in a lather of libidinous joy. The Dixie Chicks announced their displeasure with fellow Texan President George Bush and irate fans burned their CDs in what they called a patriotic display. The band went on to win a Grammy award and launch the "Not Ready To Make Nice" tour. The Grateful Dead's hippie/folk persona spawned a colorful subculture of 'Deadheads' espousing leftist politics, anti-authoritarianism, drug use, tolerance and goofy fun. Politically and socially one was either 'on the bus or off it'. The parking lot of a Dead concert became a caravanserai of folk art and crafts, while inside the stadium attendees tossed marshmallows and tortillas during the break. Paul Simon introduced Americans to the beauty and joy of South African music in his "Graceland" album and an informed wider world brought an end to apartheid. The explosion of 'world beat' recordings that make available both the popular and obscure sounds from the far corners of the globe are a testament to our growing global identity and musical curiosity, as well as the universal antiquity of musical bonding.

That music evolved in part as a courtship display is a given. Crooning love songs under balconies is in our blood. Among tribesmen of Laos, who speak a tonal language, literally 'sing poetry' to their lady loves across the valleys by blowing on leaves held taut in their fingers. The tonal contours of the song represent sentence construction rather than words. An impressive song from any culture, combined with dancing that demonstrates strength, health, creativity, coordination and self-confidence will woo a partner, as every rock star worth his salt knows. A great outfit also helps. The Rolling Stones have unashamedly built an empire on not

taking raw musical lust too seriously; "It's Only Rock & Roll (But I Like It)".

Aborigines from Central Australia were born with a deep spiritual connection to the landscape, their mothers having been impregnated by the human father and the child conceived by a spirit identified with and derived from a particular area of the land. This invests the child with a distinct place in culture's spiritual ecology. The resulting ritual responsibility throughout his life is based on the place in the landscape determined to be the location of the 'spirit conception', the place where the mother first felt the quickening. One aspect of these duties is to learn songs that represent the landscape, reflecting changes in elevation, for example, in rising and falling tones. One person's song literally 'sings' the section of land he is responsible for into existence and his song ends where another's begins. The landscape is literally bound together by ceremonial maps of sacred song, referred to as 'songlines'.

Music in human society expresses and affects our deeper being. Performing and listening to sacred music is a universal experience shared by all people through which they communicate with and glorify their divinities. Gospel music, Handel's *Messiah*, and the Balinese Monkey Chant all open channels to deities. This participatory experience serves a vital purpose; as voices are lifted together to summon or praise the deities, the communal emotions of the group are bonded in a transcendent moment of unity.

One can easily imagine the Neanderthals in the center of their crystalline ring in the torch-lit cavern of Bruniquel singing and dancing as they slipped into a spiritual reverie. In a choir of any kind, one's individuality is diminished and the group is elevated. 'Harmonizing' on all levels is the goal. Individual concerns and self-identity are lost in the larger interest of 'being of one mind' with the group. There is a transcendent experience of the loss of boundaries between self and others that unites the voices, intentions and emotions into an elevated sense of cooperation. When people join in an emotional musical ritual that reifies the deep beliefs surrounding the nature of life a peak experience can occur, unparalleled in its ability to unify and endure. This unification of spirit is an essential element of human life.

PALEOLITHIC SOUNDTRACK

Although Neanderthals undoubtedly accompanied their vocals with rhythmic clapping, drumming and blowing on reeds, there is no

firm evidence of their having made musical instruments. However, keeping in mind the Jimi Hendrix analogy mentioned earlier, the Aurignacians, by comparison, arrived with a band. Flutes have been found in Germany that date to 36,000 years ago. These were made from the wing bones of swans. An even larger cache of flutes was found at the site of Isturitz in the foothills of the Pyrenees. Some are almost as old as the German flutes and others are 15,000 years younger, dating to 20,000 years ago during the Gravettian period. These were fabricated from the wing bones of vultures and, despite the fact that there are 7000 intervening years between flutes, they are made with remarkable consistency. The Aurignacians made bullroarers and probably also drums and other music makers of fibers, skin and wood that have not survived. No doubt they made mouth sounds like hooting, whooping and whistling in imitation of the animals among which they lived and to communicate over long distances. And, most interesting for our purposes, it has been discovered that they 'played' the caves by striking musically resonant stalactites, called 'lithophones', even modifying them by chipping to alter the sound they produced and often marking them with paint. Entire cavern chambers became instruments and were given voice.

A distinction must be made here to point up a Western cultural bias. We say they composed songs and made instruments because we interpret these as conscious acts. But from the hunter-gatherer perspective the inspiration for these things may well have been received through dreaming or while in a trance state. Power songs and the need for ceremonial equipment such as particular costumes or sacred objects often come to people while on shamanic journeys or vision quests, granted as gifts by spirit helpers to facilitate the journeyer's visits to the spirit realm. The 'voice' of the cave was always there, merely awaiting release. By playing the lithophones and possibly joining in with flutes, drums and song, a spiritual circuitry was completed, channeling power from spirit cave to humans, who fed it back to the spirits, each building on the other, becoming a unity of sound.

Neanderthals had the capability to make music and may well have had a musical quality and component to their speech, yet their 'Hmmmmm' language and the unchanging nature of their culture would have limited their creative capabilities as compared to the Aurignacians. Their version of 'whale songs', like their technology, may well have remained consistent for eons, unable to adapt to the

life-changes precipitated by the newcomers. The Aurignacians, however, had adaptive lyrics to lie against music in the form of song, communication that not only was evocative and manipulative of emotions, but incorporated facile metaphors as well. Backed by flutes, drums and other possible instruments, they developed an Ice Age soundtrack that united their people, not only through the shared joy of play/entertainment, but also through the ceremonial performance of sacred music. The revelation during trance of a new ceremonial song could have given rise to a new ritual to dramatize it. Introducing these messages from the Other World to the tribe could shift the cultural focus, as did the Ghost Dance revelations of Wovoka among displaced and dis-spirited Native Americans. Tattered remnants of tribes that survived the Indian Wars were revitalized by the hope Wovoka's shamanistic visions gave them, so much so that the US Government was afraid of renewed militarism and violence and outlawed any expression of the Ghost Dance religion.

Song and poetry in preliterate cultures can be extensive mnemonic devices that allow people to remember and re-narrate myths, genealogies and stories that make them a unique and cohesive group. Bards were trained for many years to remember encyclopedic musical story cycles like the Grail legends, the Homeric epics and the Mabinogian, an accomplishment that baffles the modern mind so dependent on the written word. Songs were sung for generations, passing oral libraries of ancient knowledge along to the young, who in turn, taught their children the legends of their people and how to behave in the world. The most famous examples of this are the *Iliad* and the *Odyssey*, sung for centuries as epic oral poems. Similarly, much of the structure and significant content of Paleolithic legends no doubt endured through centuries, as did the imagery painted in the caves, and both reflected their mythologies. The art in the caves, although highly consistent in many ways for eons, reflects local preferences and shifts in symbolic significance. Like later humans, they would have adapted their mythic songs to changing times to keep them vital. The Old English "Beowulf", for example, was composed around 1000 CE but the story refers to people who lived 500 years before, and folklorists agree that the elements of the story are older still. Now it has been retold once again in a 3D film giving the enduring "Beowulf" a run of over 2000 years.

METAPHOR MAKERS

The Aurignacians flexible language allowed them to situate events in time, past, present and future, and to plan accordingly. They were adept at developing innovative hunting strategies and food preservation requiring social flexibility and cohesion. They could remember and describe complex relationships between events and things and adapt language to new concepts; in short, to communicate metaphors. To render those metaphors into visual art, a nonverbal form of emotional communication shared by members of the tribe greatly expanded the complexities of their cultural expression. Ornamentation and specific clothing amplified the body and distinguished people as having particular roles, emphasizing social status and talents. As tribal populations increased, competed for territory and became more sophisticated in ancient Europe, tribal and ethnic differences would have been critical in their clothing and accessories, clearly identifying a person's origins and loyalties.

Cave art had its 'movements', although the overall consistency of the imagery is remarkable. It is notable that the more ancient Aurignacian art in Chauvet, for example, depicts a higher number of images of dangerous carnivores and non-hunted animals such as lions, rhinos and bears than does later art. Regional differences are apparent as well; Lascaux abounds in horses where Rouffignac is full of mammoths. A particular sign called an 'avian' or 'plackard-type sign', a sort of box with wings, appears in caves in the Quercy region, at Peche Merle, Cougnac and others that are chronologically close to one another. The same area also has a predominance of the 'killed man' images, paintings and engravings of partial human-like figures with straight lines through them which some interpret as spears, and others as somatic hallucinations or energy lines. The carvings of so-called 'Venus' figures usually emphasizing robust breasts, stomachs and buttocks, however, have been found from Western Europe to Lake Baikal throughout most of the Upper Paleolithic. Recently the oldest such figure was found in Germany's Hohle Fels cave and dates to the early Aurignacian, at least 35,000 years ago. The heaviest concentration dates to the Gravettian Period from 22,000 to 28,000. Later, in the Magdalenian era, the rotund figures become more detailed and conventional and some are quite slim. These variations on the themes of Paleolithic cave art indicate cultural or perhaps ethnic distinctions in the accepted mythic and symbolic narrative.

In addition, the value of portable art in Ice Age Europe as trade

items influenced economies as well as cultural connections. Trade networks were extensive and the exchange of rare and skilfully crafted items established relationships and social indebtedness, as well as promoted the communication of iconic significance, such as the 'Venus' figurines. Multiple copies of a doe giving birth carved in reindeer antler have turned up in far-flung locations in the Pyrenees. These finds indicate a shared mythic symbolism. There was obvious joy taken in the creation of beautiful objects from all manner of materials never exploited so thoroughly before the Aurignacians, including amber, marine shells, ivory and flint that prove far-reaching trade and travel. The natural world passed through their hands and emerged transformed as art.

All of this activity fed a culture boom among the Aurignacians who ultimately ran circles around the rapidly dwindling Neanderthals. Modern humans, in direct competition with the Neanderthals for desirable living space and resources, had to have been keenly aware of the inflexiblity of the beetle-browed home team and their own biological, cultural and adaptive capabilities. They used it to full advantage. The Aurignacians' creative expression implicitly and explicitly stated who they were and the Neanderthal were not; to whom they belonged, what they believed in and what they owned that the Neanderthal did not. The metaphors broadcast by art were an indispensable part of the cultural glue that held tribes together and distinguished them from others as being unique humans, particularly in the face of competition and danger, inspiring them to solidarity and victory in the original version of prehistoric flag-waving. Extended metaphors in the form of songs, stories, rituals and myths identified them and placed them firmly within their unique cultural landscape. Most profoundly, the portrayal of iconography, in the form of both portable and parietal art on cave interiors, set spiritual belief on a delineated and common path. The Neanderthal brain was just not wired to retain mental images and manipulate thoughts as could the Aurignacian and so they were unable to create metaphoric relationships between mental images and two- and three-dimensional representations. The train that is art, packing its freight of complex metaphors, carried the Aurignacians, into the future and left the Neanderthals at the station.

Theories abound regarding the nature of the relationship between the Neanderthals and the Aurignacians. They range from wife stealing, rape and peaceful intermarriage to wholesale slaughter, although no archaeological evidence has been found of a

Neanderthal murder at Aurignacian hands. Gradual absorption of Neanderthals into the gene pool is, so far, not conclusively corroborated by the presence of Neanderthal genes surviving in our DNA. Studies at this writing are not yet complete, but generally, Neanderthals are considered an evolutionary dead end. Whether they were pushed or chose to leave areas increasingly populated by Aurignacians, at some point their thin numbers would not have required much of a shove to tip over into extinction. Their disappearance is due to a complex equation only part of which is known for certain. It may have been an unquestioned assumption on the part of the Aurignacians that the world wasn't big enough for two types of humans and it was past time for the big guys to get out of Dodge. The World Series competition for hunting grounds, resources and home territory honeycombed with caves went to the away team.

Although the articulate language skills of Homo sapiens can be complex and eloquent, there are times when the defining capabilities of everyday language become inadequate to express a unique experience. A different kind of communication is required and metaphor must take over. The archaeological discoveries at Aurignacian sites are the leavings of a culture in ferment, perpetually curious and creative, dramatically meeting the needs of adaptation with continual re-invention. Beyond the burgeoning vocabulary and refinement of dynamic tool kits, there was the need to codify and express a simultaneously developing interior landscape as well, accessed by what we refer to as the world of dreaming and hallucination, that would lead to the discovery of the labyrinth as the route to other worlds.

DREAMING AND HALLUCINATION

In tandem with the evident Aurignacian cultural eruption, occurring between 40,000 and 28,000 BP, there was an exponential advancement in contact with the metaphysical. Complex burials, abundant evidence of ceremonial activity and the efflorescence of artistic creations, particularly in the depths of caves, all speak to this. What becomes apparent is Aurignacians had developed a cognizance of a spirit world that was pervasive, growing into a deep and abiding relationship to the divine. They possessed the capability to communicate experiences through the use of metaphor that were gleaned from alternate realities entered into during dreaming, or, significantly more affecting, hallucinatory trance states. Along the

continuum of consciousness, death is the ultimate altered state. It is the point at which the spirit of life leaves the body and moves from this plane of existence to another world in which to live. A new comprehension of death evident in the burials and the requisite appropriate communication with spirits through ceremony tells us that the Aurignacians opened a new religious frontier. As we shall see, this new frontier included the complex metaphor of the labyrinth.

The combination of optics and brain structure makes the experience of hallucination a common event among mammals. Increasing degrees of hallucinatory experience begin in light trance, dizziness and disorientation, and progress into deeper levels of chaos, coma and death. All ancient humans, including Neanderthals, had the same neurological and optic system we do and all humans dream. And, when subjected to any one of a variety of experiences, which we'll discuss in Chapter 8, all humans hallucinate. Hallucinations are chaotic, fairly common, largely unpredictable and wildly illogical as commonly categorized by our Western rational minds. Neanderthals dreamed and experienced altered states of consciousness, as must have happened in the stalactite circle of Bruniquel. However, evidence so far indicates that they did not have the capability for creating or communicating complex metaphors to describe such unique experiences, nor an incentive to incorporate them into their future. If they had, it would have manifested in cultural change, evidence of which is not found. The few examples we have of Neanderthal symbolic behavior show the flickering beginnings of complex ideological thought, but they cannot be considered a cultural pattern.

The Aurignacians, on the other hand, observed ritual internments of their people in much greater numbers than the Neanderthals. Significantly, burials of women indicate that females enjoyed a more equitable and prominent status in society deserving of proper care after death. The Aurignacians buried their dead with a wealth of grave goods, including tools, shells, ochre and art objects. We can infer from the significant increase of these artifacts that these items or their essences were to be somehow transported to an afterlife and used by the spirit of the deceased. Items such as ivory or shell beads that took a long time to make from materials that may have been difficult to come by, then painstakingly sewn on to elegant garments are not buried for any practical reason. For that matter, there is no practical reason to bury the dead at all, it being far easier to leave

the body to the elements. The logic here is not a practical but a spiritual one; a transfer of valued substance to another world.

The most extreme example of early, buried wealth was found at Sungir in the Ukraine. The site dates from 28,000 BP, an Eastern Gravettian culture that corresponds to the upper end of the Aurignacian period in Western Europe. This burial of an adult male directly above two children who were buried head to head contained over 13,000 ivory beads, ivory spears, painted mammoth ivory bracelets, carved animals and spoked discs. Experiments determined that the labor involved to create the strings of beads alone has been estimated at an astounding 13,000 hours, one hour per bead or about a year and a half of non-stop work for one person. This does not take into consideration the clothing these beads decorated nor all the other artifacts found in the grave. Alongside one of the children was placed part of a very robust femur packed with ocher. None of these items in the burial were of a practical nature except the clothing and ocher. Survival in the ferocious weather of northern Ice Age Europe would have made warm and well-made clothing imperative. The symbolic significance, both social and religious, involved in manufacturing thousands of beads and then burying them with the dead apparently was well worth the time devoted to creating them. These loved ones were to enter the next world in a resplendent state.

Neanderthals were unable to make the same degree of metaphoric leap that there were other forms of existence, other worlds of spirit that coexisted with or paralleled their own, except in infrequent and tentative ways. For the Aurignacians, however, the intensity and strangeness of the experience encountered while in an altered state demanded that they define its nature within a social context, and codify mutually agreed-upon appropriate behaviors with which to respond to the experience. When something bizarre happens, our first impulse after checking for injuries is to ask 'what WAS that?' Just as the audience for Stravinski's 'Rite of Spring' needed to literally wrap their heads around the apparently dissonant music to find order, so the Aurignacians needed to somehow comprehend the bizarre reality of the hallucinatory world of spontaneous trance. Metaphor assembles a meaningful pattern from chaos. Humans can, through the imaginative application of metaphoric thinking, resolve unfamiliar or just plain strange experiences that do not conform to the normality of waking consciousness. Then connect them up with other threads of their lives to produce a cohesive and productive vision. Accepted by the tribe, a new vision can become a culturally

transforming event.

A foraging Neanderthal may have eaten the wrong mushroom and spent a peculiar afternoon. He may have told others about the experience. But they had no capacity to literally divine what had happened nor incorporate into their culture in any lasting way. An Aurignacian would have remembered what he ate, where he found it, taken some home, dried and saved it for another time, made up a story about it, and would have consulted with spiritual specialists, experienced voyagers themselves, to determine the significance of the hallucinatory journey he'd had, and whether or not he should do it again. Spontaneous hallucinatory states were cultivated, became practiced and increasingly familiar. Their weird terrains were visited and revisited and relationships developed between humans and the denizens of Other Worlds. Networks of spiritual metaphor became the Ariadne's thread, or rather a web, which bound up the multiple worlds of waking and dreaming into a cohesive responsive universe.

The unbidden revelation of a symbol-laden dreamscape, emerging spontaneously from the unconscious depths while in an altered state defies simplistic definition. This is the very foundation of mythic creation. The elements of the vision can all be described. What escapes us, and our facile language, is discovering the significance and connectivity in an overwhelming cascade of experience. Similarly, a deeply affecting dream must be translated on its own terms, through the symbolism of the elements and not conscious understanding. The logic of a revelation defies the logic of consciousness. The true communication of these emotions, the sense of having been touched by the ineffable requires symbolic language.

Representational art, stories, songs and dances are all vehicles for metaphor and therefore, for myth; for communicating and remembering a pivotal event experienced outside the boundaries of normal, waking life. This emotionally charged experience appears to come from another world, a world so indescribably powerful that it undeniably informs and transforms the everyday world. It is the raw stuff of the creative principle, the artistic urge to give form to chaotic experience, that separated us from the Neanderthals. The realization of the inevitable touch of death led the first person to seek out the wall of a labyrinthine cavern, a place where spirits dwell, and communicate with them through the ritual creation of art and so be assured of life's continuance. That person drew a spirit animal, a symbol evocative of an ineffable experience, and laid a

hand on it.

THE ARC OF DEATH

Somewhere, along the arc of human experience, Death appeared. It had of course, always been there, but had never had a name. Long ago, a sentient creature sat by the side of a child, a mate or friend and watched helplessly as the light passed from their loved-one's eyes. In that moment the creature knew he too would do the same one day, as would all creatures on the earth. A chasm of loss and suffering opened, never to be closed again, and one he must express.

We are defined by limitation, the edges of life. Death draws a final ring around life and it is within that line we come to understand ourselves and to define our world. It is the ultimate Transformation. How we cross through that membrane at the border of life and what we meet on the other side has determined the shape of human cultures the world over. Its inevitability is absolute. How do we define the essence of ourselves that makes that journey? How is that entity to survive in its new existence? What shape the Otherworld takes, who or what resides there and how we, once translated to spirit, relate to it all, determine the direction of our lives on this plane. The hinges of belief open different doors for different cultures. Whether it is the Rapture, a reuniting with the Ancestors, an eternity in paradise among a field of stars, hellfire and brimstone, or a karmic slingshot, how we face down Death gives form to our lives. Knowing we will die, knowing people we love more than life will die, makes it imperative that an agreement exists between this world and the next. The Otherworld is what it is and will not change. The onus is ours to define our beliefs and reach through that veil with the appropriate offering. For the Neanderthal, the bridge between this world and the next was built with crystalline circles of stalactites and the bones of animals. The Aurignacians cut the ribbon on a new design entirely and opened a bridge made of dreams, music, visions, ritual and art. The traffic between the worlds has been heavy ever since.

If we are to understand the grip that the symbol of the labyrinth has had on humankind for millennia, we must explore two very ancient interrelated subjects; altered states of consciousness and shamanism. Both paths illuminate another circuit of our labyrinthine journey, into the inner workings of the human brain; the darker twists and turns required to reach the paradox of the life/death interface at the Center.

Gabilliou

Tro s Frères

Trois Frères

Chauvet

CHAPTER 7

THE LONG TRIP

*"People believe what they want to believe. They find meaning where
they can. In the
end, it doesn't matter...what matters is they believe."*
Steven Spielberg's **Taken**

*"And all should cry, Beware! Beware!
His flashing eyes, his floating hair!
Weave a circle round him thrice,
And close your eyes with holy dread,
For he on honey-dew hath fed,
And drunk the milk of Paradise"*
Samuel Taylor Coleridge, **Kubla Khan**

*"If ya wanna be a bird it won't take much to get you up there...
When you come down,
land on your feet..."*
The Byrds

CONSCIOUSNESS SPECTRUM

The labyrinth is paradoxically, both a cause of one's state of mind becoming altered and an indication that one's consciousness is altered. The one leads to a deeper version of itself. A labyrinth walker notices after a relatively short time that the rhythmic movement through the pattern of swinging back and forth induces a peaceful reverie. But once one enters into a deeper state of trance, the internal labyrinth that is hard-wired into our mammalian brain appears and opens up a pathway to alternate realities. Pursuing deep altered states of consciousness is a normal fact of life in traditional societies as a way of accessing important information. Our tradition, on the other hand, has placed such emphasis on rationality and emotional control as to dismiss the regular pursuit and expression of

ecstatic states as unbalanced or even demented. This attitude is shifting however, as more is understood about the human brain.

We labor under the misconception that consciousness is a one-dimensional condition interrupted by periods of sleep, except for those rare occasions when one is laid out by a linebacker, or falls off a ladder. But in recent years brain research has revealed human consciousness to be a delicate and fluid system of apprehension, dramatically affected by something as simple as dappled light or a Mozart concerto. Our brain shifts gears constantly as the following demonstrates.

The average office-worker is roused from a sound sleep by a blaring alarm clock and her brain waves leap from a deep sleep pattern to groggy consciousness. She hits the snooze alarm and dozes, fragments of dreams floating through her head; there was something about a roomful of computers with big red lips breaking into song … Her five minutes are up, the alarm rings again, her body temperature rises and she stumbles out of bed. A shower and blow-dry help bring her around to full wakefulness, reinforced by a cup of caffeinated coffee, sugary cereal and the intrusion of the outside world in the form of grim daily news and disappointment that her favorite team has lost again. Buckled into her car and singing along with a raunchy Stones song on the radio, she fires up the engine and shifts into Freeway Warrior Mode, juggling a cell phone, lipstick, heavy traffic, anticipations of the day ahead and a travel mug of more coffee. A little anxious and late for work, she crowds into the elevator to begin the hyperactivity of stressful problem-solving crammed with conversation, ringing phones and deadlines.

By mid-morning, she stares out the window and slips into daydreaming of the romantic weekend ahead, oblivious to the supervisor standing by her desk with arms folded. The ensuing confrontation regarding her apparent lack of focus raises her blood pressure, heart rate and body temperature and heightens awareness in a classic fight-or-flight attitude. She briefly, but vividly, imagines that her boss will one day die screaming. The residual shame at seeing the other cubicle-dwellers trying to look like they weren't listening, the antagonism, tension and anger stay in the back of our office worker's mind while she works to meet the approaching deadline. She eats a fast-food lunch at her desk that leaves her stomach in a knot, while she carves small canyons through the mountain of work. She escapes briefly to a vending machine for a

high-sugar chocolate bar and a pick-me-up double latté.

After work, she fights frustration and traffic to get to the gym for a strenuous workout, while she chews over the events of the day, followed by a relaxing soak in the Jacuzzi. She finally begins to put the tensions aside. She meets her date for dinner and, over a bottle of wine, they plan their weekend getaway, which got her in trouble earlier in the day. After a romantic interlude at her apartment that keeps her up much later than she planned, she takes a sleeping pill and falls exhausted into bed where she has disconnected dreams about finding herself at work in her lingerie.

What our office worker demonstrates, besides the need to consider some lifestyle changes, is that there is really no such thing as a "normal" state of mind. It should come as no surprise that our mental state, our moods, our ability to think clearly, and what we think about are all affected by our physical condition and our environment. The mind-body dichotomy is constantly changing in response to degrees of both internal and external stimuli. Alternative states of consciousness are a normal part of every day. Stress, orgasm, affection, frustration, fear and other emotions alter our brain and body chemistry to prepare us to meet life's fluctuating conditions. Bear in mind that we, as modern industrial-world dwellers, are still only inches from the goal line following that 95-yard drive through dangerous hunter-gatherer territory.

Foods, like coffee, black tea, bananas, alcohol, and even chocolate change the way we feel and think. Add experiences out of the normal range of daily activity, and the list of neuropsychological variants becomes quite long; stroke, stress, intense pain, severe cold or heat, starvation, ingestion of psychedelic and narcotic drugs, sensory deprivation, fever, schizophrenia, depression, and blood loss to name a few.

Consciousness and unconsciousness then, are not two sides of a coin, like a light switch that is either on or off. Rather, they are at opposite ends of a continuum, one end being hyper-alertness and the opposite, deep trance, coma and death. Along the way from one end of this continuum to the other, consciousness shifts in a gradual spectrum of varying degrees and types of awareness that blend one into another. This consciousness continuum is the result of the hardware in our brains and the way our nervous system functions in response to stimulation or the lack of it. Our survival as a species depends on fast action and alert thinking, but also on reflection and cogitation. We need to play, cry, dream and get angry all as part of

121

being a healthy human.

To explain these daily ups and downs, colorful symbolic language has been created; we're frantic, psyched, torqued or hysterical, a-twitter, hot and bothered or have our hair on fire. We may be drained, beaten, wiped, spaced, whipped, burned out or somewhere in-between, chilling and kicked back. But it is the far end of this spectrum of consciousness that defies easy definition, the ultraviolet range in the palette of consciousness marked by hallucinations and visions. For that we require a special vocabulary that reaches beyond mere words to metaphor. Our Paleolithic ancestors were the first to comprehend this and to construct the cognitive pathways we continue to follow. In the next chapter we'll look at what neurological research has shown to happen to the brain while in a trance state, for while many things separate us from our Ice Age ancestors, our brain functions and nervous systems are not among them. This biological structure is the hardwiring of the labyrinth. But first we need to take a brief excursion into the social history that encouraged this research and challenged our biases.

ALTERED STATES

Throughout human history people have entered into trance states spontaneously while ill, or purposely by ingesting psychotropic plants or participating in trance-inducing activities. Some have argued that the desire for psychoactive substances is a genetically inherited trait, similar to hunger and sex. In fact, there are receptors in the brain for opiates and other psychoactive compounds. Ethnobotanist Robert Evan Schultes wrote, "few areas of the globe lack at least one hallucinogen of significance in the culture of its inhabitants." Hunting and gathering economies require the people to investigate the potential for every plant to be edible or useful medicinally. A wider definition of 'medicinal' includes those plants that facilitate contact with the spirits.

While browsing through a meadow, the Aurignacian (or possibly Neanderthal) that discovered the opium poppy, hit on a bonanza. Its leaves can be eaten like a salad and the oil-rich seeds are highly nutritious as a fat source. But it is best known for its medicinal properties that are many and varied; as a soporific, to treat diarrhea, and relieve anxiety caused by pain. But opium is one of the few Old World plants that induce euphoria and hallucinations, and an overdose can cause death. This indeed, was a valuable addition to the larder.

122

The discovery of controlled fermentation allowed people to preserve foods in new and interesting ways like cheese but also alcoholic drinks that extended the definition of 'medicinal plants'. The earliest surviving recipe for an ancient version of beer made from a fermented grain cake was in the form of a prayer to the goddess Inanna written on a clay tablet found in Mesopotamia. Modern brew masters resurrected the ancient drink and announced it to have a dense, chewy flavor but it lacked 'legs', suggesting that it had to have been drunk in a relatively short time before going bad. Images from 2000 BC show men sitting around large bronze vessels with long straws indulging in the beer. In one legend, Enki, the god of wisdom, entertained the seductive goddess Inanna with copious amounts of beer. Enki, not so wise after a few toasts, gives to Inanna the power over the attributes of civilization and knowledge including high priesthood, the throne of kingship, the In all, the tanked god gives her eighty essential powers, loads them in the Boat of Heaven and cheerfully sees her off, only to later realize his drunken stupidity in a fit of remorse when he sobers up. Seemed like a good idea at the time.

Wine residue has been retrieved from jugs in the land of Caanan, modern Syria-Palestine, thought to be the point of origin of wine during the Bronze Age. Herodotus reported on the Scythians' use of marijuana, burned in braziers in their tents, that made them howl like animals. Hallucinogens such as Thorne Apple, Mandrake and Belladonna were used in Europe in the practices of witchcraft and divination. Brandywine was cooked up and drunk in the Middle Ages. A Dutchman invented gin in the mid-1600s, originally intending it as a kidney medicine. Cheap, easy to make and more hygienic than drinking polluted city water, gin soon became the scourge of the poor, ravaging slum dwellers. Higher-class establishments served 'Pink Gin", a better quality distillation, mixed it with the digestive angostura to give birth to the cocktail. Intentionally or not, people throughout history have been altering their consciousness and trying to come to terms with the results.

At the end of the 19th century the experience of the trance state fell under the gaze of emerging Western scientific investigation. Opium was legal in Europe and America and often prescribed by doctors to cure an assortment of illnesses. A German pharmacist isolated the morphine alkaloid in 1803, the first discovered, and a milestone of biochemistry. Unfortunately, it also set the wheels in motion for what would become a worldwide plague of drug abuse

123

and addiction to a variety of opiates. The coincidental discovery of heroin and the introduction of the hypodermic syringe in the late 19th century escalated the problem exponentially. Abuse of laudanum, a tincture of opium and alcohol, became common. A draught of opium allegedly prompted Coleridge's famous poem, "Kubla Khan", a visionary journey into alternate reality. The entire poem came to him in a moment of transcendent inspiration, but was famously cut short by the intrusion of a caller at his door. Cocaine was originally considered a wonder drug and was a valued ingredient in many household remedies, along with opium. Europe was awash in mind-altering drugs but understanding the mechanics of addiction and brain chemistry was more than a century away.

NORMAL OR NOT

Reports on the use of hallucinogens had popped up in travel diaries and histories for centuries. Classical literature was rife with such references; beginning with Homer's Lotus Eaters and the krater of opium-laced wine Helen served to Menelaus, Pisitratus and Telemachus to help them forget their sorrows. There were chronicles written by the Spanish Catholic invaders about the Native American peoples' use of trance-inducing plants. The Victorian fascination with exotica fueled expeditions that sent doughty Englishmen abroad with diaries and scientific apparatus to take the measure of the world and bring pieces of it back for display, including the occasional miserable native. Intrepid American adventurers tramped off to remote corners of the globe returning with accounts of amazing people untouched by Western cultural blight. These included startling reports of shamanic magico-religious displays often involving the ingestion of hallucinogenic plants that strained the imaginations and credibility of an audience of readers raised in the staid confines of Christian churches.

But these reports were fascinating and reported by sober, reliable people in their fields, the first ethnographers who endeavored to record their observations of unfamiliar cultures relatively free of bias. An ethnography of Siberian tribes published in 1905 reported on the Amanita Muscaria, or fly agaric mushroom, the classic fairy tale mushroom with the red cap and white spots, and its use as an intoxicant. A 1916 article published in the Smithsonian Institution's Annual Report examined the mind-altering pharmacy of the Native Americans, including mescal beans and datura.

Questions arose as to the nature of the mind-altering experience

itself. The grip on hide-bound assumptions of what constituted 'normality' and 'rationality' began to slip. Those experiences that had been banished to the madhouse with white-gloved alacrity were sneaking back to be reconsidered as worthy of study and consideration. William James, well respected Harvard professor and author of *Varieties of Religious Experience*, suggested that normal consciousness, as it was understood in his time, kept company with entirely different forms of consciousness and was separated from them by the "filmiest of screens". To understand the universe in its entirety, they could not be disregarded. The physician Weir Mitchell took mescaline in 1898 and reported that he saw "delicate floating films of color... then an abrupt rush of countless points of white light swept across the field of view, as if the unseen millions of the Milky Way were to flow a sparkling river before the eye." He sent peyote to William James who failed to share his visions of another reality and just spent 24 hours being very sick.

Other researchers however, described visions they had seen with their eyes open as resembling "wallpaper designs, cobweb-like figures or concentric circles and squares", and "a kaleidoscopic play of ornaments, patterns, crystals, and prisms, which creates the impression of a never-ending uniformity". These men were inducing visions and experiences that had, in their culture, been the peculiar attribute of the mentally ill. Yet, they were finding them powerfully beautiful and transformative, begging the question, what constitutes madness and what enlightenment? Cultural and scientific assumptions were fraying. What was it about these substances that could so fully and completely replace one's reality with another never before imagined?

'Primitive' people were reported to be capable of magical healing, displays of telekinesis and extra-sensory perception, as well as shamanic trickery worthy of David Copperfield, but with far fewer props. This provoked questions about the limits of cultural and religious bias that probed at the heart of racism. Now that early ethnographers had evolved to conceive that non-Christians could be worthy of respect as humans, even if perhaps they didn't possess souls, they could begin to frame questions about human-kind in a broader sense. Fledgling ethnographers and evolutionists tried to define what culture was, and if we're so wildly different from the Hottentots or the Altai, what makes us all humans together? How much of who we are is biology and how much is environment? What goes on in our big Homo sapien brains?

CHEMICAL ADDITIVES

While the whole of Europe buttoned down for the Second World War, a Swiss expert in the chemistry of medicinal plants working at the Sandoz laboratory named Albert Hofmann began research on a hallucinatory poisoning caused by the fungus ergot of rye that attacks the grain. He'd read mysterious reports of St. Anthony's Fire, a peculiar sickness, which struck entire towns of unsuspecting villagers in the Middle Ages. Unaware of the danger, or possibly too hungry to care, they ate bread made from infested flour and suffered mass hallucinations, gangrene and death. Even the dogs and chickens went mad. Hofmann was exploring the possible chemistry behind the madness and synthesized one of the ingredients of the organic base of ergot, lysergic acid. The twenty-fifth version, lysergic acid diethylamide, or LSD-25, was particularly full of surprises. Interrupted in his normally assiduous work, he accidentally ingested a minute amount, began to feel peculiar and went home for the day to lie down. He reported that he

> *"sank into a not unpleasant intoxicated-like condition, characterized by an extremely stimulated imagination. In a dreamlike state, with eyes closed… I perceived an uninterrupted stream of fantastic colors."*

A few days later he continued his research and purposely ingested more LSD. The resulting dizziness, anxiety, visual distortions and uncontrollable laughter made it impossible for him to continue taking notes. He asked his assistant to take him home. The simple bicycle ride home and the rest of the day became, to Hofmann, epic. Glowing geometric patterns loomed at him from the corners of his room and simple, everyday sounds sparked vivid images. His neighbor lady, delivering milk, became a malevolent witch. His ego dissolved and he traveled outside his body. He thought he was dying, or at the very least, going mad. And his wife and children were due home soon. Later he was to describe his experience with LSD as "deeply religious". He had taken the first mind-blazing psychedelic LSD trip.

Initially, LSD was used as an investigative tool in psychological research and to treat alcoholics. Research scientists and psychologists wired patients and volunteers to monitoring machinery and observed their brainwaves. Psychiatry was using LSD to study psychosis and schizophrenia. But the wow factor of acid quickly moved it from the lab to the living room. The poet Allan Ginsberg, fascinated with the inner workings of

consciousness, played lab rat at the Mental Research Institute in Palo Alto, California in 1959. He shared a fascination for the effects of mind-altering drugs with Timothy Leary, then a Harvard professor and they continued their own unofficial investigations of consciousness-expanding experiences with a supply of both LSD and synthesized psilocybin from the Sandoz lab. Meanwhile, friend, author and fellow consciousness-voyager, William Burroughs was on a trek through the Amazon in search of a visionary vine called yagé. It was a matter of very little time before psychedelics became part of the fringy Beat scene that already included amphetamines, Benzedrine, alcohol, marijuana, heroin, and lots and lots of coffee. The post-WW2 Lost Generation was bent on finding itself a world that was not of their parents' making. The jazz and gritty literature emerging from the smoke-filled apartments of Greenwich Village that broke music and language into elemental, searing fragments, said that the view from here was very different.

Aldous Huxley, a highly respected literary figure of his day and son of the brilliant and open-minded Thomas Huxley, experimented with mind-altering drugs and, in 1954 wrote *The Doors of Perception*, an exploration of 'the antipodes of the mind', as a popular opening volley in what would become an on-going scientific and moral battle over the place of consciousness-altering substances in science and religion that shows no sign of abating today.

In May of 1957, copies of Life magazine, famous for its full-page photos and Rockwellian-American stories landed in mailboxes across the country. Inside was an article by banker and amateur mycologist, Gregory Wasson entitled *Seeking the Magic Mushroom*, an account of his transforming experiences under the influence of psilocybin in Mexico. The cat was very much out of the bag and roaming loose in the living rooms of suburbia. 1959 saw the publication of Andrija Puharich's book *The Sacred Mushroom* that made a case for the mystical element 'soma' in the ancient Indian epic, the "Rig Veda" to have been the Amanita Muscaria mushroom. Leary, along with Harvard colleagues Richard Alpert (later adopting the identity of Ram Dass) and Ralph Metzner composed a guidebook, a responsible and safe itinerary for an LSD trip in which, 'set' and 'setting' were paramount; always have a sober friend along and be in a peaceful place. It was called *The Psychedelic Experience: A Manual Based on the Tibetan Book of the Dead*. In Victorian times, access to exotic texts like the "Rig

Veda" or" Book of the Dead" required a four-year journey at great personal risk and expense to the headwaters of the Ganges or the heights of Shangri La and an interpreter of exotic languages. But thanks to intrepid adventurers, these, and other heady volumes, were available in the '60s at your local college bookstore.

The British military conducted investigations into the effects of LSD on their troops, who knowingly participated. In a video now available on You-Tube, the gradual disintegration of military discipline into uncontrolled laughter and disorientation is narrated by a stuffy newsreel voice. One soldier is shown climbing a tree to 'feed the birds', another hopelessly tosses his earphones into the brush, and the commander, collapsing in hysterics, declares that he can no longer control his troops or himself. Here was a potentially valuable weapon.

The inevitable cultural collision began in a more sinister way when operatives from the CIA approached the Sandoz Laboratory about buying quantities of LSD. Although Hofmann said he "perfected LSD for medicinal use, not as a weapon" Sandoz sold the CIA acid and reported to them who else was ordering it. It was, in fact, a well-financed military operation for which Ginsberg had volunteered at the Mental Research Institute. The involvement of the CIA in hallucinogenic drug research runs the gamut from shameful to bizarre. Hundreds of soldiers were unwittingly given drugs and suicides resulted from these covert operations, one young man throwing himself out of a window. The proposal to surreptitiously test mind-altering gases on unsuspecting subway riders finally raised a red flag among some sensible members of the brass. Still, by 1970, LSD was classified as a drug of abuse with no medicinal value. Psychologists and research scientists who had spent years using it responsibly as a research tool were out of business. But others were just setting up shop.

WHAT WAS THAT?

Back in California, Ken Kesey and friends were doing their own experimenting. A rabble of artists and friends formed "The Merry Pranksters" and, with musical accompaniment by the "Grateful Dead", began to have parties – gigantic parties involving hundreds of people, balloons, bubbles, toys, body paint and vats of Kool Aid laced with still-legal LSD. The playful slippage of reality during a personal psychedelic trip became a collective cascade at the Kool Aid Acid Tests, and then a goofy cultural landslide. The anti-war,

anti-establishment hippies blossomed out of the sidewalks of San Francisco, flouting every convention imaginable. The run-down neighborhood of old Victorian houses and little shops near the corner of Haight and Ashbury streets transformed overnight. Buildings were painted in wild colors, their square corners rounded with bursts of blossoms. Young people wore shoes of different colors and dressed in tribal attire, dripping in beads and feathers like their Paleolithic ancestors. The Free Store gave away everything on their shelves, once even setting out a fishbowl full of dollar bills marked 'free money' just to see what would happen, deeply conflicting and confusing the little old ladies who wandered in from the impoverished Mission District. The Diggers gave away free food. Music, marijuana, and incense were everywhere. A pagan irreverence and devotion to the simple joy of fun exploded. Photos of longhaired shirtless young men changing the Haight street sign to 'Love', and interracial and gay couples out in the open rattled parents to their cores. Terrified, self-described responsible citizens drove through the area with their car doors locked to observe the children as if they were on a tour of the Serengeti. Freedom from, and for everything, reigned and questioning authority, the architects of war and bigotry, was a commitment. The pursuit of happiness had become high art.

The art world itself began to play with the optics of color and line with the intention of purposely jangling the normal perception process and bending reality into new and impossible forms. Victor Vasarely manipulated colors and shapes to create chromatic tension that caused the eye to see flickers and pulsations in the picture itself. Bridget Riley laid vertical lines together to create optical illusions of movement and depth. Dubbed "Op Art", for optic, it was soon snatched up by the fashion world, to Ms. Riley's dismay, and people wore clothing that made them almost difficult to look at. Combined with black lights and psychedelic music, dancing bodies transformed into art objects that deceived the eye. Posters drenched in psychedelic colors and patterns pulsed on the walls of dorm rooms, record labels and MC Escher, having reached the pinnacle of his fame in the '50s, enjoyed a resurgence. The mathematical perfection of his drawings, coupled with the discovery of the one-sided surface of visual impossibility called the Möbius Strip resulted in precise fantastical architecture that defied the eye. Hallways, arches and staircases came and went in all directions and made visual sense when seen from every dimension.

But the visual art form most closely associated with the San Francisco psychedelic era was the concert poster, originally designed to advertise shows at the Fillmore Auditorium and Avalon Ballroom. Emerging from the influence of the organic forms of Alphonse Mucha's Art Nouveau, hippie graphic artists took organic to a whole new level. Images were made of letters and vice-versa. The chromatic tensions perfected by Victor Vasarely exploded off the page. Sensuous lettering dripped and ran, became clouds, breasts, smoke or anything else the artists could think of. It became a game in itself to create a beautiful swirl of advertising information that was virtually illegible and made the reader's eyes cross trying to figure it out. Toying with the optical nerve and the nature of what constitutes reality, as we shall see, was inspired by the avid pursuit of altered states.

The weekly concerts at the Fillmore Auditorium and the Winterland Ballroom were designated sensory-overload experiences and unabashed ecstatic feasts. Music of all kinds, from the gospel of the Edwin Hawkins Singers, the blues of BB King, Chuck Berry's old rock 'n' roll and the delirious psychedelic swirl of The Grateful Dead and the Jefferson Airplane pounded an equally delirious audience for hours. Anthems of the era seeped into the crowd on a cellular level and a mystical bonding seized hearts and minds as John Fogarty sang "I ain't no military son" and Grace Slick let loose a sonic blast of "up against the wall Motherf*ckers!" Psychedelic drug use was common and open and the haze of marijuana smoke filled the air. Giant spotted balloons bounced around the crowd and the occasional unlit joint sailed overhead. Light shows of squishy amoeba-like blobs filled the entire stage wall, pulsing in time to the music, mimicking the visual overlay of psychedelic hallucinations. Tolerance for everyone and their 'trip' was the moral code, unless someone crossed the line into belligerence, which rarely happened. People of all colors and backgrounds attended in droves, blissed out and swept up in the psychedelic swirl, dancing in amorphous groups on the edge of the crowd in granny dresses and fringes, swooping in dervish arcs, or pulsing in place like the light show. Collective transport to a group altered state became ritualistic for many. If the chemistry (in a variety of ways) was right, the tireless Grateful Dead in particular, would play most of the night. On your way out, the delightful alleged security guard flashed a huge smile, handed you a psychedelic poster for next week's gathering and said, "have a lovely, lovely day children!"

The spasm of lighthearted play in the Haight Ashbury neighborhood lasted about a year before collapsing into itself like a pile of cotton candy in the rain. Once "If You're Going To San Francisco Wear Some Flowers in Your Hair" hit the airwaves advertising 'the summer of love' it was all over. The idealistic and completely impractical conversion from capitalism to barter was spotty at best, and reality set in. Aimless kids with no plan, no money and no street smarts, flooded the sidewalks, as did wilier denizens to prey off them. Social services were swamped and city officials pleaded nationwide for kids to stop coming to San Francisco. Marijuana and psychedelics found themselves in the company of the darker companions of heroin and opium. Daily drug reports from the Free Clinic in the Haight went out over the airwaves of KSAN radio, warning of alleged psychedelics for sale on the street that were laced with Drano and rat poison. The specter of drug abuse fleshed out and grew fat in the Haight and madness, addiction, violence and death attended. Overburdened city officials and police cracked down.

The fragile, wilting Flower Power movement ran smack into the ugly realities of the Viet Nam War and the deadly serious Civil Rights era. At San Francisco State, across the bay in Berkeley and across the country campus riots against the Viet Nam War and Nixonian America, reflective of a discredited authority structure, exploded and inner-city ghettos from Watts to Cleveland bursting into flames. The brief flirtation with flowers and love was at an end.

Yet during its brief efflorescence, the Hippie movement along with the anti-war, Civil Rights, and Women's movements, broke open the staid hypocrisy of the '50s post-war world and laid the groundwork for significant social and cultural change. "Getting real", being honest about one's life, identity and feelings were vital to a population that had grown up in 'ticky-tacky' tract housing with the perfect families of Leave It To Beaver, Father Knows Best, and Ozzie and Harriet as impossible role models. On TV, mom stayed home, wore frilly aprons, vacuumed in her pearls and high heels, and was a sober, sensible and loving person. The worst thing that could happen to her was to get drummed out of the PTA. Dad wore suits, went to work in an office and was always mildly befuddled, but sincere and by the end of the show, always right. The children were cute little rascals who got in trouble for borrowing the car for the school car wash without asking.

The realities were much darker. Betty Friedan's "Feminine

Mystique" set fire to the assumption that women should be satisfied modeling the cardboard cutout persona of Mrs. Cleaver. The cultural divide between young and old, between those who had experienced mind-altering drugs versus drinking alcohol, became a chasm and, not trusting anyone over 30 was the rally cry of the young. Families split over questions of interracial dating, sexual orientation and opinions about the war. Parents laid down the law, affixed "America; Love it or Leave It" bumper stickers to their cars, and tore their hair out over their kids' music, clothes and lack of discipline. The kids, the antitheses of the Nelson boys, grew their hair long as symbolic freak flags, began to speak a different language, took drugs and went out of their way to point out the hypocrisy of their parents' lives. Young men were terrified of being sent to die in the jungles of Southeast Asia, sacrificed on the altar of what they saw as a lethal, failed ideology. Amphetamines and Nembutal, among others, although prescription drugs, were not restricted and could be had for the asking. Mom, dad and their friends drank a lot, and the culture of prescription drugs, booze and cigarettes was enshrined in film and song. News anchors smoked on television and singer Dean Martin based his public persona, in part, on the wink-and-nudge joke of alcoholism. How was marijuana any worse? In fact, it was better for you. Nobody ever got into a bar fight because he was stoned. The tidy ranch-style homes of America with the neat lawns out front were, behind closed doors, culture war zones and the thin veneer of respectability and familial bliss shattered. The bedrock American home wasn't at all what it appeared to be. Tectonic cultural movements opened chasms in fundamental beliefs in religion, government, and social mores.

A final blow of realization landed on the nation's jaw when large numbers of our soldiers returned from Viet Nam addicted to drugs. Cheap opium and heroin could be bought widely in Southeast Asia and making addiction easy for American soldiers was another weapon in the Viet Cong arsenal. Alcohol was everywhere in large quantities and stopping in to toss back a few, after a napalm strike, was a nerve-steadying requirement for many. Cartons of cigarettes were handed out by the truckload to our troops, provided by 'benevolent' tobacco companies. TV news reported on the wide-open use of marijuana, showing a stoned soldier in the jungle blowing pot smoke down the barrel of his shotgun at the camera, to the horror of families and politicians who saw the wheels coming off the war. Treatment for newly designated Post Traumatic Stress

Disorder quite often included detox programs. Air America, the CIA owned and operated airline, was shipping drugs out of Laos. Corruption was endemic and could not be ignored.

PURSUIT OF ECSTACY

For their 'up by the bootstrap', parents who had survived the miseries of the war years and the Great Depression, this rebellion of long-haired youth smacked of self-indulgence and air-headed philosophy. In many ways it was. But it was also a striving toward a new understanding of humanity in an affluent, post-war, nuclear-powered world on the verge of becoming a global community. The pursuit of ecstasy tried to address a deep emotional and spiritual hunger exposed by the fissures of cultural upheaval.

The 1961 a publication of Robert A. Heinlein's *Stranger in a Strange Land* introduced the verb 'to grok'; a type of understanding that implies intimate and exhaustive knowledge on a par with revelation that goes beyond mere learning; to grok is to have entered the world-view and spirit of the language and the experience has transformed one fundamentally. Profound and instantaneous insight, a hallmark of ecstasy, became the goal. Like many epiphanies of the young, it was idealistic and simplistic. But energy, drive and an often blessedly innocent sense of 'why not?' powered the social transformation the media dubbed 'Youthquake' and eventually brought along significant numbers of their elders. A new reverence for the earth emerged and environmental issues came to the fore. Young people gave up their urban comforts and moved to organic communes to be closer to the Earth's rhythms, natural food and explore dimensions of relationship. Music and the arts transformed, broken into prismatics and reassembled in new ways by the psychedelic vision. Hendrix, Joplin, the Dead, Led Zeppelin and others revisited traditional blues and folk with a whole new attitude. The Beatles as their alter egos in colorful satin band uniforms unleashed "Sergeant Pepper" during the summer of love in the Haight and the fire bombing in the black ghettos. "Hair", the anti-war hippie musical, was a sensation. The rediscovery of eastern religions, explored in part as a healthier alternative to drug use, and spurred by the questionably sanctimonious Maharishi Mahesh Yogi and his band of famous followers, challenged conventional attitudes and traditional religion that didn't speak to the validity of altered states of being. Yoga classes sprouted like weeds and the "Baghavad Gita", "Rig Veda" and "Kama Sutra" enjoyed resurgence. Eastern

medicine challenged the AMA as acupuncture and herbal treatments were explored as valid medical alternatives. Biofeedback introduced people to interactive control of their brain waves. And those people who didn't get it, who stood on the sidelines of this ecstatic, paisley culture surge with their hands in the pockets of their overalls, were derisively called 'Neanderthals'.

This pursuit and experience of ecstatic states served at least one larger purpose in the midst of all the social foment and was a catalyst to this end; that, as the consequence of universal human biology, altered states cut across assumed social barriers of race, gender, generation, religion and class and from past to future. The dissolving of social categories into the transcendent 'we are all one' made traditional boundaries petty and unenlightened by comparison. Provocative questions regarding the universality of the human spiritual experience were examined as never before. *The Tibetan Book of the Dead* and the Egyptian version as well, were examined. Sufi wisdom enjoyed a late bloom. The wisdom of the ancients was recognized as such, and not as the quaint notions of an archaic people. That these voices from the deep past held meaning, like a calm and steady hand in the midst of social turmoil, was enlightenment itself.

ENTER SHAMANISM

Carlos Castaneda, allegedly an Anthropology Grad student, was looking for a project. Taking his smarty-pants grad student attitude with him, he claimed to have met up with a Yaqui shaman named Juan Matus to study ethnobotany, the intersection of plant use and culture. The resulting psycho-spiritual butt-kicking that Castaneda reportedly endured at the hands of a brujo, a shaman adept in the use of psychotropic plants, was immortalized in "The Teachings of Don Juan; a Yaqui Way of Knowledge". In the first of a series of books Castaneda portrayed Don Juan as using a variety of mind-altering drugs, peculiar humor and psychological and physical exercises to yank Castaneda out of his ego-bound, idiotic and limited worldview and into the horizon-less universe of the shaman. Or not. Fans of Castaneda are convinced that he did everything he said he did. Others have called him abusive and an outright fraud who cribbed his stories from a variety of readily available texts. Castaneda, in true brujo tradition, remained entirely elusive, kept the truth about his personal history obscure and is now dead. His ideas have been distilled into "Castanedaism" and he continues to have a devoted

following.

In the late '60s his first book flew off the shelves and doubt about its authenticity was yet to surface. By making the character of Castaneda the butt of the endless jokes of Juan Matus and his sidekick, Don Genarro, Castaneda the author, pointed out what many people suspected and wanted to believe; that the world was infinitely more complicated and magical than our biases and limited consciousness allowed us to see. "Seeing" beyond one's cultural assumptions was entirely the point of *The Teachings of Don Juan*. For Castaneda, it required that he ingest powerful hallucinogens and enact bizarre rituals like rolling around on the porch all night to find his power spot and sewing together the eyelids of lizards. The results were terrifying, successfully psycho-shattering and definitely not fun. Becoming a brujo and 'groking' other planes of existence was dangerous and lonely work. By comparison, Albert Hofmann was a total geek in a lab coat. True or not, Castaneda's introduction of shamanism to popular American culture was a watershed moment.

In the academic community, the question whether we were the product of nature or nurture, had been debated six ways to Sunday. Freud and his student and eventual nemesis, Carl Jung, cracked open the psyche to reveal the vast terra incognita of the unconscious. How much of our personality was the result of brain wiring and how much was determined by to whom, and what we were exposed? Despite Castaneda's reports of teetering on the edge of sanity, the exotic allure was too great. Grad students (and more than a few professors) all over the country, studied and experimented with altered states of consciousness. Old ethnographies were sought out in the dark corners of libraries and dusted off. Suddenly these reports from far corners of the world on the peculiar beliefs and abilities of exotic shamans had not only merit, but profound intelligence. Reporting cultural phenomena and drawing up lineage charts from an 'objective point of view' wasn't sufficient for a genuine understanding of a foreign culture.

Unbiased ethnographic study of a foreign culture was deemed impossible, given the freight of personality and culture the anthropologist brought to the party. "Participant observation", however, allowed the observer to enter into the mind-set of the culture and empathetically understand their belief systems. What used to be derided as 'going native' became precisely the point. Linguistic immersion by an anthropologist into the culture of a tribal

group allowed entry into the logic by which, that group rendered their vastly different cultures intelligible. This made it possible for the anthropologist to discover a culture from the inside out, that is, from the intrinsic cultural distinctions, meaningful to members of the tribe. In other words, anthropologists sought 'to grok' the culture.

In a modern world that was mercilessly encroaching on the last remaining 'primitive' tribes, a flurry of new intrepid adventurers were beating the tropical bushes for their own Don Juans and the ancient wisdom of the ancestors before it was crushed under the wheels of logging trucks and oil companies. Here is Michael Harner, Anthropologist and instructor of shamanic workshops, in the introduction to his 1973 publication, *Hallucinogens and Shamanism:*

"... as more anthropologists undertake field research on the significance of hallucinogens and partake of the drugs themselves (e.g. Castaneda 1968; 1971), it will be interesting to see how 'participant observation' influences their understanding of the cultures studied and affects their personal, theoretical, and methodological orientations."

PARTICIPANT OBSERVATION

Fantastic reports such as that of the peyote cult by Weston LaBarre and Reichel-Dolmatoff's experiences with the hallucinogens of the Tucano in the Amazon suddenly resonated on a new level. Botanist/pharmacologist Richard Evans Schultes was sent to the Amazon by a grateful government to find a sustainable variety of rubber tree to replace the plantations of Indochina assaulted by blight and the Japanese army, to keep the literal wheels of the American war effort turning. But while slogging through the jungles in search of rubber trees, he encountered indigenous tribes of people living in the midst of the world's richest pharmacopoeia, and possessing encyclopedic knowledge of its uses. The discipline of ethno-botany was legitimized. Later, his student, Wade Davis, would reveal the bio-chemical component to Voodoo zombification in *The Serpent and the Rainbow*, a book that took the stuff of creepy '50s horror films and made it all the more creepy by bringing it into the real world.

The '60s saw a flurry of papers by scientists like Gregory Wasson and Stanley Krippner treating subjects such as biofeedback, chemical examinations of psychedelic drugs, kirlian photography (a

photographic technique that revealed an 'aura' of light around the subject), and plant communication, that helped fuel the flash-in-the-pan weirdness of the early Hippie movement and into the '70s. Historical reports from the 1600s of ritual plant use by the Aztecs and the drug-laced 'flying ointment' recipe used by witches under persecution from the Inquisition were reconsidered. Research into the chemical make-up of ritually used plants and the resultant understanding of their hallucinogenic capabilities helped removed the stigma that centuries of Church doctrine had placed on these reported experiences. Previously dismissed as fantasy or possession by the Devil, these reports of altered states were more clearly understood and placed into a biological and cultural context previously missing.

Christian mysticism came up for reassessment as well, as the consciousness-altering techniques of 'mortification of the flesh' such as flagellation and fasting were better understood as causing altered states of consciousness. Pain causes the brain to release endorphins, the body's natural painkillers that allow us to endure childbirth and injury. Self-inflicted pain induces the body to release endorphins as well, and creates a natural high.

As the critical mass of scientific evidence that had accumulated around Darwin's research, resulted in a profound reassessment of cultural and religious bias, similarly, on a smaller scale, the acceptance of the validity of ecstatic experience from the ritual use of hallucinogens and ceremonial activity to alter consciousness significantly transformed the landscape of religious studies. Just as Castaneda had to be dropkicked out of his reality in order to apprehend Juan Matus's brujo universe, many academicians, scientists and other argonauts of consciousness pursued the empirical evidence of alternate planes of existence. Others, despite a lack of personal experience were, nevertheless convinced this was an area of study that deserved careful exploration.

OTHER WORLDS

The discipline of archaeology has evolved from a nascent hobby of treasure-hunting, through a variety of theoretical perspectives, to a new study of the past that includes recognition that human behavior is not necessarily traceable and conclusively discoverable in the artifacts revealed through excavation alone. The new horizon of cognitive archaeology, or the archaeology of the mind, has gained considerable traction. Lurching toward a new appreciation of

Our primal selves, our reptilian brains, seethe just under the surface of civility, and we must respect and attend to the monsters that reside within. The origin of the word is Middle French, monstré, meaning an omen sent by the gods as a warning that the world is out of balance and must be righted, or unspeakable horrors will fall upon us. A hero must arise, or a heroic part of ourselves must appear. A courageous journey must be made into the labyrinth, to seek out the danger that resides there, the battle drawn and the hero emerge victorious with the sacred jewel of wisdom that saves the day.

GETTING ALTERED

The cross-cultural information that had accumulated from all those years of ethnologists scurrying around in remote corners of the world collecting bizarre information about exotic peoples, has affirmed a startling fact; whether Inuit, English, Tucano, or Ainu, when a person enters an altered state of consciousness for whatever reason, the pattern of the experience is the same. Our human biology and neurology react in the same way to certain stimuli, although the translation of the experience will be specific to the individual's cultural experience. As mentioned earlier, our fluid consciousness is continually adapting to stimuli, and trance states can be induced in many ways. Fever, hunger, pain, dancing, drumming, chanting, bloodletting, sleep deprivation and ingesting psychoactive substances are just a few. Trance states that give rise to hallucinations and visions, like the rest of the spectrum of consciousness, occur in varying stages of intensity. Hallucinations are not limited to visual manifestations but can appear in all five senses and not necessarily only, while in a trance state. Phantom limb sensations, for example, are common among amputees. Hallucinatory tintinnitus, a buzzing in the ears, is a normal occurrence when ingesting psychotropic drugs and auditory hallucinations can occur, while experiencing sensory deprivation. And the condition called synesthesia can jumble all the senses by allowing, for example, a color to be tasted or a smell to be seen.

Scientist Heinrich Kluver, drawing on his own research of hallucinogens in the 1920s and that of others, began to suspect that there were structural similarities to a hallucinatory experience. As these appeared to occur cross-culturally that would imply they were dictated by biology. He broke these into four stages of visual imagery, which he called "form constants". The first he categorized as a lattice, honeycomb or chessboard pattern. The second he described as a "cobweb" design. The third he referred to as "tunnel, funnel, alley, cone or vessel" images, and the fourth he called the "spiral".

Subsequent researchers refined Kluver's work, combining the third and fourth form constant into one for a total of three stages of hallucination, each of which, was associated with three sequentially deepening trance states. These three stages of hallucination were called "entoptic", a term from the Greek meaning "within vision". Because of their universality, entoptic imagery was determined to originate in the structure of the human optical system. The structure of the eyeball, neurological firing patterns, floaters in the eye, blood flow to the capillaries, and the visual cortex itself are, among other things, all considered players in the creation of entoptic imagery. Recent studies have concluded that, simply put, people in a trance state are seeing the interior landscapes of their brains. Precisely, which parts of the visual system are responsible for which effects is still debated, but there is consistent agreement on the end results. The information registered by the human visual system under trance conditions is universal among humans. Once seen, these images are then carried to higher brain centers for further processing through cultural filters.

LABYRINTH IN THE BRAIN

As the research has been increasingly refined the stages of entoptic imagery experienced during deepening trance states have been clarified. In the first and lightest stage of trance, people become aware of meandering lines, nested curves, dots, zigzags, grids and other geometric forms that float over the visual field like an overlay of transparent wallpaper. Those of us with checkered pasts reaching back to the '60s may well remember watching a Grateful Dead concert as if through a very thin paisley-patterned curtain. This would also explain the inspiration for a lot of those almost illegible, swirling concert promotion posters.

As a subject moves into the second stage of trance the brain tries to attach meaning to the visual hallucinations by ordering them into familiar images. We do this all the time even in our normal waking consciousness, as did the children's book heroine, Madeleine, who noticed the crack on her ceiling 'had the habit of sometimes looking like a rabbit'. But when one follows the rabbit down the rabbit hole in a trance state, decoding of a visually perceived image supplied by

swept up by a swirling tornado, which eventually dropped them in Oz. The spiraling tunnel with an hourglass tumbling inside that clues the viewer he's going back or forward in time. Bill and Ted embarked on their excellent adventures by traveling through time down wormhole tunnels in a phone booth. In the film "Run Lola Run" the heroine, not bound by the laws of time or death, revisits an event until she emerges transcendent. The movie is drenched in spirals, both images and metaphors. These are modern-day interpretations of ancient mythic imagery arising from altered state experiences. They recall the journeys of the first shamans to the gateway of the world beyond time, the labyrinth.

It is a matter of personal belief as to how the wiring came to be, just who the Electrician may have been who flipped the switch and, in a trance state, whether or not some aspect of oneself is moving though a mystical universe. In this moment, the spiritual voyager is on the very cusp of life and death, fighting for survival on the operating table, battling an illness or a deadly spirit. Some people report the experience of having to make a pivotal choice, whether to cross over the threshold or not. Others, anticipating a reunion with dead loved ones and relief from suffering, are miserable upon discovering they have been snatched back to this world. Whatever the outcome, the survivor of a near-death experience is forever changed. Witnessing the defining edges of one's existence in this life and knowing how tenuous our hold is upon it brings into high relief the preciousness of our time here. Stepping outside of Time allows us to see the eternal in every moment. As Tolle has said, one must experience death and know that there is no death. From the time our ancestors realized that Death was an unavoidable guest at the table, we have attempted to come to terms with its spectral presence, to find the comforting pattern in the emotional chaos accompanying loss of life.

There is an imperative human need to communicate what, for the cosmic traveler, has been the ultimate life-altering reality. One must tell the story of the journey in a way that expresses the depth and meaning of it and imparts wisdom learned. The symbolic language of myth, poetry and art are the vehicles of magic that can carry others in their imaginations down that same dark tunnel of swirling images toward the light and to the threshold of the spirit world. Art is the manifestation of the transcendent experience, bringing the ineffable into the waking world and giving it form. For the Aurignacians, as for all humans, an image was rendered meaningful

in the context of their lives by the symbolism attached to it. Our human capability to create metaphors, coupled with our awareness of the razor-thin border between life and death insist we have a symbol that embodies the deep ground of being. A portal through which the spirit is made manifest and manifestation is dematerialized allows the undifferentiated swirl of charged energies of the Otherworld to be rendered into form, and form to dissolve once again into potential. The symbol arises of its own accord and demands that we feel its presence and name it.

We have called it the labyrinth. This is the origin of the symbol, this paradoxical magical vortex of hallucinatory power that draws us to the verge between life and death. Spirals, meanders, swastikas and labyrinthine patterns, all represent the sensation of spinning into a deep center where one is taken out of time and profound transformation occurs. Myths worldwide tell of unavoidable, dangerous journeys through terrible darkness, underwater, into deep tunnels and caves in the earth, all inhabited by strange creatures, where death waits for the fool or hero. The labyrinth is the archetypal symbol of the journey we all must make.

But what is beyond that threshold at the end of the tunnel? Once the traveler passes through the tunnel, mesh, or vortex and moves into the light beyond, what then? What lies beyond the heart of the labyrinth? The souls of the dead pass through but rarely return. The labyrinth is the portal of the shaman, the minotaur and the mythic hero, those rarified humans who cross over the threshold, into the light of the Otherworld and then return. It was the Aurignacians who discovered the discipline of shamanic spiritual transportation and perfected the art of the Return, deep in the labyrinthine Paleolithic caves of Europe where we find ancient minotaurs dancing across the damp walls in the midst of magical animals.

STAGES OF ENTOPTIC HALLUCINATION

STAGE 1   STAGE 2

TRANSITION   STAGE 3

CHAPTER 9

THE SHAMAN'S DANCE

"I don't see nothin' new
But I feel a lot of change
And I get the strangest feeling
As I'm heading for the light"
George Harrison

"Richard made another entry in his mental diary. Today, he thought,
I've survived walking the plank, the kiss of death, and a lecture on
inflicting pain. Right now, I'm on my way through a labyrinth with a
mad bastard who came back from the dead and a bodyguard who
turned out to be a ... whatever the opposite of a bodyguard is. I am
so far out of my depth that... Metaphors failed him, then. He had
gone beyond the world of metaphor and simile into the place of
things that are, and it was changing him."
Neverwhere, Neil Gaiman

DREAMING THINGS UP

The 'Fifth Beatle", inventive producer George Martin, revealed
that the swirly sounds backing "For The Benefit of Mr. Kite" was
produced by slicing up magnetic tape of calliope music, throwing
the pieces in the air and randomly reassembling them. The
dreamlike whirl that poured out of speakers around the world
transported listeners to a strange carnival of the mind where Henry
the Horse dances the waltz.

One of the more marvelous abilities of our curio-cabinet brain is
the capacity to dream. More often than not, our dreams are a random
jumble of fragments like Mr. Kite's circus music; fragments of the
day, people we know or knew once, childhood homes, sliced into
queer bits and randomly reassembled into peculiar images and
story-lines. But occasionally the bottom falls out of this deep end of
the consciousness-spectrum and we are visited by a dream that

seems otherworldly. It has a quality to it, a feeling and clarity that doesn't exist in normal sleep. This type of dream breaks on the morning consciousness like a bucket of cold water splashing a chill strangeness in our faces. We have a sense of having 'been' somewhere else, walked with ghosts and returned with precious fragments of spirit stuff.

This dream that rattles us awake can be likened to our merely standing on the porch of the house of spirits. But shamans are intimately familiar with the vast interior. They are unique people, both men and women, who harness the power of altered states of consciousness far beyond normal dreaming to make intentional journeys into the swirling vortex of the labyrinth and then deep into other realities. There they commune with spirit beings, engage in battle against demons, seek out information unavailable through waking consciousness and, most importantly, return generally sane, intact and bearing wisdom from the ordeal.

The origin of the Western world's labyrinth is here, as we will discover, in the spiritual practice of Ice Age shamans. What began as a trance-inducing trip into magical deep caves by the first modern humans in Europe has become incorporated into mythic legend as the hero's journey. Cultural survival, hallucinatory experience and hallucinogenic underground landscapes coalesced among the Paleolithics to become a refined shamanic religion, a lynchpin of success in a harsh environment. The labyrinth becomes ever more meaningful by putting it into this context, because the fruits of these arcane expeditions into labyrinthine alternate realities remain with us today. Who were these shamans who stood apart from their tribes yet were indispensable to their survival?

DEATH ENTERS

The word 'shaman' originates from the language of the Evenk, a culture of reindeer herders in Siberia, and describes the spiritual specialists of this small group. Once a highly esoteric religious and cultural phenomenon among hunter-gatherer tribes, versions of shamanic training are now available to anyone with a ticket for a session at a weekend workshop. Anthropologist Michael Harner departed from his research and teaching in the '60s to develop the Foundation for Shamanic Studies. He is a pioneer who reawakened interest in the study and practice of shamanic techniques and now leads training seminars in 'Core Shamanism' worldwide to thousands of students. How can urban dwellers from Pocatella to

Vienna participate meaningfully in a discipline that was practiced by the cave-painters of the Paleolithic? How, in this era of nano-technology and routine space travel, not to mention the intervening tens of thousands of years and the vast array of all religious disciplines, can the experience of shamanic journeying have any attraction or validity? Beneath the universal biological experience of trance run deep currents of mythic narrative, which renders structure and purpose to otherwise chaotic hallucinations. This narrative anchors our existential fears of death and meaninglessness in origin legends that illuminate our sacred beginnings.

Many mythologies speak of an original Golden Era, a paradisiacal time of perfect tranquility when cosmic energies flowed easily and undisturbed and all creatures and elements shared a common language. The creation epic of the Tuvan people of south central Russia describes a far-off golden time filled with intimate wonders; the sacred mountain was still a small hill and the great milk lake only a pond, people and animals understood each other's languages and the horns of the mountain sheep reached into the heavens.

A similar primeval Garden of Eden is described in an ancient Mesopotamian tablet:

> *"When you were dividing the virgin earth…*
> *the land of Tilmun was a region pure;*
> *… the land of Tilmun was fresh*
> *…The land of Tilmun was bright…*
> *The raven in Tilmun did not croak*
> *[as the raven does nowadays]…*
> *The lion did not kill, The wolf did not seize lambs…*
> *The eye disease did not say, "I, eye disease,"*
> *Headache did not say, "I, headache…"*

Age, illness and death did not exist. There was no decay. All was innocence and perfection. This idyllic past, however, became corrupted and different myths account for this in different ways; greed, jealousy, power struggles among gods and the Catch-22 of original sin. The eternal net of peaceable being developed some kinks, and our world fell out of the fogs of eternity and coalesced inside Time. The world became 'mundane' and the cosmic energies that had commingled in blissful balance separated out. We lost the capability to communicate with the animals and plants. Desire was born from want and fear. People began to age and fall ill. Death appeared as the other side of life, defining our separation from

boundless being with utter finality. The world of eternal peace and delight withdrew from our reach, but the enchanted memory lingers. Myths tell of these lost gardens; Shangri-Las flowing with uterine fountains of crystalline water, milk and honey where all want was appeased, or of well-watered plains roaming with peaceable animals. After the fall into the realm of Time, a fiery angel, monster, dangerous bridge or impenetrable gate guarded the mythic lost garden. The only way to pass through the gate, to cross that threshold back into contented bliss, is through death, to slip the skins of both body and Time and re-enter the eternal realm. Yet mythic heroes pass through this membrane at the center of the labyrinthine vortex, journey out of Time to eerie and dangerous landscapes inhabited by powerful creatures, and return a hundred years later, cloaked in an aura of power. For shamans, it is their stock in trade

The first human creature that heard the final sigh slip from a friend's lips and recognized the absolute change that had occurred launched us on a perpetual quest for the magic key to unlock Death's secrets. Some animals understand death, and briefly mourn the passing of their fellow animals. And while many people assiduously avoid the topic, others paradoxically live their lives to come to terms with Death, the Master of Time, and Death's companion, Sickness. It is only through the assurance of suffering and extinction that we measure the quality and passage of our days. We find purpose in suffering, adding variations to the mythic narratives of our ancestors.

Modern medicine continues to probe at a, literally, vital detail of life; to determine when, exactly, we leave it. When does the last spark wink out? In his fascinating investigation into Haitian Voodoo, Wade Davis explores the parameters of death. Zombification, originally a social mechanism implemented in Haiti to control miscreants, has devolved into the stuff of bad horror films. The traditional creation of a zombie required careful timing and the proper dosage of a toxic potion that simulates death long enough to allow for the temporary burial of the victim, but not so long that he suffocates in the process. Before fully reviving from this suspended animation he can be dug up by his makers and enslaved.

Davis lists the diagnoses of death as "cessation of respiration and heartbeat, changes in the eye, insensibility to electrical stimuli, rigor mortis, pallor, hypostasis, and relaxation of the sphincters". He then

proceeds to demonstrate that none of these indicators is infallible. Yogis have demonstrated that both breathing and heartbeat can be reduced to a point lethal to most people. Body temperature can be affected by the manner of one's alleged death. People have recovered from burial in snow with body temperatures as low as 17 degrees C. Heart, attack victims are chilled to slow down brain processes and encourage recovery. Changes in the eye are unreliable as the muscles of the iris continue to contract for hours after death. Pallor is only detectable in light-skinned individuals. The time it takes for rigor mortis to set in, normally dependable, can be affected by unusual conditions of stress or fright that floods the system with adrenalin and delays the process. Under normal conditions, a person is considered dead if the heart ceases beating for longer than five minutes. However, if the person is subjected to unique conditions such as the effects of drugs or disease, an unusual environment like a frozen lake or, like the yogi, is trained in the art of simulating an aspect of death, these indications can also be misleading.

Davis points to only two sure-fire ways to diagnose death and the first is still not entirely infallible; a brain scan and cardiogram that require high-tech machinery and a trained technician. The second, and ultimately, the most dependable, is once putrefaction sets in, which requires time. Only when the body begins to disintegrate are we absolutely assured the spark of life that keeps it fresh is gone. The speed of this process is affected by temperature and environment encouraging the growth of bacteria and fungi. However, some bodies never putrefy but are naturally mummified in arid environments or anaerobic bogs. The Incan child mummies found at the top of the Andes and the bodies recovered from peat bogs in Ireland and Denmark are sometimes preserved right down to their eyelashes and last meals. A frozen Iron Age woman found in a sunken tomb in the Altai mountains was dressed in silks and felt, had platters of horsemeat nearby and her tattoos are still legible.

The edge of death at some point becomes absolute and irrevocable, but these examples indicate it can be a sliding scale. People have been declared dead only to horrify the mortician by rising up off their slabs in wonderment. In Japan victims of fugu poisoning, the result of eating a toxic fish that has not been properly prepared, can result in a death-like trance from which some have miraculously awakened after being pronounced dead. People who have lingered for years in the living death of deep comas inexplicably awaken. Victorian England was swept by a hysterical

fear of premature burial. Some people resorted to designing elaborate mechanisms including bells and spring-loaded coffins so they could alert others and escape should they be buried alive. Edgar Allen Poe was particularly enamored with this scenario.

Shamans, however, actively pursue and learn to control a range of altered states of consciousness, particularly deep trance, a condition poised on the border between life and death. Shamans tune the instrument of their bodies to literally dance over the edge of this precipice and return. What for us is a dead-or-alive proposition when the spirit leaves the body, to the shaman is a rigorous discipline of entering deep trance where he separates consciousness from the living body and journeys spiritually unencumbered to the Otherworld where there are other ways of living.

In the earliest Aurignacian cultures there were people who undoubtedly began to specialize in this ability, who helped define the nature of both the tribe's cosmos and its place within it by doing the impossible; perfecting the art of dying and returning to life. To speak to the dead, it has been said one must be dead. The shaman is the interpreter between these worlds, a channel for power that links these alternate realities together and negotiates a balance through manipulation of spiritual and temporal energies.

SHAMANIC DUTIES

Shamanism is found worldwide in a multiplicity of cultural guises, yet there are astonishing cross-cultural similarities among them in such far-flung places as Lapland and Borneo, Tibet and Mali, cultures that developed entirely separate from one another. These similarities have been condensed into the anthropological classification of shamanism. One would expect differences between geographically and historically remote cultures. The high degree of similarity among these distinct shamanic traditions is particularly remarkable in a spiritual practice that comes with no holy book or doctrine and has no high priest. Having arisen among nomadic hunter-gatherers, there is no Vatican or Mecca of shamanism. How is this similarity possible? Because, as discussed in previous chapters, all humans arrive on earth with the same cerebral and biological hardware. Trancing is central to shamanic practice and depends on the universal human capacity to achieve altered states of consciousness that opens on to the hallucinatory world beyond. As one in a trance moves along the trajectory of intensified experience, from light trance into deeper altered states, the sensory apprehension

is the same throughout human existence, whether one is a Paleolithic shaman or a cardiac patient on an operating table. The feeling of moving through a vortex is universally experienced as entering a portal leading to another reality, one that functions under very different rules from the waking world. Cosmic travelers universally describe journeys to alternate realities and commiseration with spirit entities, but beyond these basics, similarities diverge into a vast and complex array of culture- and individual-specific experiences.

In today's world it is difficult, if not impossible, to find a culture that has not been touched if not knocked flat by the industrial world. Despite the fading or outright repression of ancient shamanic practice under the searing light of the modern world, it is remarkably resilient and can be found entwined in every current human culture, and widespread evidence of its practice is found in ancient archaeological sites, leading to speculation that shamanism is mankind's oldest, and perhaps most enduring, religion. It is a fluid practice that functions equally well in tropical jungles, desert sands, Arctic wilderness or city apartment, and often co-exists, sometimes very uneasily, with other religions and political systems. Tibet, Siberia and many Native American tribes are examples of this delicate balance.

Since our 'mundane' world fell of its own weight from ethereal eternity into the structure of Time, marking those moments that reconnect us to divinity is the province of the shaman. Shamans may be timekeepers, custodians of calendars who maintain a respectful balance between their people and the cosmos by tracking and ceremonially observing sacred days and seasons when the veil between the worlds grows thin and the redressing of balance can be best accomplished.

Shamans can affect the weather and augur the future. Often they are adept at creating and using medicines, including psychotropic drugs. Above all else, they are experts in the arena of altered states of consciousness, having learned to control ecstatic experiences, journey to the Beyond and return successfully.

Shamanic practice among hunter-gatherers most simply maintains equilibrium in the cosmos by bargaining with both the supernatural 'Master of Animals' and the spirits of animals to negotiate the price for the souls of animals the people must kill and eat in order to live. Human food in a hunting culture consists largely of animals, both body and soul, and a ritual debt must be paid for them. Food equals

health and life. The paradox of taking an animal's soul, of causing death to preserve life, establishes a fundamental dynamic that demands the maintenance of spiritual equilibrium and harmony, the negotiated price. The shaman and his people accomplish this through ritual and sacrifice. But this is only one aspect of an immensely complex and diverse calling that encompasses most expansively the umbrella concept of healing. Ill-health in a shamanic culture results from an imbalance of energies that can originate in any number of ways. To redress the balance, the shaman becomes adept at communicating with spirits, who challenge, inform or help the shaman to resolve the problem. The shaman's role includes social work, religious practice, psychotherapy, the use of the supernatural power of plants, trickery and magic for the prevention and curing of sickness, however it is defined. The successful enactment of the responsibilities of shamans are crucial to the living soul and body of the communities they serve, maintaining the relationships which extend beyond this existence into the Otherworld of deities and ancestors.

Shamans generally do not exist in isolation, although their unique personalities and abilities set them apart from others. The Wizards and Weird Women of legend who dwell alone in the depths of the forest and work their magic are potentially evil because they are not incorporated into a social framework and their relationship to power therefore are not mitigated by social constraints. The witch of Hansel and Gretel was clearly not a social worker. Dominant monotheistic religions, in direct competition with shamans, purposely marginalized them, putting them on the periphery of society, characterizing them variously as evil, ignorant and dangerous (as some surely were) so that centralized control could be achieved. In the Middle Ages 'witches', or those judged to be, which included midwives, herbalists, healers of various kinds and rich widows whose property then was taken by the church, were famously executed in the thousands. However, the term 'witch' is accepted in anthropological literature as a less value-laden descriptor that refers to an inverted, death-seeking shaman.

A shaman today, by and large, is an integral part of his or her community and when not shamanizing goes about living just as everyone else in the group does, hunting, farming and having families. Intimate knowledge of the personal lives that make up the shaman's community makes the shaman the perfect person to effect changes for the good. The primary purpose of a shaman is to

manipulate power for the health of the people, so he must be fully aware of their personalities and relationships to be effective. Just as the small-town doctor knows the ills and secrets of all his patients, so must the shaman. Problems that arise from marital disputes and familial rivalries can fall into the province of the shaman-as-counselor, as well as the more esoteric arts of communing with spirits. These combined talents enhance and reinforce a seamless moral and spiritual universe.

David Whitley, in his book *Cave Painting and the Human Spirit* draws a distinction between more recent shamanic practices and the Paleolithic, however. Shamans of Native American tribes, as he points out, are primarily focused on healing because of the catastrophic death rate from illness visited upon them by whites. Paleo shamans, by contrast, were significantly more 'fierce', their primary concern being to maintain balance through the manipulation of supernatural power, the ultimate causative agent in the universe. As supernatural power, like nuclear power, makes no intrinsic value judgments, it can be used for good or ill and shamans could be healers or sorcerers, both curing as well as creating illness or influencing fortune for good or ill and, at times, the distinction blurs. In the perpetual struggle between good and evil, life and death, sickness and health, the best the Paleo shaman could do was to maintain a tense balance between these paradoxical forces to avoid plunging into chaos. Good would not necessarily triumph, but perhaps the cosmic wolves could be kept from the door. To these early shamans, the world was what it was and shamanic power was ambivalent. There was no vision of reconciliation between opposing forces, but rather an acceptance of the nature of forces at work in the world and a resignation that these forces, like nuclear power, would not change. The shaman's job then was to perpetually move between these dynamic opposing forces to maintain balance, by definition a tension-filled, exhausting occupation demanding great personal sacrifice. This is a significantly different approach to living from one like ours that assumes deliverance and redemption, given the right setting of our moral compass.

With this worldview in mind, the journey to the spirits was fraught with terrors and pain, and death was an ever-present companion. It is Whitley's contention that shamans often suffered from the 'shaman's disease', inherited mood disorders such as depression and bipolar disease requiring super-human struggles to maintain sanity and not be driven by despair to suicide. Shamanism,

he points out, was reported in the ethnographic literature as commonly being hereditary, with the shaman initially suffering a lengthy illness, often at a relatively young age. This was transitory but recurrent, with periods of madness followed by lucidity and productivity. During periods of madness the hallucinatory world crashed in upon them unbidden. Once it passed they reflected on this astonishing experience, its meaning, and how to incorporate it into the waking world.

Whitley suggests that Paleolithic shamans were the bearers of new genetic mutations that resulted in madness. Although controversial, this is supported to some extent by recent evidence of genetic information gleaned from the International Haploid Map, which cataloged the differences in DNA of 270 people in different cultures. Genetic scientists determined that about 50,000 years ago, when modern humans were pushing into Europe and the rest of the globe, adaptation to new environments and experiences began to skyrocket. Selection for successful adaptive mutations increased significantly with growing populations and migrations. One of these is DRD4, a mutation in a neurotransmitter receptor linked to attention-deficit/hyperactivity disorder or ADHD. The selection of this mutation as desirable for survival seems, on the surface, to be counterintuitive. But Eric Wang, a geneticist with Veracyte Inc. in San Francisco who was involved in the study states in *Discover* Magazine (March, 09), "having the trait of focusing on multiple directions might have been a good thing" during the Paleolithic. "People focused in one direction might get eaten." The traits of ADHD that lead to distraction and disruption in a modern classroom could have been highly valuable in the predator-populated landscape of the Paleolithic.

Whitley postulates the theory that the 'shaman's disease' may have provided the initial driving force behind the creation of art in the caves. The artists drew from a deep well of spirit lasting for 20,000 years derived from dreaming and ritually activating altered states, and perhaps if Whitley is right, from periods of madness as well. Integrating controlled, hallucinatory, altered states, whether experienced during the intense emotional creative cycles of manic periods or through intentional ceremony, into cultural forms would indeed be a brilliant adaptive success. Illustrated by artistic "conversations" in the subterranean caverns where iconic art closed a circuit with the spirit world, a cohesive spiritual doctrine would be revealed to those who viewed the art. This relationship with the spirits would inform and effect life above. A Paleolithic shaman who was able to control the debilitating aspects of the disease and capitalize on his creative talents would be a charismatic personality indeed, leading his people in directions never before considered. Yet he would be ever aware that the spirits could again fill him with uncontainable joy or torment, ultimately descending into irretrievable madness.

At first blush, the idea that the art of this period is the result of madness seems reductive, if not repellent, and is only one of many possible incentives. Certainly these were people who interacted with their environment at large in uniquely creative ways. However, powerful shamans fill an intensely peculiar niche in any society. A shaman, by definition, has gone through a process of psycho-spiritual disintegration and reintegration, which gives him far-reaching control of his sanity, one that allows him to venture far into other realities and bring the fruits of his experiences back to the community. A mental patient, by comparison, remains isolated in a bizarre world of his own and can be a serious danger to others. Whitley goes to some pains to state that not all shamans are or were mad, and certainly not all mad people are shamans, and what constitutes madness is defined in different ways in different cultures. Certainly not everyone who decorated the caves was mad. He refers to bipolar illness also as "the CEO's disease" and explains that the energy and creative insight bestowed during a manic phase, regardless of the era in which the person lives, when kept under control, results in an outpouring of unique and often prodigious productivity. People suffering from mood disorders are statistically highly creative people. The idea of the 'tormented genius' is a common stereotype. Consider the number of immensely talented artists and influential thinkers who have struggled with mood disorders; Samuel Johnson, Van Gogh, Edvard Munch, Robin Williams, Sylvia Plath, Virginia Woolf, Beethoven, William Stegner and Sir Isaac Newton to name a very few. We as a species are beholden to the mixed blessing of the divine 'gift' of madness for some of humanity's most remarkable creations. Whether the gift is bestowed by the gods or genes, it is a mixed blessing nonetheless.

Within the context of traditional cultures the onset of these 'illnesses' is described as 'being chosen by the spirits' to become a shaman and mercilessly tormented until one complies. Refusal to comply could result in death, often by one's own hand. Madness and power were equated and honored, provided they were kept in check.

This perspective removes all trace of modern conceptions nested in psychotherapy and pharmacology and having to do with the comforts of transcendent resolution, grace, or the mystical transport of religious experience. Instead, it lifts the lid on a primal, raw world of 'fierce' struggle, endurance, courage and creative survival.

Whitley's exploration of extensive ethnographic accounts reveals that shamans were consistently described as mentally ill and borderline antisocial. Citing references from widely separated cultures, they are described as sexual predators with no self-control, "…by and large… mad", "ailing… taken to strange places", "Shamans can't control themselves… Their power makes them act that way. It makes them crazy." "The shamans among the Chukchi… were, as a rule extremely excitable, almost hysterical, and not a few were half mad." Or the opposite end of the bipolar spectrum, "… I would sometimes fall to weeping and felt unhappy without knowing why. Then for no reason at all would suddenly be changed, and I felt a great, inexplicable joy, a joy so powerful that I could not restrain it… in the midst of such a fit of mysterious and overwhelming delight I became a shaman." The only cure for the 'shaman's disease' was to give over to the spirits, become a practising shaman and embrace this strange world.

ACCEPTING THE 'GIFT'

Think back to the sensation of utter weirdness and fear you may have had on waking from the vivid dream mentioned earlier which stood apart as otherworldly. Now imagine spending most of your life learning how to go not only there, but far beyond willingly and consciously, confronting beings whose natures are utterly foreign, nonhuman and quite often lethal. In fact, having no other option. The ancient shaman, as prototype of the modern hero, was called to embark on a life-threatening adventure through magical, dire landscapes of ice, fire, blasting winds and clashing swords, empowered by moral imperative and the driving need to survive, to do battle with powerful, often malevolent creatures and return to his community with the elixir of life, the key to 'health' that brought energies into balance.

The neophyte shaman embarked on his new life apprenticed to an established professional who was adept at interacting with the world of spirit, a guide through the strange pathways of alternate reality. Sometimes, like medical school, learning the art of shamanism requires years of training. This uniquely demanding profession

requires a unique personality to perform it successfully, one that balances personal power with spirit power, and communal values over personal ambition. A shaman must hold the attention of the people during an exhausting, riveting ceremonial performance designed to focus everyone's energy on a desired outcome, requiring hours of drumming, dancing and chanting. Often a participatory ceremony, it requires the presence and validation of members of the tribe. The community must support the shamans's visions and revelations. One could postulate the genius of theater springing from the wellhead of ancient shamanic practice. The results of a successful spirit journey were truly cathartic in the very highest Aristotelian sense; a purgation and purification leading to healing. The belief of the tribe fuels the shaman's gift to reach the Otherworld and be gifted by the spirits in turn. And there will be animals, rain, health, safety from enemies and the abundance of life.

Accepting the shamanic 'gift' of power is not an easy choice and many deny it out of fear of the social and sometimes sexual transformations that are required to become a shaman, not to mention living life partially in the spirit world. As mentioned earlier, some candidates commit suicide rather that accept the weight of responsibility, intimate relationships with spirits and lifetime commitment. Others enter training only to quit because the demands of the job are so arduous and the forces confronted so fearsome. Should a person choose to accept the calling there are two ways to become a shaman. The primary method, and the one which often produces the most powerful shamans, is when the spirits themselves choose with whom they will communicate. Quite often a future shaman who is called to the task will be hounded by ill-health and tortured by the spirits until finally relinquishing and agreeing to become initiated. The alternative is that relentless spirits will eventually drive the shaman-elect to the brink of a crazed and miserable death unless he capitulates. These are often considered the most potent shamans. The second route is that one has a predisposition for shamanic talent and chooses to become an apprentice to acquire the requisite power. In many cultures potential shamanic power is inherited from a relative and certain signs of that latent power are observed in a special child who then chooses or is encouraged to begin training.

Shamans have been described as schizophrenic, alcoholic, epileptic, psychotic, bipolar, deeply emotional and sensitive, as show-boaters and shysters. And, as Whitley and others have noted,

many who are called to the shamanic path are often socially dysfunctional, mentally or physically ill. In our culture, we think of sickness as a chemical imbalance or an invasion by a germ or cancer that attacks our bodies and must be eliminated by FDA-approved, scientifically verified drugs and cures. Illness is unnatural. The social misfit is treated with therapy and drugs and the severely ill, along the lines of the original intent of zombification, are removed from society.

In tribal societies, illness and suffering are part of a natural process involving physical and psycho-spiritual transformation. Predating psycho-therapy and anti-psychotic drugs, mechanisms of support had to be found within the culture. If a culture operates on the premise that interweaving webs of energy animate all existence, then one's illness cannot be extricated from the larger picture, a point of view to which modern holistic medicine is returning. Pulling a thread disturbs the overall pattern. The sickness that dogs one called to the life of a shaman is the direct result of the intervention of spiritual entities. Acceptance of the calling is interpreted as a return to 'health', that is, a balanced integration of psycho-spiritual elements. What modern observers describe as uncontrolled fits similar to epilepsy, for instance, becomes the controlled channeling of information from the domain of spirits. A shaman's integrity depends on his control of power, his ability to inspire and influence his people through dedicated training and moral clarity. Even though the shaman verges on the edge of insanity, he must not tip entirely over that edge. Controlled manipulation of the consciousness-altering effect of sickness becomes a vehicle for self-healing, empathetic awareness and integration with the divine. More often than not shamans report the Otherworld as a nightmarish place, teeming with monsters, demons and evil sorcerers. Shamans endure horrific pain and suffering, dismemberment and paralyzing fear. To sojourn there is not for the faint-hearted. Mircea Eliade described the practice of shamanism as controlled ecstasy, but an ecstatic state can be equally terrifying or transcendent.

Once the neophyte shaman agrees to the spirit's demands and all that lifestyle choice represents, which can take years of bitter misery and denial, he or she is healed from a spiritual and physical near-death condition, during which the spirits reveal their purpose as part of phase one of the initiation. The 'wounded healer' has been, like the shamanic Norse god Odin, wounded and suspended upside down

from the Tree of Life, learned occult secrets and returned restored and able to heal others. Experiential compassion has taken root and, apprenticed to experienced spiritual specialists, the student embarks on the difficult road to shamanism.

SEPARABLE SOULS

The fluid relationship between the body and spirit within a shamanic tradition functions as it does because the soul, or an aspect of it, can separate from the body and travel while the body is asleep or in a trance. While many cultures recognize the idea that everyone has multiple soul aspects, the shaman trains to split off the part of his consciousness that travels to other realms. The soul later returns to the body, rousing it to full consciousness. Dreaming validates this idea. A soul can get 'lost', separated from the body, through trauma, severe crisis or pain, or can wander off on its own, and may not be able find its way back, leaving the body debilitated. The life force is unprotected and in potential danger. A wandering soul is vulnerable to attack or kidnapping by spirits or evil shamans and a shamanic rescue or soul retrieval becomes necessary. Shamans enter into a trance, make the dangerous journey to the Otherworld, use their spirit helpers and clairvoyant abilities to search for the lost soul and, if possible, return it to the body. If the separation from the body is too profound, then, like Hermes/Mercury, the shaman becomes a psychopomp, assuring safe passage for the soul to the land of the dead so they don't become lost between the worlds. Should an unsettled ghost haunt the living, causing illness by desiring another soul for companionship, it is the shaman's duty to seek it out, resolve its suffering and guide it to its proper home.

People from many different traditions report that, during soul flight, or an out-of-body experience, their soul is connected to the body by a silvery cord or thin thread. This thread is very elastic and becomes thinner the further the soul flies from the body. Should this thread break, the body will die. It is important among the Washo Indians, for example, to wake a sleeper very gently so the cord of the dreaming body doesn't break accidentally and cut the soul loose.

Some traditions have souls of one sort while alive and acquire others after death. Aboriginals in Central Australia have two souls; one is a part of a supernatural being reincarnated in the body and the other is referred to as the 'mortal soul'. The 'mortal soul' regularly wandered away on its own during dreaming, experiencing adventures in places unknown by living men. Their term for

167

dreaming is 'to see eternal things.' The ancient Egyptians elevated shamanic ideas of the soul to high art, politics and grand ritual theater, breaking the soul into four aspects. They designated one aspect as the ka, a restless potential energy, another, the ba, the unconstrained spirit that passes effortlessly through time and space. The third was the 'shadow', a form of power that can bestow life on a corpse, and the fourth is heart, the vessel of 'free will' that is weighed in the balance after death against the feather of the goddess Maat to determine its purity and afterlife destination. These soul designations generated complex ritual observance, philosophical explication and an extensive funerary industry that spanned millennia.

SPIRIT HELPERS

It is our human nature to fight for life, so making a purposeful journey into a deep trance at the edge of death can be a terrifying experience. The shamanic trainee is helped with overcoming the fear of literally losing his or her soul by learning from teachers and acquiring spirit helpers to hone powers and assist in the adventures encountered as a rarified being. They may be animals that act as guides and protectors through the realms of spirit. They impart their essence to the shaman and teach their particular form of wisdom; the mouse, its ability to move through small spaces unobserved, the fish, the knowledge of the waters, a bird, its ability to fly, the eagle, the gift of vision, the bull, strength and courage, and so on. Or the spirit helper may be the essence of a plant, usually one with medicinal, poisonous or hallucinogenic properties. Castaneda fans will vividly recall his encounter with Mescalito, the spirit of the peyote. Spirit helpers can also be the souls of the dead; ancestors or shamans with great power.

Sometimes acceptance of a helper takes the form of a sacred marriage between shaman and spirit. A spirit suitor can appear in a dream and propose marriage, promising to both grant healing powers to the initiate and threatening bad luck, ill-health and misery if rejected. Like any earthly marriage, sacred marriages can run the gamut from affectionate to abusive. Denial of the marriage proposal can result in the shaman being pursued and harassed by the spirit lover for years, and the acceptance of a spirit suitor can be considerably complicated if the shaman is already married to an earthly partner. The shaman may even enter into a spirit marriage with more than one entity and sometimes of different sexes. In

Western tradition the acceptance of a supernatural marriage is not unknown. Catholic nuns accept Jesus Christ as both savior and mystical husband, becoming Brides of Christ and wearing wedding rings.

Seen from the standpoint of controlled ecstasy, a sexual union with a spirit allows someone with a proclivity for deviation from the norm to more easily enter into a transpersonal state, and one accepted by the tribe. Shamanism demands dissolution of one's identity and adoption of a new persona. If an initiate already suffers from a disturbed identity the process of disassembling the old and assembling a new one may be shorter.

A spirit helper may also be a tool, weapon or musical instrument invested with powers. Drums are common vehicles of transportation to spirit realms. In far northern cultures drums are referred to as the shaman's 'horse' and are made from the hide of a ritually sacrificed horse. They ride these 'horses' literally, musically and spiritually to the Otherworld. Mythic heroes, following in the footstep of shamans, always have magical tools and weaponry that help them perform their tasks, such as flying carpets, rings, seven-league boots, wands, mirrors and swords.

During years of perfecting a career, the shaman might incorporate, in the truest sense of taking into his body, the assistance of multiple spirit helpers that can be called on for different purposes, depending on the problem to be solved. He may also be able to send one of his helpers to make a journey in his place and retrieve information for him. As the shaman becomes proficient at entering into and controlling trance states he similarly becomes adept at manipulating energies his helpers bestow upon him. In a trance, the shaman is spirit, freed from the constraints of his body. To facilitate his flights to other worlds, the shaman may transform into a spirit animal, becoming a shape-shifter, able to rearrange his energies as he summons his helpers' powers. He is no longer bound to his human physical form and sings like the bird or howls like the beast whose form he has taken on, growling like a bear, writhing like a snake, snarling like a wolf or tiger. He enters into an ecstatic state and can then see with the eyes of the eagle, have the wily intelligence of a fox, travel through the ocean like a seal and commune with the reindeer. Through his transformation the shaman re-establishes the primordial time when humans and animals spoke the same language, before humans needed to sacrifice animals to survive, in the time before death. The ability to communicate with

all of nature opens up endless horizons of knowledge that the shaman can tap.

SPIRITUAL REASSEMBLY

Shamanic initiation is a process of death and resurrection. Destruction of the neophyte shaman's former life and personality is necessary so that he can be rebuilt to function properly in his new role. Accepting the workings of the spirit world requires the relinquishing of previously held assumptions about oneself, one's ego and the nature of being. Often this verges on a severe psychic crisis or near-death experience. The shaman must be literally torn from his former life and remade to enter a new one. Over time, coming to terms with the limitations imposed by illness and psychological crises a new breadth of personality, a deeper perception of life learned from the personal struggle to stay alive, emerges. Sometimes this includes the adoption of a new sexual identity, a third or fourth gender referred to as 'berdache' among European explorers and as 'two-spirit people' among 150 tribes of Native Americans. Erotic relationships are not considered the significant marker, although entering into a homosexual relationship is common. The distinctions are more importantly economic specializations having a spiritual/social component; domestic work and crafts for males and warfare or hunting for females. This is not necessarily a new sexual preference as much as it is adoption of an expanded gender, supernaturally sanctioned through dreams or visions. This transformation or, in some cases, multiplication of one's sexual identity, broadens a shaman's empathetic nature. They are exposed to different types of power. Liberated from the narrow confines of traditional identity, this new persona can move freely between social groups, enter into relationships, and perform specific ritual tasks otherwise not permitted. It is the genius of small-scale human societies to incorporate the different, the unorthodox, allowing for change and tolerance, which challenges adaptive capabilities.

Shamanic psycho-spiritual rewiring is often accompanied by the complete disassembling of the student-shaman's ethereal body in the spirit world while his physical body lingers near death in this one. In essence, becoming a sacrificial victim, astral nourishment for the spirits. Some shamans are seen to bleed from their joints while in a trance, as if being torn limb from limb. Some witness their spirit bodies disassembled bit by bit, some have their flesh magically

burned away, leaving only the bones, and even they are separated. The bones are boiled until purified to the spirits' satisfaction, then reassembled and clothed in flesh to create a new being of power, one now capable of enduring death and regenerating from these fertile bones.

Others are devoured by spirit animals, "digested" and vomited up again transformed. The flesh is scraped from them and scattered along the paths of the underworld or distributed sacrificially to the spirits of sickness who eat of it so the shaman will be able to cure the illnesses they cause. Then the body is reassembled. Occasionally, the spirits will implant a magical object inside the revitalized body, a crystal, or a magic stone, a sort of spiritual transistor for tuning into the subtle frequencies of the invisible universe. Quartz is widely associated with shamans, in part because when struck together the crystals glow. These 'stones of fire' are living entities, solidified light that represent and facilitate the enlightened shaman's ability to see through matter. This idea of crystals as metaphors for esoteric enlightenment is found from Australia to North America. It is easy, then, to imagine the Paleolithics' sense of spiritual transport inside a crystalline cave.

In many cultures, shamans' ceremonial clothing includes skeletal design elements that refer back to this disintegration/reintegration of the worldly body, and a mirror or other reflective surface that indicate the shaman's ability to see into other worlds.

These esoteric forays into spiritual realms are exceedingly strange and remote to many of us, yet also quite familiar in mythology and legend; strange stories of heroes, ghosts and gods tucked into our modern consciousness. Dionysus, the 'twice-born', was snatched prematurely from his mother's womb, sewn up in his father Zeus's thigh and carried to term. The Titans dismantled Dionysus, boiled him (or perhaps 'rendered' is a more apt description) and then returned him to life as the god of wine, ecstasy and enchanted epiphany. Osiris, sliced to pieces by his brother Set, was scattered all over Egypt. His shaman-priestess wife Isis collected the pieces, all but the penis, and reassembled him. He became a god of the underworld, usually depicted as black as the rich soil of the Nile delta or green as a new shoot. Although he is a god of the Dead, Osiris is not a god of death so much as resurrection, the renewing potential of life emerging from the soil. The Frankenstein story of Mary Shelley, in which a conflicted monster is constructed from the dead parts of others, takes a more

modern twist, warning of the manipulative powers of ego and technology.

TOPOPHILIA

Humans are territorial creatures. There is an unseverable attachment to the land they call their own. Many tribal names translate as 'the people', as if there were no others. Their country is often known as 'the land of our people' (a modern survival of this tribal identification with homeland is the plethora of 'istans' in Eastern Europe, land of the Afghanis, the Tadjiks, or the Uzbeks). This pervasive, passionate belonging to a place is called 'topophilia' and, in hunter-gatherer societies, this has little to do with ownership and everything to do with language and myth, a spiritual relationship to the environment, and ancestry. Their sacred sites are here, the shamanic portals to the Beyond, and the bones of their families co-mingle and dissolve into the landscape, yet their ancestral spirits remain accessible. The apparent division between the living and the dead is permeable and the separation between "self" and "other" is porous. It is clear why so many tribal societies waste away when driven off their traditional lands, as though their mystical umbilical cord had been cut. It is the shaman who talks with the extended spiritual family that cannot be separated from the land; the ancestors whose bones lie in the ground, the local spirits of the waters and the rocks, the healing plants, and the greater spirits of sky, weather and animals. The shaman is the translator who facilitates between the interior and the exterior landscapes and maintains the sacred harmony necessary for life to thrive.

Although the few remaining hunter-gatherers today live in the long shadow of the modern world, the people of the Ice Age existed long before anything resembling domesticity. The land and its bounty, or lack of it, defined their identity. The labyrinthine experience, a central mythic focus deep in the caves of their territory, gains more power in the light shed by topophilia. Consider an example of a mythic world very remote from ours that may assist us in understanding this depth of interrelationship.

T.G.H. Strehlow, a white Australian, was adopted into the Arrernte tribe in the 1930s and entrusted by the elders with the custodial responsibilities of their traditions. The trust they placed in him resulted in unparalleled saturation in Aboriginal culture and extensive linguistic and cultural research recorded in his masterwork, *Songs of Central Australia*. He reported that among

Australian Aboriginal tribes, the concept of the Dreaming illustrates this idea of topophilia. The origin myth of the older, Aranda-speaking Aborigines of Central Australia assumed that the earth and sky had always existed. The earth was originally a vast, desolate plain devoid of mountains, swamps, rivers or any other feature. Beneath this empty earth slept the embryonic forms of humans and uncreated supernatural beings that had always existed. Even the sun and moon slumbered under the surface of the earth that was only dimly lit by the distant stars of the Milky Way. These supernatural beings eventually awoke from their dreams and broke through the surface of the empty earth. These 'birthplaces' became infused with spiritual potency as these ancestor spirits materialized in every possible way, some as kangaroos, others as emus, snakes, goannas, honey ants, fish and so forth. The sun and moon rose into the sky and the earth was flooded with light. The wanderings and activities of the ancestor spirits gave form and definition to the landscape. This was the Golden Era, a time when humans could transform into animals and animals thought and acted like humans. The places of emergence, tracks of spirit journeys on the land and mythic activity would later become sacred sites where elaborate ceremonies re-enacted the emergence of spiritual beings. At the end of their wanderings these supernaturals grew tired and sank back into the land to rest but were not unaware of the happenings on the earth.

While the Dreamtime ancestors roamed over the land, rolling up mountains and carving riverbeds, they left behind them 'a trail of life'. A pregnant woman who passed over this trail could receive a fragment of this 'life' of the ancestor and her child given a defining soul of a Dreaming songline. So the children of the people had two souls, one invested by the human parents and one by the ancestor. The identity of the ancestor was paramount, because it determined the personality of the child after birth. The exact location of the 'conception site' where the mother first felt the quickening or suffered morning sickness was determined conclusively. Later, in initiation ceremonies, the child would learn his ancestor's identity and the responsibilities involved in ritual maintenance of the sacred site and the spiritual being that had sown life within him. Each member of the tribe was, then, not only the child of human parents, but was a reborn aspect of a supernatural being and that being had given specific shape to parts of the land. When the human body died the souls separated and the fragment of 'life' invested by the supernatural being returned to that being to await reincarnation once

173

again. The topophilia of the Aranda people weds the concepts of life, death, landscape and being into a complex, seamless whole, while eternally yoking the remote past alongside the present, creating a unique time category; the present-continuous.

The caves of the people of the Ice Ages were active, vital subterranean wells of spiritual power where elemental life-energy could be tapped. The conversations with the caves informed life aboveground and the joys and problems of life in the open air were addressed in the caves. Like the Aboriginal context linking life and existence to the spirits in the landscape, the Paleolithics participated in a power cycle of creation from the snows and sunshine above to the flickering magic below, and back again to the upper air.

SPIRIT WEB

All spiritual practices have, by definition, a belief in an aspect of humanity that invests it with the animating power of life, which departs the body at death and links us to an ineffable reality beyond our own. Spirit exists both within and outside of humans either as other beings, other forms of consciousness, or deities. Humans are participants in a vast network of spiritual circuitry pulsing through life and death; we act on our environment to alter it and it does the same to us. Measured reciprocity and proper behavior between the spirit and human worlds is the particular province of the shaman. During the Aurignacian period these delicate relationships were being slowly defined, century upon century, to determine the nature and dimension of this spiritual web in a way that had not been done before, and their legacy remains with us.

What we consider to be alive are things in nature that move, grow, reproduce and die. We include plants and animals, but may draw the line at rocks or weather systems, although they also grow and die. Their category of animation is considered a different classification, not one invested with life's essence in the same way as a deer, an insect or a child. In a shamanic cosmos, however, not only these, but also household objects, streams, mountains, tools, weapons, drums and so on, have a spiritual component that makes each thing uniquely what it is, all sharing in the same animating principle. A bowl is invested by spirit with the capacity to contain, a boat floats and a drum has a voice. Each plant has its unique temperament and capabilities, as any gardener knows who holds conversations with sulky tomatoes and determined dandelions. And many thoroughly rational people attach symbolic images like worry

174

dolls and 'computer goddesses' to their desktops to continue the proper channeling of energy.

Imagine spiritual power, that which is the source of life, as a form of rarified electricity. Many traditions speak of a realm of chaos where this energy exists as an infinite, restless pool, charged with potential but taking no form. The process of creation transforms this free-roaming power by channeling and focusing it, and monsters as easily as gods can result. Control of the process of creation for the good of the community demands an unimpeachable moral mastery, a right convergence of mind and energies to extract formless energy from the pool of potential and mold it into beneficent form. This is the manipulative genius of the artist and, to some extent in the mundane world, we all do this. There is the poem that drops 'out of nowhere' on to the page, the picture that paints itself or the idea for a new invention that comes in a flash of insight. We call it inspiration, literally, to take in spirit as one takes in a breath. But people can be equally inspired to create a reign of terror or a cathedral. For the shaman who trains to tap into that energy source, the moral imperative carries weighty consequences for himself and his community. Ethnographic literature, as well as mythology, is full of stories of evil shamans or sorcerers, those who succumb to the allure of power and use its manipulation for personal gain now known, thanks to Darth Vader, as 'going to the Dark Side'. In Whitley's estimation these sorcerers are those who suffer so deeply from their insanity that they enact a death wish. They choose evil knowing it will lead to their death, by execution or suicide. But until that happens they can exercise a terrible power.

The idea of a mystical web of energy that empowers creation is not really as esoteric as it may appear when it is applied to the miraculous world of biology. Over millions of years of evolution and specialization, unique relationships of amazing specificity have developed among species to insure life and propagation. Consider the web of life surrounding the Brazil nut tree. Towering 160 feet above the jungle, a single tree is home to literally millions of species, including a spider the size of a dinner plate. The tree is central to these species' continued existence. Its cannonball-sized nuts fall at speeds of up to 50 miles-per-hour, but don't break on impact with the earth. The only creature capable of opening the nut is the agouti, a shy animal the size of a rabbit, which has teeth like chisels. They chew open the husk, eat some of the nutmeat and, squirrel-like, bury the rest. Equally squirrel-like, they forget where

they put them all and small trees result. But for the nuts to appear in the first place it requires the services of the orchid bee to pollinate the tree's flowers. The female orchid bee doesn't settle for just any old bee. She is a very romantic and discriminating lover. Before she will mate her partner must be bathed in the scent of the orchid flower, which sounds good to me. But should the jungle be disturbed, logged for example, and the orchids gone, there will be no bees, no pollination and no Brazil nuts to feed agoutis or fuel a million-dollar Brazil nut industry. As with most things in the world of life essence, one cannot draw a straight line from the agoutis of the rainforest to the economic wherewithal to purchase a pair of designer shoes in Rio, but one can follow the spokes of the web.

As George Martin selected and assembled bits of tape to create unique music, the shaman taps into a reservoir of potential to create harmony. But where Martin's selection for a linear tape loop was random, the shaman's is the result of carefully considered, organic inspiration. This naturalistic reality envisions all existence as varying intensities of spiritual energy, a luminous web of power that the shaman learns to use and is entrusted to maintain in harmony. The idea that all existence shares in this web of power gives phenomena an expansive fluidity. The Sioux conception of the Whirlwind Complex, as discussed in Chapter Three, is indicative of just such a fluid universe. No line of demarcation is drawn to separate people from animals or spirits. Manipulating power then becomes a matter of comprehending the nature of different densities and formulations of energy and acting on them in such a way as to bring about a desired metamorphosis. No easy task.

This idea of metamorphosis is one we will return to, for the portal of the labyrinthine web leads ultimately to the shaman's reservoir of power, the unformed source of life energy from which all existence is drawn, and makes metamorphosis not only possible, but inescapable The realm of the sacred lies just beyond the veil, guarded by the shamanistic Minotaur, in the Center of all possibilities.

CHAPTER 10

FINDING THE CENTER

"Here the night overflows with stars.
Man is too numerous. Endless generations
of birds and insects, multiplying themselves,
of serpents and the spotted jaguar,
of growing branches, weaving, interweaving,
of grains of sand, of coffee and of leaves
descend on every day and re-create
their miniscule and useless labyrinth.
It may be every ant we trample on
is single before God, Who counts on it
for the unfolding of the measured laws
which regulate His curious universe.
The entire system, if it was not so,
would be an error and a weighty chaos."
Jorge Luis Borges, ***Poem of Quantity***

COSMIC MAPPING

The chaotic pool of energy beyond Time has been tapped for eons to bring endless numbers of worlds into being. With a multiplicity of spirits in an inexhaustible universe, how does a soul traveler find his way home? For that matter, how do those of us on middle earth orient ourselves as residents in this endless universe? And how do we understand our departure from it? Like spiders, we weave a sacred geography by following the vibrating threads of energy in the web of life to the archetypal sacred center of the labyrinth.

The spiritual topography of every culture on the planet is marvelously unique, an integral part of the natural world of that culture. Each has a mystical map whose pathways are marked by a shifting continuum of celestial movements, unique environments, guardian/ancestral beings and topophilia. Every plane within a

single spiritual system and its relationship to other worlds within the same system possesses its own cultural logic and are bound together by consistent symbolism. Although the spiritual maps of the Amazon jungle will be decidedly different from those of the far north of Alaska, the biological unity of human experience ultimately melds with the ordering principles of the natural universe, regardless of how we attempt to alter or ignore it. The most obvious of these is the consistent rising and setting of the sun and moon that, for most of humanity, mark the east and west, and by inference, the north and

south, quartering the earth and sky. Cultures in the Arctic and around the equator divide the year into seasons of darkness and light or of wet and dry. Time and season are anchored at each quarter of the year by the solstices and equinoxes, and the waxing and waning of the moon measure the months. This simple orientation becomes increasingly complex when interwoven with wheeling skeins of constellations and wandering planets that mark seasonal patterns of life, death and ceremony.

The other worlds are mapped as well as shamans find their way from the middle world into the mystical landscape. The Amazonian Cosmos, for instance, is surrounded by a void. Beneath the sky, the Earth is divided by the Amazon into the Land of the First Ancestors. From there one moves through the Worlds of the Vulture and Condor into the Half World and Place of Thunder and Lightning where the Mother of Thunder resides. Beyond is the Celestial Lake and House of the Wind. Beyond this lake not even the most powerful shamans can go. Here the dead reside in the sky with the celestials, the Pole Star, the Moon and Sun and evening Star. Here too, at the farthest corner of this universe, is where the Great Primordial Shaman dwells.

The indigenous Siberian cultures usually divide the cosmos in three, with humans occupying the middle world. To enter the sky world, one passed through a small hole into a landscape full of animals. Above, there were more levels, in some cultures as many as 16. The lower world is the land of the dead. These realms were similar to the middle world, having water, mountains and animals. The Nganasan people believed the realm of the dead to be very cold, while the Yakut believed the upper worlds to be frigid as shamans returned from their sky journeys encrusted in ice.

In hunter-gatherer and early agrarian societies of more temperate zones, the symbolic cosmos is most commonly divided by four roads that correspond to the four cardinal directions, and sometimes

include two more, the sky road and the path to the underworld, designated variously by color, sacred animal, manifest power and eventual destination. All of these roads converge at a Center. Imagine a mystical overlay of spiritual cartography on the landscape of one's homeland; a white road leading to the north, home of the cold winds, a yellow road arcing off to the warm south and the generative power of the herds, a red road to the east, the morning sun and the beginning of all things, and a black road to the west, the way of the dead. Where these ways of power intersect is the radiant hub of being, the driving wheel of time. Yet its unmoving Center exists outside of time.

The shaman moves from one world to another along a route at this center called the '*axis mundi*', a spinal cord of power that branches from the underworld, through the middle and into the sky world. The world tree, Yggdrasil of Norse legend, is such a magic tree whose roots stretch from the lowest depths of existence, through the axle of the middle world, and in its branches are hung heaven's stars. Yggdrasil was also the 'terrible horse' that men rode down to their deaths and that became the shaman/hero Odin's gallows during his nine nights of sacrifice to wisdom. Buddha's Tree of Enlightenment is another, while the Mayan Bible, the Popul Vuh, has its ceiba tree. Along similar lines, the Omphalos of Delphi, the 'navel of the world', is a channel through which creative power passes. However, a strict geometic partitioning of the universe is more liable to be the result of a Neolithic mindset where divisions of property, fields, towns and constructed ceremonial centers birthed a mathematical ordering of the universe. The Paleolithics and other pre-Neolithic cultures, moving so completely within the rhythms of the natural world, would have probably used a more abstract or organic aesthetic of the universe as their paradigm. We will discover this to be profoundly true in the cave art of the Ice Age.

Shamans will ritually create a world tree in ceremony as a path to the sky or nether world by erecting a pole and infusing it with spiritual power. It may be carved with potent images, have steps on it, be decorated with feathers or flags, have holes drilled in it that allow spirits to enter, or it may have a platform at the top from which the spiritual specialist can shamanize. The platform symbolizes the horizontal intersection of the world of appearances by a vertical channel to the sacred. At the place or moment of convergence, sacred mystery is made evident. The Center is the zone in which the veil of the mundane shivers, fades and reveals the

holy. In this light, the image of a sacrificed Jesus on the cross resonates with very ancient traditions.

The two trees in the Biblical Paradise are likewise, each an *axis mundi*, linking the sky world of God through the middle earth of Adam and Eve, with its roots in the underworld represented by the serpent. Eating the fruit of the Tree of the Knowledge of Good and Evil allows Adam and Eve to become wise, their eyes are opened and they can see. No longer innocent, they are capable of distinguishing a moral universe. Before the serpent tempted Eve with the sacred apple they were blissfully unaware of the second tree, the Tree of Life, because it was 'hidden' from their limited sight. Now that they have gained 'insight' they are cast out of Paradise for breaking the rules. More to the point, before they have the chance to eat the fruit of the Tree of Life, which would make them immortal and therefore indistinguishable from God and the angels. Awareness of the Tree of Life is not easily gained. Adam and Eve have effectively brought the middle world of humans into existence by having drawn the boundaries between human and divine. The Fall into Time and out of the Eternal Garden brings with it labor, pain, suffering and death, but also wisdom. It is this moral discrimination and self-awareness that makes the transmutation of energies and metamorphosis both desirable and possible. Indeed, the gods and angels would wish to keep this from us.

Cherubims and a fiery sword 'which turned every way' are posted as guardians to prevent man from gaining access to the ultimate mystery. We think of cherubs as pudgy rosy-cheeked, naked babies with wings only useful for holding drapery that hides the anatomy of immortals or assisting the Virgin's ascent to the celestial realm on puffy clouds. Not a very frightening spectacle even armed with a fiery sword. Before their Baroque makeover, cherubim or kerubh were Babylonian guardians, composite beings with eagle wings, bull heads, lion feet and serpent tails. As representations of the sacred animal of each of the four cardinal points, they were guardians who protected palaces and temples from threats that came from any direction. Posting cherubim and an omnipresent fiery sword around the World Tree of Life sends the undeniable message that this is sacrosanct territory of the highest order, the Center of the eternal Mystery and mere humans who carry the stench of mortality are not admitted. Besides, they would just muck things up.

THE SACRED HEARTH

Traditional homes in many cultures reflect the cosmic layout of the universe, a constant reminder of the family's connection to the natural and supernatural, their topophilial universe. A Turkic yurt, like a Plains Indian teepee, is oriented with the door to the east, the direction of the dawn, and the place of beginnings. Many cathedrals also have this east-west orientation and Christians are buried facing east so that on the day of resurrection they will rise up in their graves and behold the glory of the resurrected Jesus returning to the earth. Among the Navaho, the hogan is an eight-sided structure symbolic of the entire cosmos, four sides oriented to the four sacred directions and four to the cross-corner points, with the fire in the center. The door always faces east. When a death occurred, a hole was cut in the north wall of the Hogan, the direction the Navaho associated with death, through which the body was passed for burial.

The fireplace, source of light, heat and food, was the domestic and spiritual center of the home. It extended down into the underworld where the ancestors reside and so, into the past, and simultaneously the smoke lifted upward into the abode of the spirits. The hearth is an access route to the spirits of the air, the underworld and the ancestors who dwell there and is often the site of domestic ceremonies. The tending of the fire as the center of family life was a sacred domestic duty. Allowing the fire to go out through pure negligence was unthinkable, an affront to the spirits, as well as impractical. Only at ritual times, such as at the turn of the year or during times of mourning, was the fire purposely extinguished.

The ancient nomadic people of Europe had a central hearth with a smokehole in the center of the roof. Shamans and others desiring communion with deities envisioned their essence ascending through the smokehole of the house and riding the smoke up this ethereal *axis mundi* to the upper world. Any spirit visitors who would enter the house would use the same route, descending into the home by following down the stream of smoke.

The connection of magical flight and smoke was seen during a Midsummer ceremony among the Eveny people of the far north. On this magical day when the sun seems to roll around the horizon like a marble on a plate, the people created a gateway to the sky by stretching a rope between two larch trees. Two fires, burning fragrant rhododendron wood, wafted purifying smoke through the gateway. The people each walked counter-clockwise, or against the

181

sun, around the first fire marking the end of the old year and burning away its illnesses, then clockwise around the second in the direction of the sun, to welcome the new year. During these prayers for fertility and success in the new year each person was said to be carried into the sky on the back of a reindeer to the paradise of the sun where they received blessings and renewal. Although most of the people rode on the backs of these sacred animals, the shamans became them.

We see a modern echo of the fireplace as spirit conveyance in the use of 'floo dust' to assist the wizardly transportation of Harry Potter via the fireplaces of England and Hogwarts. During Obama's inauguration, a Washington D.C. transportation official, anticipating the unparalleled crowds expected to attend, wished in vain for a pile of floo dust. In Ionia, wine and oil were poured through the center of a ring-shaped cake on to the fire at Christmas time. This practice echoes the ancient custom of making offerings on the home altar/hearth to the goddess Hestia. She was an eternal virgin, wedded only to the phallic fire and her sacred duty of hospitality. To mistreat a guest of the house was a direct insult to the goddess. Ever the image of domestic sanctity and tranquillity, she never took part in wars or disputes.

In Roman times, the goddess of the sacred hearth was Vesta. The hearth fire was the sacred center of the earth as well as the center of family and clan life. As the Roman Empire grew, the sacred center of the capital city of Rome was the temple of the Vestal Virgins who maintained the altar fires of Vesta. Her temple at the foot of Palatine Hill is one of the oldest in Rome, the first possibly built in the sixth century BP. Despite many renovations and reconstructions, some due to the obvious danger of fire, the doorway always opened to the east and the flaming sun. Should the fire of Vesta go out, it was believed that the Empire would fall. The temple was round, reminiscent of the prehistoric round houses or tents of the Roman tribal past with the fire at the center. The Latin word focus means 'fireplace' and later, 'fire' itself. In modern English, 'focus' has an optical connotation in terms of being able to see clearly, but also to attend to something important. For tribal people whose domestic focus was their fireplace, their attention was on things of the spirit seen with the inner eye, a focus that kept them grounded in the waking world.

The hearth as *axis mundi*, the traditional route to other worlds, resonates in the legend celebrated every Christmas in which a jolly

old elf of considerable girth manages to squeeze himself down chimneys all over Christendom to deposit gifts in the space of one night. Then, according to Clement C. Moore's famous poem, by 'laying a finger aside of his nose' he rises back up the chimney. He is then whisked away into the sky realm by flying reindeer, spirit transportation of the Siberians from time immemorial, although Santa's pull a sleigh. Whether the link between Santa and shamans is valid or purely poetical, it has a magical resonance that has made him a central iconic symbol of Christmas.

Santa shares the holiday with the miraculous birth of the baby Jesus, foretold by signs and portents. A living symbol of resurrection and spiritual redemption, Jesus is a mystical sacrificial offering, as was Odin, Osiris, Adonis and Tammuz, each a mythic promise of the fertile cycle of life, eternally springing from death. Jesus's birthday coincides closely and purposely with the Winter Solstice, when the rising morning sun has reached its lowest point on the horizon and begins to gradually move higher in the sky each morning, bringing with it the heat, light and life of the growing season. The Minotaur is likewise a sacrificial creature, but his original Paleolithic identity has been overlain with a mantle of monstrosity. Still, as we will see in Lascaux, he is associated with the cycling seasons and return of life.

The fireplace as potent focus of family spiritual life was also celebrated in old Europe by the placing of a Yule log on the hearth at the time of the winter solstice. The hearth fires were ritually extinguished and rebuilt, representing the end of the old cycle and a new beginning at the hinge of the year. The Yule log was usually a heavy chunk of oak, which was worshipped as the King of Trees by Celtic pagans. The word 'pagan' literally means 'rural' or from the countryside, but became a contemptuous term for nonbelievers and bumpkins. As Christianity made inroads into the old beliefs, overlaying traditional pagan observances with their own, the sacred oak became the foundation of the New Year's fire on Christmas Eve, rather than the Solstice. Its size and location, fitted into the floor of the hearth under the fire proper, assured that it burned only very slowly and would last the entire year. At the new year, the ashes and remaining fragments from the previous year's log were considered to be a source of vigorous fertility, having been charged in this concentrated power spot all year long, and were spread on the fields to encourage the crops. Any remaining charred pieces of the Yule log were used as a wedge for the farmer's plough, because its

potency transferred to the soil and seeds and made them thrive. The ashes were believed to have curative properties for both people and cattle, and if remains of the Yule log were steeped in water and given to the cattle to drink it would help them to calve. The oak tree was further connected to fertility as it produced prodigious amounts of acorns to fatten the pigs. Clumps of the parasite plant mistletoe found growing in the branches was considered a magical cure-all and has been shown to have some medicinal properties in the treatment of some cancers and high blood pressure.

Oak ashes spread on the wheat fields would prevent mildew and a piece of the charred log placed under the bed would protect the house from vermin. Some people carried a bit of the log in their pocket to protect them in the fields against hail. Because of its deep roots and durability the oak can survive lightning strikes and fires to grow to a venerable age and enormous size and was revered for its strength. Because of mystical properties of oak connected with the god of thunder, the Yule log was also thought to protect the house from lightning and the inhabitants from sorcery.

Consider these connections of oak, lightning, flame, fertility and protection from Celtic tradition in relation to the Sioux Whirlwind Complex that combined invisibility, metamorphosis, buffalo, spider and cocoons, and the strangeness of the unfamiliar dissolves. The related categories have a cultural logic, weaving together a pattern of thought and behavior in which we still find some comfort, although the logic escapes us. A mythic vision of the interconnectedness of spirit is not so deeply buried in us as we may think. Although we have lost the ancient pagan meanings under centuries of 'progress' and Christian overlay, and no longer build circular houses that necessarily face east, the powers still resonate, and fragments of the rituals are still observed. Many of us celebrate the ascent up the world tree via our sacred hearths by a spirit figure every year at the Winter Equinox, the return of the light. We decorate our homes with symbols of life; 'evergreen' trees, representative of the eternal *axis mundi*, are ornamented with sparkling stars and angelic spirits, the denizens of the sky world. This tree is set apart from all others as sacred, having been 'made special' by virtue of its decorations that reflect our individual ideas of the sacred and family traditions. The seasonal colors are red and green, symbolic of life-blood and renewal. In a display of familial and social sacrificial commitment we pile gifts for friends and family that often we can't afford at the foot of this *axis mundi*. We

gather around the roaring fireplace with cups of cheer and, even if we don't sing communally any other time of the year, we lift our voices to sing songs about the Yule season. The spirit of generosity and abundance prevails. In *The Christmas Carol*, Dickens's Spirit of Christmas Present, balanced in Time between ghosts of the nostalgic Past and the fear of death in the Future, makes his jolly appearance amidst a mountain of food and wealth.

The word 'yule' is possibly descended from the Indo-European 'qwelo', or 'go round', the source of our English word for cycle and wheel. The Yule log represents a magical connection with the completion of one yearly cycle of life and the beginning of a new year. The wheel of Time will spin again and we pray that protection, unity, strength and abundance will be ours surrounding the sacred hearth in our homes. The smoke will ascend to the Upper World and bear our requests to the spirits who dwell there, while, at the still Center, eternity abides.

THE CENTER

The mystical center of the world that orients us in our spiritual landscape is relative and mobile and resides where the focus, or fire, of sacredness is the strongest. Every people has its own center and it can be created and re-created as tradition and ceremony demand, or it may be a specific geographically designated place of power on the earth, or both; a cave, mountain, cenote or lake. The Dome of the Rock, Mt. Sinai, Borobudur, the Omphalos of Delphi and the Lakota Sun Dance pole are all such places. Shrines are often built over or near places of unique geological power such as springs or volcanic vents. This sacred architecture serves to align cosmological energies so that the upper, middle and lower worlds are brought into power-generating harmony along a single axis, which unifies the natural divisions between emanations of energy; the directions of north, south, east and west, as well as sky and underworld. This supernaturally charged alignment opens a portal when awakened by appropriate trance-inducing ritual or ingestion of psychotropic drugs, and draws back the veils between worlds, allowing for an exchange of power between them.

The Center is a whirlpool, a spiral, a wheel in continual motion, a vortex of power. Yet the center of the Center is utterly still and unmoving, the hub of the wheel. A shaman, in a heightened trance state, makes the passage from one direction to another, from human consciousness to spirit consciousness and back again, through a

The encroachment of the modern industrial world on traditional cultures, with its narrower, linear world view and its high-speed lifestyle, has brought about a retreat of the spirit world, and denial of its existence. Ireland, the Celtic bastion most remote from Roman and Christian dominance, was the last holdout of the ancient Western pagan tradition of Druidic nature worship. Many of the faerie stories, in which faeries disappear from their usual haunts or become diminutive or merely pesky creatures, reflect the shrinking of the spirit world. Lugh, the great Celtic god of the sun and patron of arts, was known in Ireland as the embodiment of creative energy and adept at many crafts, including shoemaking. As the old ways were driven underground, Lugh, a dynamic creative being, became diminished until he was just a faerie craftsman called 'Lugh chromain' or 'little stooping Lugh'. The great Celtic creator-god had been shrunk into a leprechaun. Similarly, the tales that recount the stealing of human babies by faeries like Rumplestiltskin to replenish their depleted stock, or the ill-fated children born of forbidden marriages between faerie and human such as in the story of Melusine, suggest a failure of the folk-spirit world to thrive.

The mythic three-tiered cosmos of the shamanic world in which movement between the realms was relatively facile has faded. The reciprocal perpetuating mechanisms of belief and ritual observations that reinforce belief, nested into a lifestyle that makes space and time for them, is vanishing. We must clap our hands and believe to bring Tinkerbell back from the brink. These tales, although reduced now to the province of the nursery, bear the mark of truth, the symbolic power of ancient wisdom traceable back to the shamans of the Paleolithic. What you believe, or allow yourself to 'see', is brought into being. We actively alter our reality through the processes of belief and naming, for belief and truth are the same thing to the believer. What de la Valle did not 'see' in the cave of Niaux as he wrote his name next to an ancient painting, and what the contemporaries of de Sautuola stubbornly refused to see at Altamira, was fully visible to his little daughter. As the scales fell from their eyes and the evidence became undeniable, the world shifted on its scientific and spiritual axes. The antiquity of humans was evident, their expression of art eloquent, their spiritual commitment sophisticated. Their humanity became approachable; as they reached out a paint-smeared hand to meld with the magical wall of their cave, so we reach out a hand to them to touch the mystery. In so doing, the labyrinth, an echo of their primeval

shamanic world, is re-emerging in our time, actively being sought out and condensing into our reality.

MYTHIC WORLDS

Travel to other worlds is the central component in legends of heroes and gods. The ancient heroes that survive in literature today are probably the enduring collective memories of talented shamans who traversed the *axis mundi* vortex in antiquity. The classic steps of the hero's journey as outlined by Joseph Campbell in his book, *The Hero With A Thousand Faces*, parallel the shaman's journey; the call to action, refusal of the call, gaining supernatural help, crossing the threshold, enduring trials, apotheosis and magical return. That George Lucas followed Campbell's hero road map to the letter is one reason the first *Star Wars* films were so popular. The spiritual validity of this archetypal human experience resonated on a deep level with movie fans, whether or not they recognized its mythic foundation.

What are these other worlds, the upper and lower realms visited by heroic humans? The Underworld takes many forms, but a common element is darkness or, at best, a feeble light. This cosmic realm often is similar to our waking world, having streams, mountains and a pale sun and moon. But the rules are different. The spirit traveler must carefully and respectfully navigate these mythic landscapes through wary attentiveness, courage and proper ritual to be able to successfully return to this plane intact.

Shamanic transportation to the lower realm is usually accompanied by the somatic sensation of difficulty in breathing, or being squeezed. Shamans tell of being drawn down tree roots or through narrow rivers, pulled through holes in the ground or cracks in rocks, all versions of passage along the *axis mundi* and through the center of the labyrinth.

The eerie tale of Beowulf tells of the Germanic hero's journey after being implored to save King Hrothgar's men. Dressed in full armor he pursues the monstrous mother of Grendel (described as suspiciously Neanderthal-like) into a smoking, churning, frost-rimmed pool where Beowulf slays a parade of water monsters on the way down through the vortex. He emerges into a magical den at the bottom where the creatures reside and confronts them. Mourned as dead by his warrior-friends, he emerges days later, bearing a dwarf-crafted jeweled sword hilt, the blade having been dissolved by the toxic blood of Grendel's mother.

The mythic Mayan Hero Twins journey through the underworld of Xibalba and do battle with such colorful characters as Pus Master, Jaundice Master, Bone Scepter and Stab Master. These shamanistic contests occur in terrifying places such as Razor House, which is full of voracious flying stone blades, Cold House, where hail falls continually and hungry jaguars roam, and Bat House, where they must spend the night squeezed inside their blowguns. Only the Hero Twins' courage and wiles get them through these trials. Although they may be the sources of disease and putrefaction, the lords of Xibalba are fortunately not very bright and the trickster Twins eventually re-emerge victorious into the middle world of humans.

The ancient Greeks envisioned the dreary, dank kingdom of Hades lit with dark fires. On rare occasions the living visited there as well. The entrance was a cave guarded by the fierce three-headed dog Cerebus. Theseus, our presumptive hero of the labyrinth, attempted to steal away the Queen of the Underworld, Persephone, was captured by her furious husband and imprisoned in a blazing-hot chair. Hercules rescued the hapless kidnapper by wrenching him free, but in the process left some of his buttocks behind.

The Mesopotamians envisioned a perpetually gloomy land where despairing spirits eat dust and mud. The goddess Inanna journeys to the land of the dead after she 'opened her ear to the Great Below', to lay claim to her dark sister Ereshkigal's throne. On the way she passes through seven portals and at each she is stripped of one more symbol of her power in the sky-world until she is reduced to a skin hung on a peg. Two professional mourners journey there to release her. They strike a devious deal with Ereshkigal, sprinkle Inanna with the food and water of life and the goddess is restored to her splendor. Eventually she returns to her rightful place in the heavens, having learned, but not claimed, the mysteries of the netherworld.

The Norse god Odin, a shape-shifter of terrible power who rode a flying, eight-legged horse named Sleepnir, was wounded with his own spear and hung on the World Tree, Yggdrasil, for nine nights. He mystically traverses all the realms of death so as to learn words of power, sacred poetry and the secrets of the runes. Each of these mythic characters enters another world by means of some form of portal, encounters or endures death and returns with mystical wisdom that will improve the lives of those who depend on them. The drapery is different, but the body of the myth is the same, and the journey is the same as reported by shamans around the world.

190

On the other end of the spiritual/somatic spectrum from descent into the underworld is the experience of weightlessness, expansion, hovering and leaving the body to soar to the upper world, a celestial world of brilliant light. Shamanic journeys to the sky realm are made on the backs of flying reindeer or birds, by climbing enchanted trees or ascending by way of magical bridges of smoke, lianas or ropes into the sky. The shamans of legend soar to the sun or moon, brushing the stars out of their way. Nepalese have wondered if our astronauts met their dead on the moon, and others were amazed they needed so much technology to make the trip when their shamans fly unencumbered.

The journey to the Upper World is told in the ancient Mesopotamian Epic of Gilgamesh. Devastated by the death of his friend and keenly aware of his own mortality, the hero Gilgamesh sets out in pursuit of the secret of eternal life. He must pass the guardians of the gateway, the Scorpion Men, then walks for days through the black darkness of a tunnel. He finally emerges into the glittering garden of the sun god, Shamash, where the plants are made of jewels. The Aztec hero, Quetzalcoatl, departs life in a boat made of serpents which beaches in the country of Red Daylight. There he is dressed in garments like the sun and immolated in a sacred fire that transforms his heart into a star and his body is changed to light. The Egyptian god Horus, not content at birth with merely a place in the Sacred Boat of the Sun along with other deities, bursts into life as a savior in the guise of a falcon and takes control of his destiny. He flies beyond the stars and all the souls of the old divinities that inhabit the constellations on the eastern horizon, beyond the boundaries of the divinely created universe to return with the power of light to defeat Seth, who holds dominion over the terrors of darkness and death.

There are always exceptions and one is the Southern Aranda-speakers of Australia. According to their mythology there was, in ancient days, a casuarina tree in the Simpson Desert that reached to the sky. Another casuarina tree several miles away leaned against it at an angle and so provided a ladder for people to climb into the sky and live eternally. But this tree was chopped down by a gang of 'Blood Avengers' so all hope of eternal life was severed forever. The supernatural beings and the celestial ones, the sun the moon, the Seven Sisters and the Evening Star, although born from the earth, neither care about nor attend to activities on the earth. When the Dreamtime totemic ancestors sank into the ground to rest, their

essence rose into the sky and never looked back.

Along similar lines, the Ik of Uganda were forbidden by their modern government to hunt in their traditional lands, which had become a wild animal reserve. They were forced into an agricultural lifestyle that imploded their culture and resulted in widespread starvation. They told of their sky gods who climbed a rope into heaven, then pulled it up after them.

Myths that speak of journeys to the underworld or flights to the stars arise from the complex human biological processing of the effects of altered states of consciousness in the same way. Whether one's spirit is actually making this voyage is a matter of personal belief, but the equipment with which we perceive it is universal. The neurological and somatic experiences encountered during trance states are at the center of the shamanic universe. They are also increasingly familiar to modern ER patients who report the near-death experience of traveling down a tunnel, encountering departed loved ones and almost crossing over the final threshold to join them. Although many people point to this empirical evidence as proof of an afterlife and find great comfort there, its disturbing, mystical implications are just as often deflected. 'Going for the light' has become a catch phrase for seeking heavenly access however it is attained. Bob Dylan, after surviving a brush with death from a serious infection, quipped that he almost met Elvis, a modern iconic spirit whose own layers of metaphoric potency are laid down year after year like nacre on pearl. Whatever shape the story takes, the archetypal vortex endures, wired into our brains, a whirling bit of sand at the heart of the spiritual pearl, gateway to the beyond.

SPEAKING POWER

That worlds are literally made of words, that one can summon and enter worlds beyond our own through the ritual use of words, is fundamental to religion. Sound is simply vibration at various frequencies, and the magical use of ritualized sound to transcend waking consciousness is as old as humans. Just as the clear high note of a soprano can shatter glass, the right pitch and endurance of ceremonial sound can shatter assumptions. Chanting, singing, prayer and magical spells are some of the vocalizations that summon those parallel realities and open portals between them. Accompanied by rhythmic drumming or other music, the shaman is transported, or 'rides his drum like a horse' to the Beyond.

The world is, quite simply, made of stories; the stories we tell

ourselves, and those we tell others. Or, perhaps more precisely, the languages that compose those stories. The Aurignacians who invaded the stronghold of the Neanderthals had a linguistic facility that transformed that primal world into their own, and resulted in the inevitable extinction of the primitive humans who had dwelt there for hundreds of generations. The very structure of our languages, the words we invent and adapt to describe our existence create the world as we see it. The world in which we find ourselves needs to be communicated. If there is no knowledge of tapirs, we have no need of a word for one. Yet, should we discover such an animal our first compulsion is to name it, as did Adam in Eden. As concepts, novel experiences and technology come into our lives, they are named and change the way we see the world. A brief list of words minted in the last few generations demonstrates this; A-bomb, TV, desegregate, X-rated, Ipod, Frankenfood, space shuttle, sexism, shopaholic, mallrat, virtual reality and designer drug. We weave our existence from words that explain its origin and nature and how we are to move in it as beings of a certain type.

The Aranda-speaking tribes of Central Australia possess a lyrical linkage of relationships between the land, spirit and language. As mentioned in the previous chapter's discussion of topophilia, the Dreamtime ancestors created the landscape and everything to be found on it. During this process of impregnation with life energy, myths were likewise laid down in a network of song-stories that covered the land; songs of the ancestors' emergence, adventures and where they came to rest. These myths literally arise from the landscape and are as much a part of it as are the rocks and water. A man who claims a particular totemic ancestor has an intimate relationship with the ancestors' Dreamtime landscape and the animal or being in whose form the ancestor was incarnated. An initiated man was responsible for learning the myths and songs that tell the story of that piece of land and for participating in sacred ceremonies that perpetuate its fruitfulness. His sacred songlines link to others that connect geographically so that the landscape is crisscrossed with lines of song that reflect the variations in the geography itself, rising and falling in tone with the hills and valleys and leaving off when his mythic song and sacred landscape meets that of another. Their world is literally made of song and the voices of humans reify its creation.

In many ancient origin tales, the world is brought into being by the power of spirit-voice or breath. Once released through the potent

creative force of articulation, thought, energy and breath unite, coalesce and condense into tangible substance. Existence takes form and is animated by the pneuma, the spirit of breath. "In the beginning the world was without form and void and the spirit of God moved over the face of the deep. And God said 'Let there be light'..." God speaks and the world comes into being. The Biblical Adam, the first man, completes God's creation by naming the animals, anchoring them in the world of Eden. In the Quiché Mayan Bible, the Popol Vuh, "Sovereign Plumed Serpent and Heart of Sky spoke together. They joined their words and thoughts... and then the earth arose because of them, it was simply their words that brought it forth." The ancient Egyptian Memphite Theology survives on a badly damaged inscribed stone, itself a copy of a much older worm-eaten text. This is how it describes the beginning of everything:

"The sight of the eyes, the hearing of the ears, and the smelling of the air by the nose, they present to the heart. This is what causes every completed concept to come forth, and it is the tongue that repeats what the heart thinks. Thus all the gods were born...Every word of the god came into being through what the heart thought and the tongue commanded." (Shafer 96)

The world is what we believe it to be, and we believe it to be what it is because we have sensory perceptions of it through the instrument of our body. And we have told ourselves stories that explain its nature and validate our experiences. The stories we tell relate the experiences of our lives, the lives of our ancestors or our gods and so we pass legends on; which makes the shaman's conversation with the sacred deer or spirit of the peyote plant no less genuine than my grandfather's mystical moment at the fountain of Lourdes. Science tells us carefully researched stories of DNA and the Periodic Table, but when approaching the nano-realities of string theory and quantum physics the straight lines of reasoned theory begin to blur. Light is both a particle and a wave. Space bends. All bets are off. That humans hallucinate and are fitted with brain wiring that makes the vortex available to them is a given. What we believe that vortex to be and why is another issue entirely.

Like de Sautuola, who never thought to look up to see the paintings of bison on the ceiling, we in the modern world are constantly, busily involved, scuffling about to reify our view of the world. Yet what view is that? We are 'stressed', 'under the gun', and 'up against a deadline' (deadline being a particularly interesting image – cross it and you're dead, but not in any shamanic sense of it

194

being a valuable experience from which you can return enlightened). We are flooded with images and interpretations from the media "telling it like it is" or, like they say it is, edited for brevity and maximum impact, listing the things we need to most fear up-to-the-minute. It is purposefully de-Centering, or perhaps constantly refocusing on ephemeral centers that momentarily serve the broadcasters' purposes.

Soundbites is another interesting word. We are so assaulted with information that we only have time for a mouthful of sound at a time before moving on, leaving most of the substance on the plate. Everything is abbreviated. Text messaging, twittering and emoticons shortcut the need for words to express emotion, reducing communication to a few keystrokes. The slow cooking of measured criticism, the extended observation of process, the graceful dignity of carefully distilled ideas and thoughtful comment that bring worlds into being seem to be things of the past. We do not 'take time', but rather fill it. By being so absorbed in the paradigms of the modern world we can easily deny that the world could be other than what we are told it is as it whirls past us in a blur.

Our word 'monster' originates in Old French as monstre, 'to warn'. It meant an omen, a warning from the gods that something is out of kilter, literally 'off-center', and required immediate attention to set it right. The metaphor of a horrifying creature in our midst wreaking havoc is potent and requires the intervention of a hero, often a reluctant one, to heed the warning of the gods and return the world to order. The form of the monster was, by definition, gigantic and unnatural; a dragon, an ogre like Grendel, or the Laidley Worm of folk tales. Today, monsters take the form of tyrants who cause wanton death and destruction among innocent people, usually the very people they are entrusted to protect, or those who live quietly in your neighborhood and prey on children or store human body-parts in their freezers. The truth of the metaphor is unchanged and the speaking of it and the naming of it has brought its true nature into being in our minds where it didn't exist before. The name of Jeffrey Dahmer will provoke a quiver of fear and revulsion as long as his crimes are remembered. Something in the world falls out of balance when a monster appears, a serious kink in the web of energies, a disturbance in the Force, and chaos threatens. It needs to be righted or the gods in some form will intervene and it won't be pretty. The implication is that we have both the capability of right-thinking and the responsibility to act appropriately for the good of

the group. But dire situations call for a hero, a leader of exceptional gifts with the courage to confront the monster, act and realign the collective moral compass. Among hunter-gatherers there were warriors of great bravery and resourcefulness who became legendary heroes. But, when confronted by a monster of otherworldly dimension, the hero was the shaman.

The ripples of Paleolithic shamanism are still evident in the world today because they resonate among us like a rock thrown in a deep well. An Ariadne's thread, they guide us through the labyrinthine vortex of altered consciousness as recorded in their art. We are made of the same biological stuff as they, and our neural pathways are indistinguishable from theirs. It is no wonder that the power of their images affects us so profoundly. Their spiritual specialists learned to ride the energy currents of altered consciousness to the planes of existence beyond our own. In fact, it may be that it was the human capacity for hallucinating and, more importantly, the need to integrate that experience into a cohesive cultural system that sparked the evolutionary leap to modern humans. Training and manipulating the sensory apparatus of the human body, they exalted the spirit and transcended the mundane. As we will see, the deep caves manipulated their consciousness and they, in turn, conversed with the spirits in the caves, establishing a dynamic spiritual relationship. Those people who were more adept and courageous in their explorations of these psychic realms would have exerted significant influence, becoming healers and leaders who could, at will, tap into the currents of the spirit world and define it to those who chose not to make the journey. If David Whitley is correct, many of these people suffered dreadfully from what today we call bipolar disease, but they knew as spirits. Unwitting bearers of a mutant genetic code that sentenced them to enduring years of grim torment, horrific hallucinations and the yearning for death, followed by brilliant creative outbursts, those who embraced the spirit world and danced on the edge of madness and death found their way into realms of power to become healers and charismatic leaders. As only one small element in an untamed natural world animated by the same spiritual agency, it was for humankind to live gracefully within it. The journeying Paleolithic shaman stood at the intersection of paradoxical opposing forces deep in the labyrinth, maintaining a dynamic balance between them, preventing either from overwhelming the other, which would release chaos on the world.

The realms of wonder and spirit will not be ignored. They thrust themselves into our tidy world when the hinges of power open and admit an unbidden vision. A blessed birth or a tragic death, or a tragic birth and blessed death, show us the borders of our reality and force us into the mystery beyond it, the place where souls fly in and out of our lives. We are 'taken' to the timeless Center and shown the place where all roads meet. Time is shattered at such a moment and Eternity invades. When it emerges into our lives from beyond the veil, much as that cave ceiling swirling with bison that we have only to look up to see, we are jettisoned out of our categories and made to understand that the world is a much more complicated and wondrous place than we ever imagined. Like the baby set down uninjured by a tornado, the world is filled with the paradoxically strange. The emergence of the labyrinth in our midst is such an epiphany, a primal symbolic link to our Paleolithic forebears, to the essence of the human spiritual quest leading to the still Center of being.

How do we make the journey from our frenetic modern lives to the deep labyrinthine caves of Europe and find meaning there? How do we begin to discover the mind behind the painting? For that we must return to Africa and what may be the world's oldest surviving culture.

CHAPTER 11

THE BRIDGE BETWEEN THE
WORLDS

*"But how does it happen," I said with admiration, "that you were
able to solve the mystery of the library looking at it from the outside,
and you were unable to solve it when you were inside?"
"Thus God knows the world, because He conceived it in His mind,
as if from the outside, before it was created, and we do not know its
rule, because we live inside it having found it already made."*
Umberto Eco, *The Name of the Rose*

THE SAN

An unlikely but pivotal link connecting our modern labyrinth
with one of the world's oldest tribal groups was discovered by way
of mythic images recorded on rocks from Zimbabwe to South
Africa. In the 1870s a German linguist named Wilhelm Bleek
traveled to Africa to compile a Zulu dictionary. While in the British
colony of Natal he discovered the existence of the Bushmen tribe,
denizens of the Drakensberg Mountains, and became fascinated
with their language, which incorporated tongue clicks and other
unusual sounds. Later in Capetown, he learned of a group of /Xam
Bushmen imprisoned in the local jail who were put to work on the
harbor breakwater. They were a different tribal group from those of
the Drakensbergs, though culturally related. They called themselves
the /Xam, the slash indicating a vocal click sound. The Zulu
dictionary was forgotten and Bleek made arrangements to have the
/Xam men released to him. They moved to his home and settled in
to teach Bleek their language. The /Xam were keenly aware that not
only their language but their beliefs and entire way of life was
endangered by the encroachments of colonialism and were eager to
have it recorded. They were the last of the /Xam people to follow
their traditional lifestyle, others having been absorbed into other
groups. Later, their families joined them. Eventually they became

199

known to the world as the San.

While Bleek learned the San language and compiled a grammar and phonetic dictionary that could capture the unusual sounds of the speech, his sister-in-law and co-worker, Lucy Lloyd recorded personal histories, activities of daily life, myths, and rituals. Unfortunately, Bleek died well before his time and much of his understanding of the San mind died with him. Lucy Lloyd, continued to document as much as she could until 1884 when the last San informant departed. The generation of San informants who worked with Bleek had all been witnesses to the invasion of their ancestral lands by colonial whites and black farmers alike, and the accompanying devastation of the wild herds and vegetation they relied upon. But their parents had lived a traditional existence as stone-age hunter-gatherers, although there had been contact with farmers for perhaps 2000 years. Some of their parents had both painted and engraved rocks, passing the mythology down to their children, and were probably the last of the San to do so. By the turn of the 20th century San culture was well on its way to complete absorption, the people having been dispossessed of their territories and transformed into servants and farm laborers.

Although the Bleek team failed to collect information from the San women, which would have probably provided important and different insight into the art and culture, they were able to snatch back from the brink of extinction an extraordinary wealth of information. The language is extinct and many of the stories, the glue that holds a culture together down the generations, were no longer remembered. But the surviving San people of the Kalahari still follow a shamanic tradition today, and often many members of a single tribe, as many as half the men and a third of the women, become shamans. The efforts of Bleek and Lloyd to understand and record a vanishing human culture have gifted us with a window into the stone-age world of the Paleolithic mind through the miracle of the San people's rock art; pictographs, or paintings, and engravings of exquisite beauty and detail. In particular, they were able to establish connections between their oral myths, the process of painting and the images in the rock art.

David Lewis-Williams, Professor Emeritus and Senior Mentor in the Rock Art Research Institute at the University of Witwatersrand, Johannesburg, discovered the Bleek research collecting dust in storage. Lewis-Williams insightfully applied the San premises of shamanic-based image-making to Paleolithic cave art and found one

of the most significant keys to unlocking the secrets of the cave art of France. We'll investigate this idea later in the chapter, as it leads us to the archetypal labyrinth.

The appreciation of San rock art had some major historical and cultural hurdles to jump. It is charitable to say that the white colonists 'pushed' the San off their traditional ancient homeland. It is more accurate to say they were forced to assimilate, systematically exterminated and hunted for sport. The occasional cattle rustling by the San was met with swift and terrible retribution, including the slaughter of the men and the capture and indenturing of the women and children. The colonialists validated their invasion with racist notions that these were treacherous, lazy little subhuman heathens who were so primitive as to be unable to grasp the concept of a Christian god. The next assumption, by this logic, is that they were doing these poor people a favor by bringing them civilization. Their art, in the best light, amounted to child-like renderings of their simplistic life.

A one-two punch was completed when the Abbé Breuil visited Africa. The Abbé is enshrined in the annals of prehistoric research as a tireless recorder of cave art who proposed a sweeping theory of its origins and purpose. Unfortunately he worked largely from a position of scholarly isolation and personal bias that taints his work today. He was in Africa to search for evidence to support his Euro-centric theory that art was born in the caves of Europe and therefore, there should be indications of European influence in Africa. Europeans who preceded Breuil were hard-pressed to reconcile their racist ideas of the San with the elegant rock art and determined it to have been created by ancient Europeans, East Indians, and even Babylonians. Waving his wand of universal theory, Breuil declared San rock art, if it was theirs at all, to be art for art's sake and, of course, hunting magic. After all, there are all those images of bleeding elands, a type of large antelope.

In a perfect example of 'what you believe is what you get', Brueil identified a San rock art figure as 'the white lady of Brandenberg'. A very cursory examination of the image reveals that it is, as Lewis-Williams has famously put it, neither white nor a lady and certainly had never seen Brandenberg, but rather an indigenous San hunter with a penis, in body paint, carrying clearly identifiable traditional hunting weapons. Ignoring entirely the cultural context of the art, Breuil determined the other figures in the panel to be of Mediterranean and European extraction, which validated his self-

fulfilling theory. He was a man of his times on a mission and unable to see the pictures, or the San for that matter, for what they were.

ART THEORIES

From the time the modern world admitted that Paleolithic paintings were, in fact, executed by 'cave men', theories as to why they were created have accumulated like old *National Geographics*. Initially, the image of prehistoric Ice Age people, emerging from the deeply held bias of a Judeo-Christian mind-set, suffered from two extremes; either they were ignorant brutes with no spiritual aspirations whatsoever, or they were the 'noble savages' of Rousseau, uncorrupted by the evils of civilization who dwelt in a land of idyllic plenty. The art itself is testament to the sensitivity, talent and intelligence of the Paleolithic people. But the disproportionate number of children's skeletons suggesting high infant mortality and adults that rarely exceeded 40 years of age exhibiting severe arthritis and painful dental problems stemming from a tough diet demonstrate that all was not bucolic in this land of ice and giant predators.

Certainly not every artistic creation was prompted by deep spiritual purpose. The sheer joy of creation is often evident and the beginner had to start somewhere. Yet the idea that, because prehistoric people lived in a romantic time of plenty requiring that they slaughter a mastodon only once every six months, they had lots of time on their hands during those nippy Ice Age winter nights to sing, dance and decorate their caves is completely unrealistic. This implies that art was something people indulged in when their bellies were full and they weren't out grubbing around for edible shrubbery or stalking elusive reindeer. But the opposite has been shown in ethnographic studies; that people are equally liable to have ceremonies and perform rituals when times are tough, food is scarce and supplications must be made to the Master of Animals so the game will return and allow itself to be slain.

The burnished image of the Rousseau savage at the turn of the 19th century took a tarnishing hit when new ethnographies proposed a downgraded view. 'Primitive' people were not really strong, carefree, unsullied savages, but rather, they were puny creatures trying to scrape by in a hostile world. Robbed of their feral glory, the newly minted troglodytes had little recourse to survival but to lead brutal, bloody lives, red in tooth and claw. One bet-hedging option emerged; sympathetic magic. This is the Abbé Breuil's

202

concept that through the creation of an image of an animal one captures an essence of that creature, and by manipulating the image some form of power can be exerted over the subject for desirable ends. So, by creating an image the hunter captured a part of the animal's spirit, becoming its master, and could hunt it successfully. Images of animals punctured with holes or overlain with spear-shaped lines seemed to bolster this argument.

Hunting magic was so appealing an explanation that it was expanded upon through the years and found its way into popular imagination through the tireless work of the Abbé, who recorded and reproduced volumes of cave art. Unfortunately, Breuil was alone in his field, completely dominating the study and interpretation of the images for many years with no small degree of subjectivity. He recorded images selectively, excluding some and focusing on others to the point of elaboration. He operated on the assumption that cave art was a random compilation of images having no relation to one another, composed by simple individuals over millennia. The creations in the caves took on a utilitarian aspect, the practical application of limited power to wrest some modicum of control from a dangerous world. Paint equaled food and safety. Animals were ritually slain by the insertion of arrow-shaped patterns or lines representing a spear, or they were caught in nets or traps as represented by grid designs in near proximity to the animal. In addition to enticing food animals like aurochs, deer, ibex and horses to be killed, sympathetic or hunting magic was said to have a destructive capability when directed at animals dangerous to humans like lions or bears, as well as the ability to bestow fertility on desirable animals through the representation of sexual scenarios between creatures. The abundance of 'goddess' figurines was assumed to be a magical plea for the increase of the tribe itself.

There are many reasons why this spiritually mechanistic theory is limited or wrong. The number of sites discovered since Breuil's time has increased greatly, as has the systematic, statistical recording of the images, the number of people from widely different disciplines with pertinent information now involved in the field and the resources available to them. The self-contained bastion of doctrine that Breuil supported in splendid isolation has, as a result, crumbled in the face of overwhelming numbers. The majority of images show no indication of ritual slaughter and coupling animals are few and far between. A horse, engraved into the clay on the walls of the cave of Montespan, is stabbed with holes and was used

to bolster the hunting magic argument. But the area around it is likewise pierced. If control over the animal's spirit was the point of ritual representation, the alleged hunter had a very bad aim.

In addition, a century of ethnographic studies shows that hunter-gatherer tribes have complex cultural constructs in place to limit the number of children born, including infanticide, abortion and a requisite length of time to nurse babies, a natural form of birth control that prevents the mother ovulating. To feed, care for and carry too many infants can jeopardize the health of the mother, limit her capability of finding food and affect the tribe's ability to move easily and quickly if need be. Both natural and ritual birth-control methods are employed to maintain a viable number. The large number of 'goddess' statues has something to do with females and feminine power, but it probably wasn't to promote human fertility.

THE STRUCTURALISTS

Until the 1950s the doctrine of Breuil held sway and cave art was understood as a chaotic assortment of images created whenever a male member of the tribe felt the need to exert magical power over an area of his life. That a woman may have been an artist or hunter literally never entered into the early illustrations of cave life. They were always shown out front scraping hides and caring for the children. Multiple ethnographies, however, demonstrate that women probably provided the bulk of the food, gathering wild plants and snaring small animals. And some hand- and thumb-prints in caves are probably female. Then the Structuralist movement emerged in France and shined its light on cave art. Andre Leroi-Gourhan, Max Raphael and Annette Laming-Emperaire led the charge against the crenellated assumptions on which Breuil based his opinions.

In direct opposition to the venerable old man of cave art, the young turks postulated that every fragment of art was related to a contiguous whole and no stray mark should be ignored. The art, they proposed, was not random, but rather, highly structured mythograms that could be read like the mythology of living peoples if only we could crack the code. The 'nets' and 'traps' of hunting magic went out the window and returned through the door of the Structuralists, newly defined as meaningful signs that somehow related to the animal images, if only their meaning could be discovered. Everything was purposely and intelligently arranged to convey a complex worldview. The fallacy of this view is that, despite being separated by perhaps thousands or tens of thousands

of years, one picture meaningfully related to others nearby. This implied that, before painting an image, the artist thoughtfully considered the mythograms already placed on the walls, understood them, and continued the idea.

The study of single isolated images that Brueil had done, assuming that each was created individually, was a dead end. The Structuralists saw compositions and patterns in the multiple pictures. They set about counting and documenting not only the art itself, but also its location in the cave, relative position to other images and the surface on which it was painted. The frequency of relationship, one animal to another, was noted. The regular occurrence of bison and horses together, for instance, couldn't be by chance. At bottom, the system of organization revealed itself to Leroi-Gourhan as based on sexual symbolism and all animals and signs had either female or male values; bison and aurochs were female symbols while horses were male. Spear-like designs were penile while enclosed signs like ovals and rectangles were womb-inspired.

This neat theory of dynamic opposition and complementariness dismissed the relative proximity of one animal to another and assumed that animals some yards distant were nonetheless related. The gender that was depicted by artists who had intimate knowledge of the beasts was ignored in preference for formula – if it's a horse it must be a female sign. The postures of the figures were not considered, the number of animals, nor the way they were rendered. Why, for example, draw a panel of complete and detailed bison and then include a bare charcoal sketch of a mammoth's head? The Structuralists had replaced one over-arching theory of hunting magic with a different abstract theory that similarly didn't address many issues. Their theory implied that artistic symbolism must have endured unchanged for tens of thousands of years over the whole of Europe. Critics charged that their theory was excessively broad and really explained nothing in terms of why the images were created in the deep caves in the first place. Further, it was based on a purely subjective interpretation of what signs and symbols may have meant. To equate a rectangular figure with a vagina was a stretch, if not a fantasy. To assume that pictures created over many centuries informed others nearby was unfounded.

Yet the Structuralists have passed on an important legacy; the importance of recording each human-made image, however seemingly insignificant, as it appears and not as we might wish to

see it, as well as a thorough documenting of every other human impact on the cave environment. This approach allows us to gain a total picture of artistic activity within a specific cultural context and how that relates to other Paleolithic activity through the era. The painstaking detail with which Paleolithic art is now deconstructed has revealed secrets of its creation the good Abbé never dreamed. We'll return to this later, but for now it's important to note that current research, inspired by Structuralist methodology, documents an exhausting amount of information which includes the nature of the surface on which the art appears and whether it was prepared beforehand; the chemical makeup of the pigments and therefore the origin of the raw materials; or, if an engraving, the tool employed, the style and technique of its creation; the way the light falls on it from different directions; where the artist was standing at the time; whether there are aural effects that may relate to the art; the discovery of artifacts and the mapping of their relationship in time and space with others in the same cave; and how that art relates to art in all other decorated caves over a vast time period.

Recent discoveries of additional decorated caves like Chauvet and Cousac as well as improved dating, information collecting and recording techniques provide a complexity of relative measurement unavailable before. Research by legions of specialists with whiz-bang machinery has made it possible to compile a jaw-dropping avalanche of information. The Paleolithics are no longer consigned to one polar extreme, either stupid savage or flower child artist, but rather, as the wealth of new evidence reveals, they emerge as complex, efficient societies.

SAN CULTURE

The 12,000 pages of information compiled by the Bleek team, while largely unpublished, have been mined by David Lewis-Williams in a more enlightened era than they were written. By contrast, Breuil's Euro-centric conclusions would be all the more quaint were it not for the appalling damage such bias visited upon the San and other traditional peoples, confirming them to be of little interest or value and as standing in the way of 'progress'. Quarrying the ethnographic information collected by the Bleeks made possible a perspective allowing for much deeper understanding of the subtle yet powerful relationships between San art, culture and religious practice. Lewis-Williams and others have made elegant use of this new approach to inform our understanding of Paleolithic art and the

origin of the symbol of the labyrinth.

It is vital at this juncture to point out that cracking the door on the subject of San culture is to invite a subject as vast as the teeming Serengeti to spill through. The decimation of the San people in the 19th century left enough survivors and informants to entice later ethnographers to attempt an understanding of their world view. These new ethnographers recognized the imperative of an interpretation of the San spiritual world on their terms. The simplicity of their material culture in no way implies a parallel poverty of their interior lives. Far from being simplistic and childlike, as European colonists assumed, the San perceptions of life and the spiritual power that infuses it are deeply complex, utterly foreign and perhaps, as Peter Garlake states, ultimately beyond our understanding.

San tribal people created rock art over a period of thousands of years and vast areas of southern Africa where granite outcroppings occur. There are no limestone caves here as in Europe. Some have been dated by charcoal used in the drawings as ranging from 13,000 to 5000 years ago. Because of exposure to the elements many have disappeared. The extensive study of DNA from blood samples around the world point to the San as possibly descending from the earliest humans in Africa. Other African tribal groups who likewise carry ancient DNA markers share the language of clicks that so entranced Mr. Bleek. These may be some of the most ancient cultures on the planet; their memories, carried in language, art and ceremony, cast far into the mists of the past.

The people Europeans found in Africa were not, as they assumed, an untouched 'primitive' people. The San have interacted for centuries with farming cultures and did not live in isolation. There are still San people who live a lifestyle approximate to their ancestors, maintaining a cultural continuity against overwhelming odds. Possibly many centuries and thousands of miles separated the informants who shared explanations of their art and culture with Bleek from the ancient artists, and yet their understanding of the rock art was largely intact and consistent with their existing mythological construct. They could read the symbols.

There is no single San culture, but many separate language groups in ecologically different part of Africa that each relate uniquely to the land, the animals and plants specific to their respective regions. Where the eland is the most sacred of animals to the Drakensburg San of South Africa, the elephant appears to fulfil

that role in Zimbabwe. This demonstrates variations on the theme of 'San culture', just as the French, Germans and English demonstrate differing aspects of 'Western culture'. But the most significant hindrance is that we derive our language and thought forms from a European cultural tradition that values clarity, precision, analysis and categorization. We cannot begin to truly 'grok', for lack of a better word, a culture so fundamentally different. In the words of Peter Garlake, "they have no dogma, seek no definitions, create no distinctions or boundaries, demand no consensus, accepting apparent anomalies and contradictions. Belief is a lived experience, one open to individual exploration, personal expression and debate. Submissive wonder is more important than analysis". An intellectual analysis of the San culture may be doomed, by definition, from the outset. Yet we can gain some interpretive traction by exploring some basic ideas. What follows then, will be a mere dipping of the toes into the deep well of San culture and art, peeling away only a few layers of meaning. And, as Lewis-Williams has discovered, a rich source of interpretive potential for Paleolithic cave art.

CULTURAL ASSUMPTIONS

What the Abbé Breuil and other Europeans assumed were paintings by Phoenicians, Babylonians or other ancient peoples from the classical past, or that were dismissed as childlike images of primitive hunting magic, we now can begin to understand as keys to the portals of other worlds visited by the ancient San. Consider for comparison our assumed comprehension of the symbol of a man hung on a cross and the levels of complexity it presents. The central mystical event of Christianity can be understood to variously mean sacrifice, resurrection, salvation of the soul from sin, ultimate elevation to a blissful eternity and a mystical communion with God through a miraculous conjoining of three spirits and a sacred meal of God's body and blood. The assumptions underpinning these broad-brush symbols run so deeply in Western culture that they are often not even recognized as such.

Whether one has been raised in a Jewish or Christian environment or not, the ideas of the Judeo-Christian traditions have been subsumed into the culture as a whole and surround us like the water surrounds the fish. The idea of sin implies judgment and the idea of original sin has colored women's roles significantly, to say the least. The potential to be delivered from evil suggests what is required to attain deliverance. The Supreme Being is generally

208

assumed as a remote single male who must be appealed to through the intercession of priests and saints. Time and existence came into being in six days at his hand and will be taken out again at the end point of a linear time scale. This Supreme Being placed man in a garden, that paradise before Time and Death when talking with the animals was possible and, that's precisely what Eve did when she had that chat with the snake. But paradoxically, man was given 'dominion over every living thing that moveth on the land', a vestige of Neolithic farming that set man outside and above the natural world. These are deep structure thought patterns that are ingrained in Western thinking and belief and constantly reappear in various guises to be reconsidered and redefined in whatever current culture war is being waged.

The iconography of religious art represents these themes and, during the Middle Ages when few people could read, the art of the cathedrals served to educate the congregations about the tenets of doctrine. The stained-glass windows depicting St. Peter on a rock holding the keys to Heaven, statues of the Virgin Mary in her starry robe poised on a slice of the moon, the stations of the cross posted on the walls mapping Christ's simultaneous physical and spiritual journey to crucifixion and resurrection, and the central altar crowded with saints, gold, flaming candles, heady incense and flowers all radiate from the focus of power, a bleeding Jesus on the cross, or sometimes just the cross alone, with the shadowy implication of God the Father hovering overhead.

Now, imagine that you are a San Bushman dropped into the middle of a cave-like Chartres Cathedral that is pierced by rays of multi-colored light sifting in through magical glass. The dizzying concentration of potency would certainly be impressive; what D.H. Lawrence described elegantly as an involved seed. Although our San would recognize he was in a sacred space, with no reference to the symbolic content, it would remain only that. And although the San built no cathedrals or gold statuary, their art is as deeply laced with interweaving sacred metaphors, and as essential to the survival of their culture, as the Vatican is to a devout Catholic. Gazing at the images of San rock art is for us, the uninitiated, equally mystifying.

The energy of San art is striking. The exotic bestiary crowded with antelopes, elephants, giraffes, kudzu, zebras and rhinos explodes with life. People leap and dance, sit together and sing, make love, hunt, fight, rejoice and kill. These elements we can easily recognize, as the San tourist beamed into Chartres would

know the Holy Mother was a kind woman and something serious had happened to the man on the cross. But what are we to think about the people with hooves and antelope ears, the woman who appears to be disintegrating into small flecks, the one-legged man with wings, the grossly distended bodies poised on zigzag lines, the mysterious, bulbous animals speckled with dots, the boat-shaped signs reminiscent of bees nests or saw blades and the strange partitioned ovals exhibiting the character of enchanted vegetables? We are deep in the land of San symbol and myth without a tour guide. In fact, a San person raised to value the idea that 'submissive wonder is more important than analysis' has a better shot at understanding the Christian concept of the transubstantiation of the soul than we do of recognizing the significance of a magical rain animal.

TRANCE DANCE

Key to the art is the dance, the solar power of the San universe. They are a people who dance often for many reasons, children's games, entertainment and re-enactment of events being among them. Some dances are reserved exclusively for women and only old men are permitted to dance the rain dance. Some dances are a performance opportunity to demonstrate acrobatic talents. Others are ritualized and choreographed and performed only once every few years at significant life transitions. But when there are tensions in the community, when illness has appeared or 'it feels right', they dance the trance dance, the central sacred activity of the group, which can take place as often as every two or three days. Both men and women can be shamans and many members of the community will enter into varying stages of trance during this dance. Spiritual power is available to all who choose to seek it. They often dance themselves into the far range of consciousness, to the border of life and death, to deep trance.

It begins when women light a fire in a central clearing and begin to clap rhythmically and sing songs. Rattles of seed pods tied around the ankles shake with every step and enhance the rhythm. Some wear animal tails, others a hat with animal ears attached, and some use walking sticks to support them during the dance. Gradually the rhythmic and emotional intensity builds as more people join in. They form a line and dance very closely together, some fluttering their arms. The dancing, singing, focused concentration and hyperventilation increase the concentration of power until one or

210

more shamans will enter a deep trance state. Through the now-vanished language of some branches of the San we are introduced to the concept of !gi:ten that translates as 'full of supernatural potency'. This is a kind of spiritual electricity (sound familiar?) endowed by the trickster god /Kaggen upon humankind and some animals and natural events deemed special; honey bees, gentle soaking rain, animal fat and, in the Drakensberg Mountains, the eland, and in Zimbabwe, the elephant. When a shaman enters a dance-induced trance state, this spiritual potency churns and swells in the abdomen, is tapped and 'boils' up the spine along channels in the body to the head where the energy explodes and allows the shaman to be transported into a rarified spiritual state. In a particularly deep trance a shaman will sweat profusely and hemorrhage from his nose, going rigid, staggering or collapsing and shaking. This nasal blood and sweat is not only charged with supernatural potency, but is potency itself. Others will protect them from harm and take them a safe distance away from the danger of falling in the fire. Here, cared for and fully charged with spiritual potential, they can shamanize.

Trance dancing in this communal forum is not an occasional social event, but rather a fairly common yet spiritually transcendent ritual activity that is incorporated into all dimensions of San life. The experience of dance, shamanic trance and their revelations inform the rituals performed for boys' hunting initiation and the onset of first menses for girls. It underpins the main themes of the mythology and, most important for our concerns, is the well from which springs their art. Trance dancing, the wilful passage into the far end of the consciousness trajectory, calls up hallucinations and focuses the electric power of the supernatural. The entire company and everything around it becomes charged with potency. Sacred animals gather on the periphery of the firelight and spirits hover. Powerful trancers can focus this energy into invisible arrows of potency and, like crossing crackling electrical wires, shoot them into the reservoir of a novice's abdomen to help elevate him to a more intense experience. In this light, Paleolithic cave art that depicts arrow-like forms passing through animal or human bodies could be interpreted as a spiritual event rather than a hunting scene.

The deep trance state is not understood among the San as merely a metaphor for death. It is death itself. To speak to the dead one must be dead. The shaman in deep trance has separated his soul, leaving an aspect of it in his physical body to maintain life, while his

journeying soul is taken into another realm. His body has become transformed into a conduit of power and, although physically he is perhaps shaking and unable to stand, his spirit is rarified and supercharged. His vision has taken on supernatural capabilities and he is not bound by the constraints of time, distance or waking consciousness. The shaman's spirit leaves his or her body through the top of the head and visits distant relatives, observes the formation of rain clouds, determines the ripeness of fruit in a remote valley or the movements of game animals. He or she may travel to the spirit world to battle spirits of the dead or even the gods themselves to request that evil visited on the group be expelled. The potency-charged trance allows the San shaman to visually penetrate a patient's body and see the cause of illness. Disease can result from spirit arrows of sickness sent by an evil shaman or malevolent spirits. A person can harbor these arrows in their body and not even know it. The adept healing shaman will conduct a form of laying on of hands, drawing the sickness into their own bodies. They bathe the patient in the magical fluids of their sweat and blood, the most powerful of curative agents, sniffing and sucking out the evil objects and then releasing them, with a shriek, through a hole in the nape of the neck, at the top of the spine, the channel of boiling spiritual potency.

In the deepest trance states, like shamans everywhere, the San transform into animals, perhaps an eland, bird or lion. The line of demarcation we of the supermarket culture draw between animals and humans is erased in a hunter-gatherer culture. The animating principle is universal. At the time of creation the supreme being of the San created, according to Garlake, "a single living form, the people of the early race among whom differences between all living creatures were obscure: animals behaved in a fully human way and shared all human virtues and vices, emotion and reason, lusts and ambitions, plots and plans". (114) One assumes they spoke the same language. Later, the god separated out different species and assigned them purpose and specific behavior patterns. Man is not master over nature, but must be a worthy participant and contributor to the natural moral order, all having evolved from the same source. The distinctions between them are superficial and external.

This fluidity of being allows one to become the other, animal can become human and human can transform into animal. The San say that during deep trance 'lion's hair' grows out of a trancer's back or that the shaman is 'walking on hair', a metaphor for paws. The

shaman's transformation into a lion or other animal is a central fulcrum on, which the San spiritual life turns, for this is the most profound level of potency and healing potential. He or she is closely monitored in this condition because the surge of power can either cure or harm. Evil shamans can in their lion incarnations, 'take bites out of people from the inside' and cause serious harm. Lions are dangerous, powerful beasts that prowl the edges of the firelight and attack without warning, while people are asleep. In contrast are the 'hoofed' creatures, the eland and other herd animals that do no harm live in communal groups and provide meat. This distinction between 'pawed' animals and 'hoofed' animals is primarily behavioral, rather than a physical characteristic. Crocodiles and snakes are categorized as 'pawed' predators, as were the colonial white men.

ROCK AS MEMBRANE

Entering into a deep trance, is certainly not an evening's entertainment that we, in the modern techno world, would contemplate indulging in, a few times a week. And not one lightly entered into by the San themselves. The sheer weirdness of it is too baffling for most of us to begin to approach. But, entering into the strange terrain of San culture requires a spiritual roadmap. The principles of shamanism based on control of altered states of consciousness and the art-as-treasure-map are our guides. Perhaps treasure map is the wrong analogy for there is no "X marks the spot" here. Mr. Bleek did not leave behind a Tut's tomb of relics to pore over, but rather drew a lot of fascinating lines on our map that all tend to run off the edge of the page. We'll try to connect them up and show them leading into the vortex of the labyrinth.

It is David Lewis-Williams' contention that much of the art of the Drakensberg San illustrates aspects of the ecstatic central experience of their culture, the trance dance. (Garlake, by comparison, feels that little of the art of the Zimbabwe San is trance related, yet he devotes considerable time to that which does occur.) By altering their consciousness dramatically, and controlling the charged energy within the confines of their rituals, the San enter into the spirit world to gain wisdom and assist the community. The impact of this hallucinatory experience pervades the culture. The flow of appropriate energy must be maintained. Others in the group have important roles in the experience, novices must be trained and the earth kept in balance, the web of life and death kept vibrant and alive. The power, and its effects, must be remembered through time

CHAPTER 12

DESCENT INTO THE LABYRINTH

"I would venture that, more than any other single quality, it is the relentless moment-to-moment forgetting, this draining of the pool of sense impression almost as quickly as it fills, that gives the experience of consciousness under marijuana its peculiar texture. It helps account for the sharpening of sensory perceptions, for the aura of profundity in which cannabis bathes the most ordinary insights, and, perhaps most important of all, for the sense that time has slowed or even stopped. For it is only by forgetting that we ever really drop the thread of time and approach the experience of living in the present moment, so elusive in ordinary hours. And the wonder of that experience, perhaps more than any other, seems to be at the very heart of the human desire to change consciousness..."
Michael Pollan, **Botany of Desire**

"A few cave walls were painted and some rather fine hunting weapons were made; but there were no events that influenced the course of future history, that which created the modern world."
Steven Mithen, **After The Ice**

"Evoke the forms. Where you've nothing else construct ceremonies out of the air and breathe upon them."
Cormac McCarthy, **The Road**

THE VISION

The man had danced for a very long time, a galloping step that rocked forward and back in place, making the strings of shells on his clothes rattle rhythmically, until his legs ached. He had made music with his flute, sending the breath of his life and his prayer through the instrument of flight, the carved wing bone of a vulture, the creature who fed on death yet through whose bones life could be summoned. Shells-that-were-stone had been brought north from a

221

distant valley, were perforated and strung on his necklace along with a polished ivory horse that told of his status and worth. The pouch at his feet held his magic things; pyrite, medicines, the tooth of a dead man, the carving of a pregnant woman, an ivory blade and crystals. All of these contained the seeds for transformation.

The wounds in his arms where he had opened them for the blood offering throbbed, but he no longer noticed. He had been in the womb of the earth for a very long time and now he sat on the floor of the cave praying and singing in a hoarse whisper. He was stiff and cold and he had eaten little, but his stomach was used to the craving emptiness and did not complain. The world of light above, bitten hard by the cold and folded deep in winter snows, suffered more than in any memory or legend. Tools broke in the cold, creatures hid from men's spears, there was sickness and the children grew hollow-eyed and listless. He reached his cold hand to a crack in the cave wall, at the borderland where the stones thinned, the floor dropped down and the spirit horse fell eternally into the void. He wedged a stone blade into the crack, insuring that the path would be open and the spirits beyond would expect and accept him.

The small oil lamp finally guttered out with a hiss. He did not relight it and the sudden darkness enveloped him, a palpable substance settling around his body heavier than the dust of night. Although he could no longer see them, he knew they were there, the animals. He felt their eyes watching him. The rituals above and below had been performed and the powers aligned. He called out with the practiced voice of spirit the chant he had been taught to help him find his way out of sickness. It spoke through him, using his fevered body to say what must be said, echoing back to him, magnified many times by the glittering walls of the cave. The power was in him and beyond him, through and beyond the rock, called by the sacrifice and song, charging his blood and bones with coursing potency.

Struggling to his numb feet once again, he shuffled a slow dance step. He opened his eyes against the velvet pallet of utter blackness. Sparks of color erupted and began to swirl. The musical water, the sacred fluid of the earth that binds all life, seeped through the living rock of an alcove and filled a pool at his side. The watery voice sang to him its strange percussive song, murmuring and gurgling deep in its stony throat-blending with the visions that wheeled before his eyes, each enhancing the other. Pulsing circles appeared within circles, beginning as small, wavering rings of light that expanded

outward to surround him and move past. He was being pulled down a long tunnel of the cave. His body stretched painfully till he thought his joints would rip loose and the air sucked out of his lungs, leaving him gasping, drowning in the dark. He knew this spirit place well. With each hypnotic droplet of water echoing from the grottos of the cavern, dots of color materialized, elements of spirit that arranged themselves in patterns and lines, joined and separated, not yet coalescing into solid form. Power spears appeared and stood in rows before him, then wavered and fell, crossing one another to become the webs of a net that stretched to the ends of the world, each corner tied to a horizon and holding all things in its strands of power. The four corners began to draw together as if the net was gathering up around him.

Like a fish in a weir, he was pulled into the mouth of a spinning portal and the walls were the net. As he moved deeper into the vortex, the metamorphosis began. Here was where things of this world met the other, where he split from his skin, his spirit emerging, his being dividing; leaving his body behind while his awareness took on new form. His spine flexed, pressed from all sides by the web whirling around him. The bones softened, twisted and gathered up into a hump on his back. Soaring energy flooded up his spine and horns shoved through his skull like strong shoots. The ears of a bison sprouted from his head, twitching and alert, hearing the other world beyond the vortex. His bearded jaw stretched and the scent of sweet spring grass was on his breath. He felt thick, black hair curl from his flesh, matting his back and chest with a warm coat. Snorting through velvet nostrils he danced on his human feet, arms shod with hooves outstretched, praying for an emanation to come closer, to make itself known.

The humming in his ears was a thick chorus of angry bees thrumming from the other world. It thinned and stretched in tone and intensity and the watery cave song accompanied their glittering flight around his head. He felt the sound pulsing through him, through every vein as the gold-winged bees swarmed in the channels of his body, coursing from his twitching ears down his spine and along the sinews of his muscled neck and hump, swarming in his lungs and stomach, down his arms and into his hooves so that they radiated light and sound, into his legs, pushing the exhaustion of dancing ahead, out the soles of his feet and into the crystalline floor. His hair rose up in black spirals around his shaman's horns and a corona of light ringed his head. His skin

223

on bellies, hands and knees, through tight, slippery passageways and Arctic wonderlands of stalagmites, smashing calcite curtains to reach the chambers beyond, repelling into pockets of invisible toxic gas, slipping around bottomless collapsed pits and lowering into deep shafts, wary of cave bears, and all with the most minimal of equipment. Amazingly, no one has yet found the body of an accident victim from the Ice Age.

Despite the stirring but outmoded image of mystical male ceremonial initiations happening in the caves and the fact that the sacred was sought and found in the deep caves, it seems everybody who wanted to wandered into them for any number of reasons. A baby's handprint was found in the depths of Bedeilhac. The footprints of a two-year-old survive in the clay depths of Tuc d'Audobert a mile underground with very difficult access, obviously taken in by the parents and perhaps set down for a moment's rest. The footprints of an eight-year-old child, probably a boy, were found in Chauvet beneath where the child paused to wipe the excess burnt fragments off a torch so it would continue to burn brightly. At least thumbprints and possibly handprints of women adorn the famous Peche-Merle horses as archaeologist Michel Lorblanchet discovered. As he attempted to duplicate the mural, he found it is impossible for a man's thumb to bend the way a woman's can. It was probably a woman or perhaps an adolescent who created the pointillist bison out of handprints in Chauvet. Under what circumstances all these people of various ages and both sexes were in the caves, ceremonial, social or just exploring, is impossible to know. But clearly it was not an exclusively adult male-dominated ceremonial space.

These subterranean chambers are worlds of illusion quite distinct from that of the upper air. In the perpetual darkness time loses meaning and only increasing hunger and a guttering lamp mark its passage. Paleolithic cave exploration was an extremely dangerous undertaking for these visual animals of the light. Ancient explorers held the supreme darkness at bay with small, fat-burning lamps and juniper torches as they traversed unpredictable terrain, the shadows leaping and fleeing before them as darkness instantly closed in behind. Some walls, draped in cascading calcite and leaking water, appeared liquid, wavering in the uneven light. Some caves are little more than dimples in a hillside. Others, like Niaux, unwind for miles beneath the earth and art is found in the farthest depths, even beyond tunnels drowned in underground opalescent lakes.

The cave of Rouffignac is so enormous that modern tours take an electric train into its depths to view the art. Before the floor was excavated, the room called "The Grand Plafond" (French for 'expansive ceiling') had a very low ceiling, requiring that the artist lie on his back to make an image. The artists would not have been able to get far enough away from the pictures to see the panel in its entirety and would have been unable to see the nose of the animal while they engraved the tail. The act of making the image was more important than the viewing of it. In a visionary state, it may be that the artist/voyager, in 'releasing' a spiritual image through the membrane of stone, didn't need to 'see' the image with fully terrestrial vision. The cave of Cussac is quite long and can be walked through upright most of the way, but it can take up to four hours to move from the entrance to the farthest reaches and back again, having only small lamps or torches for light. Yet the Cussac's soft limestone walls are deeply engraved with mammoths, horses, women and even a goose.

Quite apart from the casual visits of the curious, a ceremonial sojourn in underground realms was not entered into lightly as we'll discover. The arduous purpose of the journey complete and the lamp running low, to once again near the entrance to the upper world, feel the air change and smell vegetation and at last, to re-emerge into the sunlight, must have felt akin to rebirth.

SENSORY DEPRIVATION

The shamans were obviously unaware of the neurological firing that we can watch crackle across the brain of a grad student volunteer on a laboratory screen. But they were master electricians of spiritual circuitry. They had a keen awareness of the behavioral switches to trip that would link them to the power grid of eternity and they certainly took full advantage of the mind-altering environment of the caves, an ideal model for the labyrinth.

The deep caves are perfect sensory deprivation chambers, conspiring against our biological apprehension equipment that allows us to function during normal waking consciousness. The strange chthonic atmosphere invades our sensory receptors. All our afferent conditioning that channels information from outside to our inner nervous system, honed in the upper world of movement and light, is altered. It undergoes a dramatic adaptation to an enchanted landscape underground, one that literally captivates the spirit. Vision is restricted to a tiny pool of flickering artificial light. One's sense of

smell becomes a mostly monotonous experience of damp earth occasionally punctuated with a whiff of minerals. It is sterile, the smell of stone without the loamy odors and perfumes of plant life. Hearing is strangely distorted. The temperature is constant, cool and damp. Even gravity seems akimbo as the floor suddenly drops away or a tilted tunnel spirals up and around. With all of our normal references under assault, merely spending time in a deep cave will, of neurological necessity, alter human consciousness. It would be impossible to spend much time in this environment and not be affected.

The restless human brain, deprived of the natural stimulation with which it is constantly bombarded, its sensory receptors isolated in a still, dark place, begins to search for something to do. It hallucinates. Sparkles of light appear and voices come out of nowhere. Leaping shadows catch the eye and visions take on meaning. Eventually, these hallucinations can become a palpable presence. Combine this conspiratorial environment with ritual and ceremonial activity and a shaman couldn't ask for a more perfect time-suspension machine to carry him to the far end of the consciousness trajectory.

An explorer moving into a deep cave discovers that sound becomes a personality of its own as it is transformed by the rock surface. The feel of each chamber and passageway is very different. Sound is, in some places, swallowed by the absorbent rock as if by deep snow. Softer surfaces of decayed limestone and clay lend an auditory closeness to the walls, giving a powdery feel to voices. Someone speaking just around a corner can't be heard until, rounding the corner, the channel of rock carries the cascading sound to the ear. But in a chamber glazed with glassy calcite, sound has a brittle echo that reflects and magnifies as it is thrown back off the resonant surface. Voices in a large cavern arrive at the ear from a distance after bouncing along the uneven surfaces as a garbled, unintelligible effervescence.

Contrasted with the frequent storms of the Paleolithic, the whirling glacial dust and stinging snow, or the sunlit, noisy activity of the tribe and the vibrant animal life, the caves must have been a miracle of strange peace; a still, mysterious warp in the world. In the absence of wind and animals, the only motion in these subterranean recesses aside from the occasional rock fall is flowing water. In the profound quiet of the cave a hushed symphony of water plays in the darkness, an aquatic arpeggio of gurgles and drips. During rainy

seasons there are floods here, underground streams that sluice through the caverns as they have for millions of years, swirling bones and debris into eddied piles. The caves have a constant cool temperature and dense humidity, some as high as 90 per cent, creating an indoor rainfall. It is the water, the slow dripping, seeping and coursing of this vital fluid through the arteries and veins of the earth, the patient gnawing and garnering of minerals that makes a subterranean cavern a living and transforming environment, one whose animation is ponderous and deliberate in the extreme. To those delicately attuned to the animate in the natural world, the caves were a living presence.

The spiritual professionals seeking a more practiced level of consciousness alteration may have sought out the deepest chambers of some caves where there are no running underground streams. Carbon dioxide gas collects in pockets here during certain seasons of the year. It is colorless, odorless and undetectable to a novice caver, but experienced speleologists today notice a dry acidic taste in their mouths. The unexpected effects of this invisible toxin are increased pulse and breathing, dizziness, clumsiness, headache and even death. It does not conduct heat away as rapidly as normal air. Standing in an invisible pool of CO_2, a person would feel their lower body strangely warmed in the typically cool air. Interpreting their response to a CO_2-laden chamber through the cultural filter of a Paleolithic hunter-gatherer, a chamber that affected them this way would have had particularly potent qualities in an already intense environment. There is some conjecture as to whether this might have been a bonus for the shamans, who may have briefly entered into this cloud of chthonic effluvia for a boost along a mind-altering path, or to tip an initiate just a bit more off center.

MIND-ALTERING TOOLS

The peculiar auditory qualities of caves were familiar features to the spiritual specialists. The most fascinating instrument to create music in the caves and the one that leaves no evidence was the human voice, singly and in concert. Significantly, it has been found that in some caves, up to 80 per cent of the art is positioned where an echo resounds. Chanting repetitively, even by a single person, would have folded back on itself and multiplied to become a cascade of sound. Rhythmic hand clapping would have been deafening. However they understood the mechanics of an echo, the effect would have been powerfully moving and, at least in some

caves, the sound and the art were mutually evocative. In a calcite chamber of Cougnac an artist saw a relief of the natural stone as the neck and chest of a megaloceros, a giant deer with enormous antlers, and a relatively infrequent subject in cave art. On the megaloceros's shoulder is one of the famous "killed man" torsos, a naked figure in black, appearing to lean forward while three lines extend from his back and buttocks. Other images of a mammoth and ibex are found in this resonant chamber as well. Almost half a mile underground in the gigantic cave of Niaux is the enormous vault of the Salon Noir, so named for the panels of black animals that adorn its walls. Here, the smallest sound reverberates around this domed chamber. It is inescapable that this resonant, magnificent space was a sanctuary that could accommodate large groups of people and its sonic quality was a significant element of its holiness. Any orchestration of voices and instruments would have been deeply affecting and, as mentioned earlier, ritual speech and music help create sacred space.

Music of a sort was made by striking calcite draperies and stalactites to produce a wide range of vibrational booming sounds, enhanced by the cave architecture. These early percussive instruments bear the marks of having been 'played' and of also having possibly been modified by chipping to alter their tones. These 'lithophones', as they are called, were sometimes marked with ocher in recognition of their unique auditory qualities, lending further significance to the idea of orchestration.

At a site in Eastern Europe near Kiev, a xylophone made of mammoth bones and painted red was discovered. Rituals in the caves were quite possibly performed to the accompaniment of wood instruments and skin drums, the traditional instrument of most shamans, that have not survived. But bone flutes from the Aurignacian and Gravettian eras have been found, and bull roarers as well, a simple but eerily effective instrument made from a flat piece of bone with a hole in one end and a string through the other so that when it is whirled around the head it makes a whooshing, roaring sound. Put a few of these together, add the weird echo of a cavern and the results would have been spine tingling. The already mesmerizing atmosphere of the depths was fully manipulated to create a higher level of strangeness.

The most significant sensory input for the creation of cave art is the utter lack of light. Any light in all but cave entrances was artificially introduced by people and manipulated to enhance the

environment. The introduction of light brought the underground world out of its black sleep. Yet, in the grand chambers it would have been impossible to see from one wall to the others and have a visual sense of the total space without posting torches at regular intervals, and that would have provided at best a wavering and uneven light. The high dome of the Salon Noir of Niaux is well beyond the power of a torch to illuminate. The small space visible around torch-bearing explorers vanished completely as they moved on, swallowed by the velvet black as if it never had been. Archaeologists studying the earliest lamps determined that Paleolithic communities producing lamps were restricted to areas where cave art was most plentiful. The suggestion is that lamps weren't used much outside of the caves. It would have taken quite a few to light a large space and they would not have produced smoke as torches would have. The number of lamps required was also dependent on the composition of the cave surface. In Lascaux, for example, the Axial Gallery has a highly reflective surface that needed fewer lamps than did the Shaft, a lower geological layer of much darker, light-absorbent material where many lamps were discovered.

The steady, well-lit panorama we can see of the Salon Noir with lamps and the visual spatial arrangement from the upper gallery of Peche Merle down to the magnificent spotted horses below was unattainable then. But, although steady, dramatic lighting in the caves today allows us to take in a stunning chamber in its entirety, the power of electricity can be a significant hindrance to reading the caves as they did. Modern tours stand staring at a blank wall in the gloom while the guide explains a fine point of cave art. Then, with a practiced and dramatic tilt of the guide's flashlight, animals leap from the wall as the light casts shadows on the engraved lines and the tour gasps with awe. It is easy to imagine the Paleolithics controlling the light in the same way for the same effect. Paradoxically, bright, direct light can erase an engraving altogether by washing out the shadows that give it form just as effectively as darkness. A Paleolithic open-air site in the Côa Valley of northern Portugal was not discovered until the 1990s because the engravings were so difficult to see. Similarly, a photograph, taken with careful lighting and designed to fit a flat, square page gains in detail, but loses the organic contours and natural shading of the original surface that define the subject's character and enhance its purpose. The natural bulge of the stone that suggested the muscular swelling

of a bull's shoulder to the artist can be lost in the well-lit photograph. The cave itself and the spatial arrangement of images seen from one end of a chamber look entirely different from the other and this disorienting feeling cannot be replicated effectively in a photograph. The horse 'masks' drawn on protruding rocks in Altamira, for example, can only be seen from one angle.

In the Salon Noir, light tipped at the proper angle casts a shadow over an edge of the natural rock to create the back line of a bison. The underside of the animal is drawn with a red line, but the animal is mostly made of light and shadow. Other paintings incorporate a trick of light by using a natural concavity as the bulky body of the animal. The shadow cast by a light creates the illusion of convexity and the animal is suddenly three-dimensional with a full, rounded belly. Move the light up and down as a flickering flame would have done (another tour-guide trick) and the animal becomes animated, seeming to leap from the wall. These optical illusions may, from our jaded standpoint, appear like a form of game, like the 3D books one stares at until the squiggles on the page suddenly transform into leaping dolphins. But for the Paleolithics when art was new to the world, these creations represented the unfolding of a mystical relationship conjoining them with the cave's unique personality, spirit animals, and the revelatory magic of shadows and light. The miraculous potentials of the mind-altering Underworld linked them through direct sensory experience with spiritual transformative powers.

The palpable darkness adds a peculiar dimension to the sense of space; in this hallucinogenic realm, the encasement of the body diffuses, the interior human spirit blends with the interior of the cave. For a hunter-gatherer who would have been intimately acquainted with a very large territory above ground, and the resources to be found there at every season, the ability to hold a detailed mental map of the location of images in a cave and their relation to one another is reasonable to assume. The knowledgeable cave visitor would know the terrain in terms of both subterranean and spiritual space. As they had no alternative, it may have became immaterial whether all the pictures could actually be seen together or not, as we can see them with dramatic lighting. It was enough to know they were there; inner visions charted, along with the interior landscape of the cave and the topography of their belief, comprised a cartography of spirit.

CONVERSATIONS WITH THE CAVE

Anyone who has spent a lazy day watching clouds float by has had the experience of assigning meaning to the random swirls of vapor. After a few days touring the caves of France I was beginning to see reindeer in the patterns of the hotel floor tiles. For us it is a carefree pastime, but in the context of the ritualized Paleolithic cave environment the visions appearing before them were communiqués from the spirit world. The hallucinogenic qualities of the deep chambers produced revelations, the inspired result of a complex conversation between the people, the architecture of the cave and the beings beyond the membrane of stone. Natural formations revealed a being existing just beyond the surface; a crack becomes a bear's back, vertical stalagmitic ripples become the wooly coat of an ibex, circles are added to a long, rectangular rock and it becomes a horse's head with eyes and nostrils in place. A black oval-shaped hole in a wall is transformed into a stag's head with the addition of a few lines to indicate antlers. Another becomes a pool as a deer drawn next to it dips its head to drink. Stone pillars present the massive legs of an improbably leaping mastodon.

In the recently discovered cave of Villhonneur the calcite-covered skeletal remains of a young man, dated to about 27,000 BP, was found. This in itself is unusual, but above the body was a startling piece of art. The natural calcite had formed in two flows that suggested long, shaggy hair parted down the center. On the rock 'face' between the flows someone drew a simple vertical line and two horizontal lines to form a nose, an eye and a mouth. The head appears to tip forward slightly in three-quarter view, the eye shut. One is struck by how similar this is to mourning graveyard angels as guardians, keeping watch over the dead. The caves offered both the vision and the vehicle required to attain it. They are a protean, elastic world of shape-shifting potential where metamorphosis is the rule.

There is one other sensory experience to consider and that is touch. The modern visitor who dares to even appear to try touching a Paleolithic painting will be scolded unmercifully. The ancient artists, however, entered into the surface with their breath, fingers and hands. Manipulation, the removing and adding of materials with hands and tools, created the art. Where the surface is covered with a layer of the moist clay resulting from degraded limestone, they ran their fingers through it in patterns of swirls and waves called finger fluting, as if the sensory, tactile act of this graceful patterning were some sort of dance their hand performed with the cave. Cosquer, the underwater cave near Marseilles, is covered with these trailing lines made with two, three or four fingers, so high off the ground in fact they must have used ladders. Everywhere the mud exists on the surface it is covered with these patterns. They are curved, zigzagged or squared, reminiscent of or evoked by entoptic forms. Some were drawn and drawn over again to assure their proper form. This was no idle pastime but purposeful creation. In Peche Merle these markings appear on most of the accessible clay walls. The smaller hands of an older child or a woman can be detected here among the larger tracings, and small footprints left behind confirm their presence. In Cosquer these flutings underlay all the images as if this were some primordial preparation for the emergent representational art, a quickening of the pregnant potential. Perhaps these markings helped activate or permeate the membrane and make the other world accessible, reaching through to touch spirit.

Reaching through or beyond the veil is found in rock and cave art the world over in the form of handprints. Both negative and positive prints suggest a sort of signature or relationship of a very intimate nature. Positive prints are made by painting the hand and pressing it on to the wall to leave a handprint. In Chauvet someone with a small hand pressed a red-painted palm to the wall over and over again until, from a distance, one can make out the pointillist image of a bison. As Valerie Feruglio, a cave art specialist who plotted the prints by determining the ghostly outline of fingers, has said, there are easier ways to get paint on a wall. This was a repetitive symbolic act resulting in the magical creation of a bison coalescing from the beyond.

Negative prints are made by placing the hand on the wall and blowing liquefied pigment on to it from the mouth, a form of Paleolithic airbrushing. The hand, covered with paint, disappears in the color field. When it is removed, a negative imprint remains. Recall the sacred San pigment, quang quang. Its production required an extensive ritual involving journeying to a remote mountain to obtain the sparkling red hematite and a prescribed ceremonial preparation that imbued it with sacred qualities, including mixing it with the blood of the sacred eland. When this potent substance was used to create a handprint, the subject covered not only his or her hand with it, but sprayed the rock as well, creating a solid surface of magic conjoining the human and the divine by dissolving the barrier between. Occasionally, fingers will be folded down in various

combinations so the prints left behind hint at an ancient signal, a sign to the gods or human observers. Children and even babies had their handprints put on the walls. Jean Clottes discovered that the painters in Niaux and La Vache used a unique mixture for their pigment, grinding together minerals that don't naturally occur together. Whatever symbolic weight was attached to these ingredients, they found a particular recipe, no doubt after much trial and error, that extended the pigment, flowed easily and resisted cracking when it dried. For some reason, they changed the recipe after a thousand years.

However it was done, the result is that a reflection of one's hand, a deeply personal statement, remains behind. The artist bonded with the rock. If we reflect back on the Oglala Whirlwind Complex and its many layers of interconnection, this Paleolithic interweaving of sacred breath, magical pigment, saliva, the intimate and manipulative human hand and the realm beyond the stone membrane suggests a complex spiritual web of logic; a materialization of prayer, the word made flesh.

It seems almost an intrusion to witness the results of this ritually intimate act of touching spirit, what may have been the sealing of a private covenant between souls. Yet human hands seal many bargains, some quite fierce. The prints may have indicated the achievement of having reached man- or woman-hood and this landmark required the recognition of spirit. It may have indicated some sort of supplication, or contract, an agreement to dedicate strength to a divine or earthly purpose. There are many possibilities, but all, ultimately, speculative. Once the hand was sealed into the wall with the powers of the paint, its removal left a void, a portal opened through which communication was established. Some handprints have been found scraped off or over-painted as if to obliterate that connection, but the vast majority have endured for millennia.

Imagine the ancients standing on the high trail of Peche Merle. A scene intended to take the breath away is about to be revealed, framed in sparkling stone draperies that drop from the ceiling like the curtains of a Baroque opera house. The torches only reveal the immediate area; expectant wide-eyed faces and these stone curtains, waving in the torchlight, which appear to open on the Abyss itself. Below, across a deep gulf of blackness, the eerie lilt of a bone flute wavers through the dark air, joined by the low whine of a bullroarer and mesmerizing drumming that builds and rolls off the walls from

somewhere in the distant darkness, waves of sound that become almost palpable, pounding in the chest, hearts answering. Then below, flickering fires are suddenly lit to reveal life-sized horses emerging from the slick floor of the cave. They appear to leap in the dancing light, materializing out of the ground. Handprints framing the figures seem to beckon them through the rock surface. Large black and red pointillist spots on their coats spread beyond the animals to the visual field around them, wavering in the uneven light, making them appear to be either coalescing or evaporating. Not anchored by their small or nonexistent hooves, the animals seem to hover. And, where the eye first sees two horses standing back to back, another suddenly appears as the wedge of rock on which the pictures are painted assumes the shape of a third horse. Adding to the surrealistic, subterranean vision, a vague red fish floats across the bodies of the horses. The illusion is stunning.

This magician's sleight of hand using the darkness and light as an ethereal pigment was brilliant and intentional. A sophisticated use of illusion perfected as a powerful tool of persuasion could be understood as the manipulative power of art to persuade, and may well have been. The magical revelation of this sacred art, echoing mythic stories, defined them as a people of that land moving through life together, the images anchoring them in a spiritual landscape. Yet the architecture of each unique cave spoke images to the artists who, in conversations with the cave, were gifted with the undeniable presence of the spirit world. Photos of these images in a book, made with the best modern lighting possible, cannot begin to do them justice. One must breathe in the atmosphere.

SUBTERRANEAN TRAINING

Possibly many types of ceremonies took place in caves. Having such an intense environment at hand would have answered a variety of needs, both spiritual and adventurous. Shamans had the ideal consciousness-altering environment at hand to contact beings from other worlds. Some caves were intensely used and the traditions of cave art were created and re-created with amazing continuity for 20,000 years. There had to have been a consistent and compelling school of art, a vital element of Paleolithic life perpetuating this cultural engine of expression for millennia which provided continuity to their spiritual needs up to the beginning of the Mesolithic. The caves were perfect for initiation ceremonies that consecrated young people as members of their tribe and instructed

them in the iconic imagery. Children growing up with knowledge of the caves, that people went in and later emerged quite changed, would internalize cultural expectations of a ritualized cave experience. Witnessing and possibly helping groups of people prepare scaffolding, pigment, make stone lamps and torches and then carrying them into the depths would have certainly excited interest and no few questions.

Deeper mysteries, including powerful mythologies and secrets reserved for adulthood, would have to wait until proper initiation to be revealed, but preparation for such experiences would have been gradually introduced over time. Pueblo and Plains Indian children, by comparison, were raised and many still are, with the expectation that a vision quest is an unquestioned rite of passage for young people. Awareness that deep caves held the portal to the Otherworld where one encounters the spirits would have sifted early into a Paleolithic child's mind, guided by the timely release of pertinent information by adults, whispered tales from older friends, observation, and perhaps a forbidden journey underground, as the footprints of three children across a sand-bank in Niaux suggest. This honing of the sacred, the systemization of hallucinogenic experience into a form of doctrine answering to cultural needs and expectations, reinforced by instructions in the proper interaction with the spirit world to assure harmony, was passed to the children, and so carried down the generations. Those young people chosen by the spirits or who exhibited a desire to shamanize would be induced to enter training. The experience of the subterranean labyrinthine journey as a metaphor for confronting life's challenges, leading to a union with the divine and culminating with the successful return to the waking world, became a keystone in the mythic temple of the sacred.

After lengthy ritual preparation in the upper air inducting them into the mysteries of the chthonic world, shamanic experts who had intimate knowledge of the sensory-altering qualities of the chambers and the hallucinatory world on to which they opened, may have led well-primed initiates into the uniquely beautiful cave of Cougnac. Imagine them guiding hushed, expertant young people into the inky blackness where the shaman could conduct every element of the ritual for maximum effect; the light, the sound and the tolerances of his students.

A glittering forest of stone forms drips from the ceiling and is mirrored by stalagmites reaching up from the floor, absorbing

sounds of the people passing through, soaking up voices and footfalls like new-fallen snow. But the path dips down, rounds a corner and a salon opens up that resounds like a parking garage. Elders, transformed by costumes from their normal appearance into mythic beings, including a dancing shaman wearing a bison robe and horns, awaited the initiates with lessons they would never forget. Those experiences that jar our normal sensibilities, that cause the heart to race and palms to sweat, which are endured in deprivation, pain and strangeness, are imprinted on our minds in high relief. It is a basic tenet of all initiations into adulthood that the rituals embody elements of fear, pain and sacrifice, to alter consciousness and brand vital cultural information on the mind and soul of the initiates.

In the calcite echo chamber of Cougnac, voices ricochet off the walls and tumble together into a layered, multi-dimensional chorus, giving this space a dramatically different presence from the entering pathway, as if having walked through a curtain of sound. In ancient times the wall opposite the entrance was cleared of the stalactites that hung from the ceiling in front of it and the surface that reflects voices was painted with images. The initiates would be indelibly saturated in the eerie aural magic of an echo amplifying a long-lost rite of passage, the voices emerging from the painted rock portal singing the sacred myths that bind them eternally to their gods, their land and their people.

These children were forever changed, their childhood identities had died and they took on a new status. Like shedding a pupa, they crossed over into adulthood, a metamorphosis that requires induction into the powerful secrets of tribal responsibilities and the endurance of those mysteries.

HONING THE SACRED

The need for ritual behavior runs very deep in our species, far back to the wellspring of humanity. The hint of an accompanying ceremony is suggested by the presence of ocher in very early human sites. Ceremony is implicit in those rare cases, indicating care in the handling of human bones. In the Middle Paleolithic the evidence of deliberate and intentional burial is conclusive. The placing of antlers, flowers and arranged bones in a few Neanderthal graves suggests our early ancestors' belief in another world to live in beyond this one. But ceremony was a major component of Aurignacian life and the subsequent cultures of the Upper

Paleolithic.

David Whitley proposes that a mutant gene carrying the double-edged blessing/affliction of mood disorders such as bipolar illness appeared in these early modern humans, injecting into culture the potential for raging creativity driven by hallucinations and degrees of madness that was passed on through families. Those shamanic sufferers who survived the maniacal terrors of their illness did so by 'answering the call, the ritual obligations of shamanizing, finding structure and strength in the creative impulse of art. The genius on display at Chauvet, the oldest art of this magnitude found so far, proves there was no long period of progress from stick figures to magnificence, but a full-blown revelation of immense talent. Although the evidence of their creative genius survives primarily in cave art and carvings on bone, there would have been those exceptional people who manipulated music, clothing, ceremonies and other untraceable artifacts of culture, setting in motion social and spiritual changes never before seen. These charismatic individuals would have offered adaptive alternatives to lead their people to succeed through challenging times.

Thirty-two thousand years ago, the initial imperative to make art, to separate out that which was to be 'made special', reflecting the desire to touch the sacred, attained a critical creative mass. The magical images the people had long evoked on surfaces above ground now had an entirely new palette, surfaces enclosed in an enchanted subterranean underworld. Underground was a focused power unseen before now. One frozen day long ago, a call was heard from beyond the veil, a voice that beckoned from the telluric depths to be released from the wall of a deep cave. The early humans of the Upper Paleolithic brought with them the talent, desire and inspiration to evoke iconic images of great symbolic significance. With the caves as their sacred cathedrals, the first modern human arrivals in Europe set about inventing religion.

Forty millennia elapsed between the arrival of the first fully modern humans in Europe and the warming climatic shift to the Mesolithic that led them to abandon the sacred caves, their nodes of spirit. It is Professor Mithen's contention, quoted above, that 'nothing much happened' during this time. But then, his excellent book, aptly titled, *After The Ice*, focuses on just that; how and why human society set the wheels in motion in a newly warm and more inviting world to carry itself forward from hunter-gatherers into the revolutionary era of settled villages and farming called the

language and demanded translation and interpretation upon re-entering waking reality. Through instruction and initiation, a body of cosmic understanding was created and, simultaneously, the on-going formation of a successful, cohesive social structure to accommodate it. The neurons and synapses of the uninitiated, hallucinating Paleolithic brain, firing in all directions, were gradually trained into learned, controlled pathways that promoted tribal unity and survival in a dangerous and difficult environment. Discipline and cooperation were vital. These imperative spiritual conversations were conducted both in the caves and with the caves, where small, determined bands of people literally drew lines in the sand and on the cave walls that defined Homo sapiens as a new, spiritually conversant species.

Beyond the construct of worldly social dynamics there existed the parallel augmentation of the Otherworldly. People were not consciously sitting down to design rituals to make their societies function better. The impulse to enact ceremonies and express the sacred arose out of their psycho-spiritual landscape organized by their cosmology and fed by the revelatory visions of the specialists and the visions so revealed gained in power. The spirits appeared and told them what needed to be done. Increasing familiarity with the hallucinations encountered during altered states and the process to attain them sharpened the relationship between the shaman and the spirit world. Conversance with strange beings and experiences helped spiritual voyagers to master the fear of these mysterious worlds, define alliances with spirit helpers, defeat evil shamans and accumulate spiritual power. The prolonged cosmic communion among the people, the chthonic chambers of the caves and the spirits was a circular, reciprocal event.

PEOPLE IN THE CAVES

The spiritual specialists of the Ice Age blazed the first trail of the heroic/shamanic journey into the labyrinth, marking out its turns and twists, identifying and encoding the entoptic landscape of altered consciousness, traveling to the Center and returning, and teaching the Journey to others. Their psychic scaffolding endures in our own myths and cosmologies today. Here we find the lynchpin that joins the dots of shamanism, altered states of consciousness, mythology, sacred art and the labyrinth. Lewis-Williams' resuscitation of Bleek's San Bushman ethnographic material, in concert with Clottes team's exhaustive approach to the study of the decorated caves of

France, knits up the final Ariadne's thread that will lead us to the revelation of the symbolic labyrinth in Lascaux.

Lying at the nexus of this horizontal axis of land and people and the vertical axis of sacredness that joins the chthonic, middle earth and upper worlds, is the vehicle of transition, the labyrinth, the *axis mundi* that links all existence. Ritually traveling through the deep cave veil, a melding of the physical, social, mythic and spiritual worlds was realized; a catharsis of being. The art emerging on the surface of the cave was a fulcrum upon which their world turned. During times of mystical transport they were simultaneously walking through the cavernous material counterpart of their deep psyches and experiencing the sensation of being drawn into a spiritual vortex in their bodies and brains. The spirits residing beyond the membrane of rock called to them with other worldly voices, blending with their own in a prismatic cascade of sound. Power was tapped and released through creation of a picture, magic channeled by the revelation of art. The transformative mythic 'hall of mirrors' so awakened reflected the upper world upon the underworld, the waking on the dreaming, the body on the spirit, the eternal present on the future and past, ancestor on child, individual on tribe, in a multiplicity of potent images, driven by song and story, bound together with the common thread of maintaining cosmic balance.

The inner light of spirit, striking the lens of the labyrinthine paintings, emerges through the wall and is bent and focused by a psychic refraction of the human personality, as pure sunlight is captured and magnified by water, embroidering the river rock below with color.

CHAPTER 13

THE LABYRINTH OF LASCAUX

"Color is the deeds and sufferings of light."
Goethe

"...a flame is a living gem, endowed with all the transporting power that belongs to the precious stone... This transporting power of flame increases in proportion to the depth and extent of the surrounding darkness. The most impressively numinous temples are caverns of twilight, in which a few tapers give life to the transporting, other-worldly treasures of the altar."
Aldous Huxley, **Heaven and Hell**

"Only a few truly memorable years of severe cold or hunger would sear themselves into legend, to be passed from one generation to the next. But the people always knew that ... the endless passage of the seasons would bring more plentiful ones. Ultimately, they believed their survival depended on the potency of the animals they hunted, on the powers of the supernatural world, and on the reliability of close kin."
Brian Fagin, **The Great Warming**

TELLURIC GIFTS

The small hunting party crunched through the snow, following the tracks of a lone bison. Driving winds scoured the snowfields, sending sparkling whirlwinds over the ground and hitting the skin like needles. Their smoking breath frosted into a brittle, crackling rime on the fur hoods pulled tightly around their faces. If they could bring the bison down it would fill their families' bellies for a long time and there would be a new robe to keep the children warm. The cold this year had a tight grip. It felt like it would never release them. The snows still came, long after the melting should have

begun.

The bison tracks led up a sloping hillside where low shrubs and junipers bowed under the weight of the snow. The bison had stopped here briefly, pawing for frozen grass beneath the snow and leaving deep spear-shaped grooves. A hunter called the others to come see. The bison's hoof-marks pointed to a dark void against the stark white snow, a passage that vanished into the earth. Breaking dead limbs from a nearby pine to make torches they slid inside for a quick look and a break from the cold. In the stillness, out of the wind, a large chamber opened out before them. They had never seen such bright white walls, a dark horizon running beneath, and the ceiling billowed above them like a cloudy spring sky. It was a hushed world awaiting creation, a spiritual landscape empty of animal gods. Their low voices rumbled in the empty chamber as they reached out slowly and touched the surface. It was covered with tiny reflective crystals that sparkled in the first light ever to shine here.

Their dancing torches lit the rim of a portal at the far end of the chamber. As they entered, it drew them in deeper, down a narrow, sloping corridor where the smooth, arched ceiling was a miracle of white stone. They felt they were spinning, being pulled down the tunnel although their feet were firmly planted. It was a place unknown to them. Yet it was very familiar. The bison had brought them to this sheltering womb and now it would wait outside for them, and let itself be killed. They would live. The spring would return and with it, the reindeer. The children would be fat again. Summer would follow, mantling the meadows in flowers. They vowed to return here and give praise for the gift of this place.

The first Paleolithic shaman/artist to behold the space of Lascaux must have fallen on his or her knees in thanks for this blessing of natural perfection. Here, indeed, was a magical gift. Unlike the huge, open porches of caves above the river that announced their dramatic presence from miles away, the entrance to this cave is relatively disguised on an undistinguished sloping hillside. It opens into a spacious, oblong room large enough to contain an entire tribe. A darker layer of rock around the base of the walls creates a natural ground line. The ceiling is clabbered with rounded rock. Between is a pristine white pallet, encrusted with tiny calcite needles that grow in all directions and bounce the light in a way unique to Lascaux. The optical quality of this stone occurs rarely in France, and then only in small patches in a very few caves. Here, the entire surround is reflective, catching light and magnifying it. But beyond lies an even more valuable treasure.

At the far end of this room, later named "The Hall of the Bulls" or "The Rotunda", the expansive chamber funnels into a keyhole-shaped portal. Passing through, one enters a narrow tunnel, just over 72 feet long, which gradually slopes down. The lower half of the walls bubble with dark, brown cauliflower-like stone and rises to form a defined shelf, the 'legs' of the keyhole. But above arcs a white vault of rice-grain calcite, fine-textured and highly reflective. The passageway narrows even further at a major constriction of the wall. Near the end, the vault of the ceiling drops precipitously, deep fissures appear at the base of the left-hand wall and dark cavities give the impression of a bottomless void. The space becomes very confined, allowing only a single person to pass. The floor drops down considerably then cranks to the left, almost inscribing a full circle around a tight corner. Water has worn away the soil beneath the stone that forms this corner and it appears to hang, weightless. Beyond this 'false pillar' is a narrow space with a vertical wall on the right. The tunnel becomes very low and narrow and silts up a little further on, effectively dead-ending and one must return by the same route, past the suspended pillar, up the confining slope, into the spacious Rotunda and out to the upper world.

By their mysterious nature alone, other caves decorated by the Paleolithics encouraged and enhanced shamanic visionary journeys. Lascaux's particular gift was the geomantic parallel to the labyrinthine experience; the natural, telluric expression of the journey to the far side of consciousness. Here was a chamber that precisely mimicked the look and feel of that deep, trance state. In stark contrast to the roomy, communal Rotunda, this narrow passageway called the Axial Gallery was an invitation to the solitary shamanic journey through the *axis mundi* followed by a return to the Rotunda before re-entering the upper world. It awaited only the release of the guiding spirit animals beyond the veil to activate it.

LGM LIVING

The Hall of the Bulls tunnels off to the right as well, a branch called the Passageway, where the surface changes to a powdery material lacking the optics of the Rotunda. This angles off to yet another area named "The Apse" and, plunging off the edge of the Apse is the Shaft, a narrow, deep space requiring a rope to get down to the floor. At the bottom of the 16-foot well is the most famous of

all Paleolithic paintings, a man and bison confronting each other in a rare scene, one to which we shall return. There are a total of eight recognized areas of Lascaux. For now, our focus is on the Hall of the Bulls and the Axial Gallery. The final chapter will explore the others, each having a unique sacred purpose.

More than 100 lamps, many tools, sea shells from a western French beach, some perforated and worn as jewelry, and a pebble carved to resemble a shell, manganese used for pigment, a needle and awl and a block of molded clay still impressed with fingerprints were found in Lascaux during early excavations. The discovery of so many portable objects in a painted cave is rare and the presence of a needle that would be categorized as an aboveground tool is puzzling. Some of these items like the needle and spear heads clearly had no practical function at the bottom of a well in a deep cave. And many artifacts found here are decorated with images repeated on the walls. Symbolic nested lines carved into stone lamps, and cruciform and star-like patterns on bone spearheads also appear on the flanks of horses and cows and hover around bulls, marking a significance we cannot know. We can only say a small tribe of Ice Age people understood their importance and that the symbols on tools and paintings alike were, like the iconic animals, consistent with a category of magical powers available both above and below ground.

Dating Lascaux has been problematic as studies at various times have yielded dates from 8380 BP to 18,600 BP. Charcoal from hearths was disrupted by trampling and washed around by flooding waters and the artists, possibly in recognition of the unique surface of the cave, left no torch-wipes on the walls as occurred in other caves. As the paintings contain no charcoal from which a precise date can be extracted, a number of other techniques have been used to determine when the paintings were executed. Stylistics, comparison of thematic images with other dated sites, the type of animals represented on its walls, the tools left behind, and a radiocarbon date from a reindeer antler baton found in the Shaft, all point to the range of 18,600 BP, pushing back the previous date of 17,000 BP. This new date places Lascaux deeper in the midst of the Last Glacial Maximum (LGM), straddling the end of the Upper Solutrean culture and the beginnings of the Magdalenian, an interesting place to find oneself.

This time period around 18,500 BP was the coldest of the Upper Paleolithic. The Last Glacial Maximum encased much of the

northern world in ice one last time before the climate began to change erratically. The ice sheets ground mountains into dust, sending it swirling through the air on blasting, frigid winds. Cold, dry tundra extended across most of Europe. The grim cold and relentless winds generated by massive glacial barriers prevented movement to the north into Scandinavia. Leafy woodlands disappeared, replaced by sparse, sturdy junipers. Bitter semi-desert conditions prevailed across southern Europe. Permafrost reached as far as central France, where desert animals such as the Saiga antelope roamed. Brief but drastic fluctuations in temperature from era to era would have driven migrations of both people and animals to find food and refuge from the cold; from summer grasslands stretching across Ukraine to winter in the Mediterranean south and back again as the temperature pendulum swung. The grassy tundra would have resembled a chilly Serengeti during the short summer, roaming with enormous herds of animals. But the first night of killing frost heralded the onset of nine long months of deep snow and freezing days. Year to year, brief periods of stability would again give way to fierce cold followed by thawing.

This climate flipping must have put unique stresses on the people whom we call the Solutreans. Their culture emerged at the height of the Last Glacial Maximum when efficiency, cooperation, discipline and determination extended the razor-thin margin between life and death. There may have been only 40,000 people, sprinkled in tiny bands across the whole of Europe. The loss of a hunter to accident or wild animal, or babies to illness, cut that margin even closer. Hunger was familiar. Endless winter weeks confined in smoky, close quarters with the family must have produced unique social pressures, to say the least. Escape into the warming spring days of food and freedom must have dawned like a miracle. The journey out of these close dens to seasonal meeting places where new faces, stories and trade goods abounded restored the spirit, cemented new relationships and ended others too strained to endure.

The tools the Solutreans developed employed pressure-flaking techniques never seen before and produced an array of particularly beautiful leaf-shaped flints for light projectiles and elaborate tanged arrowheads, narrowed at one end, the better to fit into a shaft. Bone implements were developed and more commonly used because they tended not to shatter in the great cold as does stone. This graceful technology and the people who made it had a brief flowering on the planet, appearing about 20,000 BP and disappearing rather mysteriously about 18,000 BP, possibly overwhelmed by sheer numbers of invading Magdalenians, on the move to find secure hunting grounds in the teeth of the undependable climate.

During this liminal time frame of monumental transition in climate that affected every aspect of human life and the animals they depended upon, the need to codify and transmit their belief system and rituals, the glue that holds societies together particularly in difficult times, was paramount. At this juncture in time between the Solutrean and Magdalenian, on the edge of the Last Glacial Maximum, an apparent cultural need to create a concentration of painted caves took hold among people who shared a common vision. Lascaux, like other caves of the same period, is an unpretentious opening in the ground of a gently sloping hillside. These caves, Gabillou, Saint-Cirq and others are not easily detected and don't announce their presence like later Mid-Magdalenian caves such as Rouffignac, Les Combarelles, and Bernifal, yawning openings in the cliff-sides with grand porches out front. Eschewing the Ice Age antebellum architecture for the more inconspicuous was a clear choice on their part, for the more prominent caves could not have been missed by people so well acquainted with the neighborhood. It indicates a preference for a certain kind of territory over another, perhaps one that could be concealed or, at least, not very easily found.

Not only were they chosen for their inconspicuous entrances, but also stylistic conventions and unusual themes are shared among them, indicating a common purpose. Grid patterns are found at most, and the image of a confrontation between man and bull or bison is revisited in a variety of ways, from simple depictions to the mysteriously evocative composition in the Shaft of Lascaux.

Life events remembered in stories and myth was their record of survival, reading the secret signals of nature and compiling a mnemonic diary of the years; the times of deep cold, sickness and ragged living, the year the snow was chest-high and the ice broke late on the water, and those short summers of fat animals easily caught, the seasonal moons when the berries grew ripe, the numbers of salmon exploded in the rivers, and the reindeer moved like a dark roiling flood through the valleys. Their stories weaved together a multiplicity of maps; of the geography, the plant life, the weather in both difficult and graceful times, the movements and personalities of animals, the social relationships and obligations to people seen perhaps once a year, the existence of others never seen but who

provided exotic goods such as fossil sea shells and obsidian from lands beyond the mountains. Ever-present in the midst of summer feasting was the ghostly collective memory of desperate want and vicious winters past that must never be forgotten. These legends of hard times that took the lives of strong hunters as well as children and the old were burned into the mythology, not as cautionary tales, but as real as snarling wolves that prowled beyond the ring of firelight.

Underlying all of these mental maps and mythic diaries ran the deep structure of spirit, the connective tissue of a cosmovision woven on a loom of sinew and animal bone. The stories and songs of the waking world had an underpinning of spiritual logic arising from the hallucinatory shamanic network of energy. At the center of this web of life was the *axis mundi* of the labyrinth, the portal of metamorphosis that opened on to the world of spirit, survival, healing and wisdom. The person who moved through that portal and into the weird hallucinatory world beyond, who attained metamorphosis, was immortalized on the walls of deep caves. This was a vital story these people of the Last Glacial Maximum lived, shared, told and retold so its lessons would not be forgotten. The mythic theme of confrontation between man and bull or bison recorded in the Solutrean/Magdalenian caves became, at certain times, a collision, melding the two beings into a single potent creature at the center of the labyrinth.

Yet, at the time of the Last Glacial Maximum, this mythic being was already ancient. He presided over the deep and fecund gallery in Chauvet, 14,000 years before in the company of his goddess-consort. There is more raw urgency about this minotaur's energy. He looks over his shoulder at the intruder as if caught in an intimate moment. By the time the minotaur appears at the icy edge of the Last Glacial Maximum, the rough sexual energy has been transformed into a controlled ecstasy found at the center of the labyrinth. Shape shifting has become a practiced art for select adepts, a process has been perfected, and the role of shamanic spiritual specialist refined. The route through the labyrinth has been mapped and, in Lascaux, the sacred space illustrated.

Lascaux was planned and created during the Last Glacial Maximum, possibly within the time-span of a single generation, some paintings probably executed by one exceptional artist, the Picasso of his time, although people visited the cave on many occasions over the millennia, even building a fire at the entrance

during the Mesolithic. Aujoulet's extensive study of the cave has determined that the cohesive aesthetic of images and signs, the brilliant artistic renderings, the uses of polychrome color and the art's agreement with the natural features of the cave itself confirm that nothing about the art of the Axial Gallery is random. Whether the images were made at a time of fierce cold and deprivation as a plea for survival, or in gratitude for a more gracious season of hopeful plenty, there is no way to know. Even if there was a firmly dated charcoal drawing, there could never be a conclusive connection made between the narrow window of time during which Lascaux was decorated and a particular weather cycle, nor can we know for certain the Solutrean/Magdallenian response to it. Early excavations, primitive by today's standards and tainted by hundreds of eager visitors, were unable to preserve information with the kind of detail available to archaeologists today. Abbe Breuil, in a well-intentioned but archaeologically cringe-inducing attempt to drain off the standing water on the floor of the Rotunda, cut a hole in the calcite floor. He succeeded in draining the water, but also managed to flush into the depths below whatever debris and artifacts may have been left behind as well.

Excavations conducted in 1979 support the wide swings of climate variation at Lascaux during the Last Glacial Maximum, colder periods followed by warmer in succession, as indicated by pollens from a variety of plants discovered in a cross-section taken from near the entrance. Each type of pollen is unique to each plant species and is densely structured. It can survive in soil for many thousands of years. Recovered in archaeological digs, pollen reveals what plants existed at a particular place, what the ecosystem was like or what season it may have been when a layer of soil was laid down. In the cave of Lascaux, the pollen could have been blown in by wind or carried on animal fur or people's clothes. Yet, archaeologists also say that at some point people carried flowers or blossoming plants into the cave during the warm season of the year.

It used to be assumed that people celebrated rituals when living was easy and time and energy allowed for the elaborations of ceremony. But the opposite, in fact, is true. When life is most desperate is the time people turn to the spirit world for answers. The execution of the monumental works of art in the Rotunda and Axial Gallery was of paramount importance to a group of people perhaps inspired by a charismatic shaman/leader, demanding inspired planning, design, lamp making, accumulations of resources,

transportation and construction of scaffolding inside the cave and the final execution, all requiring dedication of significant time and resources. The labyrinthine journey into deep trance replicated and assisted by the cave and its art was vital to the continuation of the people and the blessings of the land above.

The Hall of the Bulls, the Axial Gallery and the Meander, taken together, are nothing less than the rendering of the shamanic spiritual journey, from the world of human culture, through the vortex of the labyrinth to the Eternal, the source of life, and the shamanic return from death to the upper air. It is the crystallization of the metaphor of transformation, of the fluidity of life as it passes through Earthly existence and out of the realm of Time, but with the promise of return to the temporal community. The mythology that bound them to their gods and land, to the weather and life, to the ancestors and spirits, is illustrated in Lascaux with purposeful intent.

The grand sweep of geologic time, millions of gallons of water frozen into relentless glacial juggernauts, thousands of years of human culture and the gods they worshipped, are suddenly telescoped here into the intimacy of a small tribe of brilliant, dedicated people who together enhanced a naturally gifted sacred space to capture their most profound symbolic beliefs and channel them in a spiritual reactor, resonant under the earth. Here, art is serious business.

TIME MACHINE

The perfect canvas of Lascaux's walls took on art at a prolific rate. One-tenth of all known parietal art in France is here. There are nearly 2000 figures, far more than any other of the great sites of Ice Age art, including caves that are much larger. The unassuming and relatively small Lascaux gallery called the Apse contains over a thousand figures, an intensity of creation unseen in any other Paleolithic cave. Norbert Aujoulat, author of an exhaustive study of Lascaux, calls this chamber "a sanctuary at the heart of a sanctuary". These people had many artistic conversations with the Beyond, more than any other group, and apparently, in a fairly short period of time. Aujoulat's careful consideration, meticulous research and reporting, and his admonishment to not allow one's imagination to run away with oneself, makes his comment that "the iconography of this cave is, above all, a fantastic ode to life" all the more powerful.

Aujoulat's dedicated years of often solitary study has revealed an accumulation of evidence that is meticulous and extensive. Sheer

Map of Lascaux

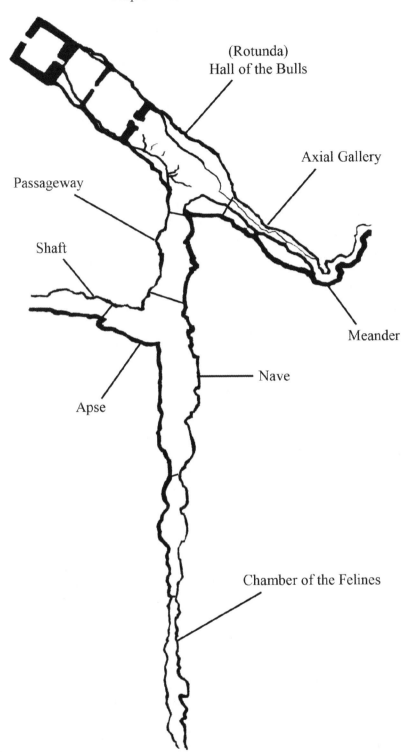

(Rotunda)
Hall of the Bulls

Axial Gallery

Passageway

Shaft

Meander

Nave

Apse

Chamber of the Felines

numbers alone would suggest the Lascaux painters were people of the horse as it is the subject most frequently pictured. The number of horses is closely followed by that of bovines and stags. These three species comprise 97 pe rcent of the total animals in the Hall of the Bulls, 93 per cent in the Axial Gallery and 71 pe cent in the Nave. The regularity of their appearance made it possible to determine which animal was drawn first, which second and so on, based on which was painted over, to some extent, by another. Wherever they appear, the horse was first placed on the surface, followed by the bovines, and finally the stags. This consistency demonstrates their creation was intended to convey a symbolic relationship. Groupings of a single species were produced with remarkable uniformity of color and technique, regular spacing and identical orientation, indicating the same person created a particular frieze during a single time period. The clues continue, adding up to the fact that Lascaux was planned and executed by a few people over a short period of time for the intentional purpose of communicating a sacred symbolic message, a prayerful rendering of the inevitable cycle of time.

The subtleties of the message are lost to us as if we had found the sheet music but not the words to a sacred song. We have the soaring melodies and rapturous phrasing, but not the libretto. What Aujoulat has deduced is that each of these three animals, significant enough by their overwhelming presence and the consistent order in which they were painted, horse, bovine, stag, appear in the seasonal attire they would have worn at the height of their species' mating seasons. The horses were given the coats they wore in late winter, early spring. The bulls and cows appear as they would in summer when the grass was deep. And the stags all sport elegant antlers as they do in the fall when battling other males for mates. Recall that these three species were painted in strict order; horse first, followed by cattle and finally, stags. The logic of their creation on the walls corresponds to their biological seasonality, spring, summer and fall, so consistently that it can be said that they are iconic representatives of the progression of the seasons. Taken together, they symbolize the cycle of time itself. No iconic symbol of winter has been identified, possibly because few, if any, large animals are driven to mate in the depths of winter. The common thread is the renewal of life.

The rendering of these animals at the height of seasonal mating, when they were most fierce, most potent and driven to create new

feature and an even more remote black stag, indicated by only a few lines that hint at antlers and a possible nose. Its back is also a natural formation of the wall. The artist quite possibly meditated on the blank wall, its formation, lines and features, and this group of stags presented themselves.

And then there are the bulls. They dominate most of the sweep of the paintable wall. The most monumental work of Paleolithic art, the white summer bulls of Lascaux are a breathtaking vision. Potent and gigantic, one measuring 15 feet long, their presence is overwhelming. The implication of masculine power is pervasive. They preside over the hall, spanning both sides of the entrance to the Axial Gallery. The up-and-inward vaulting of the ceiling and the massive bodies balanced on tiny hooves give the observer the sensation that they hover. There are twin images of bulls with red cows and their calves, one on each side of the Axial Gallery entrance. The cow on the left, like her sister on the other side, faces the opposite direction from the bulls. Her head, neck and shoulder are contiguous with the calf's head and the bull's testes.

The second family appearing on the right side flanks the portal to the Axial Gallery's deeper mysteries with the message that the sacredness of familial unity and its continuance through time is not only paramount, but life itself. This cow is followed closely by her calf. She appears between the fourth and fifth bulls, her mid-section under the hooves of the fifth bull and facing his hindquarters. She is a vision in red, a vivid color of life. Her hooves disappear into the imaginary ground line, but her body is thickly painted. Her calf is the identical color, its head overlaying her flank. The calf's head is distinguishable in this swath of red by a slight variation in the application of paint; the front of its face is a heavier line and it is set off from the cow by a slight blank space between the brow of the calf and the mother's flank. Joined together in a field of color, the artist obviously intended to emphasize the relationship between the two. The age of the calf indicates that it is a few months old, reinforcing the symbolism that this is a summer-time scene. While the spring horses in this chamber almost exclusively face into the cave and the stags of autumn consistently face outward, the summer bulls and other bovines face both into the cave and out, as if somehow transitional.

This mural of bovine fecundity, bull's testes, emergent calf and dominated cow speaks volumes. These are families, the essential social unit; the distillation of life's elemental manifestations. These

images are a summoning of the divine, archetypes of their species invested with complex symbolic power. That they appear in a dual tableau of relationship indicates that they are representatives of divine kinship as expressed in the natural world. In hunter-gatherer cultures, the concept of family is inclusive to everyone in the tribe; all aunts can be mothers, all uncles, fathers, which relates all children as brothers and sisters. But only certain cousins can marry others, based on clan affiliation. The extended family, a network of people whose relationships were defined by custom as those to be relied upon for social support, mutual defense, marriageable partners and food sharing among many other possibilities, embodied vital cultural life and the promise of its continuation over time.

Yet the nuclear family during the Paleolithic was life's continuance pared to the bare essentials. In the Rotunda we see both. The Western ideal of the rugged individual probably did not even exist in this archaic and dangerous world, and being cast out of one's social circle was anathema, probably akin to a death sentence. Tolerance allowing for creative categorizations of behaviors was inclusive, as in most tribal groups, even for those who deviated from the norm as the shamans may have. Social skills, interdependence and intelligent, complex communication on many levels, guided and disciplined by precepts and rituals of an over-arching cosmology, are what allowed people to succeed in this difficult environment. The sacredness of the family was imperative and cooperation under times of extreme duress was essential. Each of these iconic animals bore a wealth of symbolism for the people who painted them and viewed them. Placed together in a cultural context and in this chamber multiplies the meaning exponentially in ways we can only imagine.

The majestic aurochs that dominate the Hall of the Bulls and appear in other galleries as well present a fascinating part of the puzzle of Lascaux. These giants, six feet high and 11 feet in length, needed the milder temperatures of summer when lush grasslands sustained them. Bison today, like their ancient ancestors, are undaunted by freezing temperatures and snow and will paw through it to the grass below. In deep snow they have a method of pressing their noses forward and swinging their great heads back and forth to tunnel down to the grass, pawing at the more stubborn frozen chunks to dig as deep as four feet. Modern cattle, on the other hand, will not do this, and herds marooned by deep snow survive only because ranchers deliver bales of hay to their pastures. Wild cattle

The Axial Gallery
North Wall

Meander

paradoxical illusions of inside/outside, humor and potential tragedy, solidity and tenuousness set the visitor off balance. Replace the humor with awesome seriousness of purpose and that is the disorienting feeling one has upon entering the Axial Gallery. The name describes the sensation; one is literally sent spinning around an axis. The strangeness suggested by the Unicorn now begins to make itself known. We are loosed from our terrestrial footing and tumble into a world without gravity and without time. The same rules that apply in the open air do not apply in the chthonic universe. We are embarking on a journey into another reality.

Lascaux, and particularly, the Axial Gallery, stand apart from almost all other decorated caves in the use of color. The overwhelming majority of images in decorated caves are monochromatic or without color at all, relying on shadows and light to make engravings visible. Very few caves, among them Font de Gaume, Lascaux and Altamira in Spain, make use of multiple colors in a single figure. The painters made the most of Lascaux's miraculous even, white surface by using multiple colors and deftly shading them into the natural white to achieve even more chromatic range. The polychrome technique in Lascaux, achieved by applying paints with brushes, pads, and by blowing pulverized material on to the walls, reaches a luminous pinnacle unparalleled in Paleolithic art.

Making one's way through the portal, under the hooves of the great bulls of the Rotunda, one enters what has been described as the Sistine Chapel of Paleolithic art. To describe it in detail is beyond the scope of this book, for the entire tunnel is a gallery of exemplary genius. A few illustrations will make the point. The visitor is immediately aware of an elegant black stag. Although other stags appear elsewhere in Lascaux, this powerful specimen is the only stag in the Axial Gallery and, unlike his brothers in the Hall of the Bulls, this autumnal symbol is facing intently towards the deep cave. In a state of great agitation, he lunges forward, his muscled back enhanced by the swell of the wall, the strong chest fading away towards the front legs, his body not revealed. His head and magnificent rack of super-sized antlers, however, is carefully detailed. The aggressive pose, the rolled-back eye, open bugling mouth and thrown-back head announce unmistakably that this is the time of rut. The visitor is entering a potent place and the power, like water, flows downhill into the depths. His black color, in contrast to the warm reds and yellows of the other figures here, makes him

uniquely elegant. He is a transitional figure between the Hall of the Bulls and the Axial Gallery, a herald posted at the door to announce the next event. Around his muzzle is a light spray of red, a feature seen also on another lone black stag in the Hall of the Bulls that seems to emphasize the breath, the bugling call he is making, a summons to battle competitors and create life while his blood is hot, before the deep winter snows chill it. Beneath him runs a line of black dots just as long as the stag, that ends in a small black square under his throat and one larger dot, an underlining that punctuates the stag's sexual frenzy. In an altered state of consciousness, aural hallucinations are an integral part of the experience. It is very possible that, through the use of natural echoes as well as by visual content, images 'spoke' to seekers. A visitor in an altered state may have been introduced to this stag accompanied by bullroarers or vocal imitations of a bellowing stag. But the image is so intense that one deep in an altered state would hear secrets bestowed from this spirit animal, just as we can almost hear them today from this vivid messenger.

On the opposite side of the ceiling floats the Red Cow With Black Collar, like the Unicorn another seeming misnomer, as her entire head and horns are a dense black. She lacks an eye, but her lower lip and tuft of hair between her horns is detailed. Her legs drift down the wall from her substantial body. Without hooves to stand on she is not rooted in space. She hovers, her excessively long tail trailing out behind her. The effect is as if she has materialized from the smoke of campfires, a red, cloudy being that has become solidified. She provides us with important information about the intention of the artist. From the perspective of the painter up on his scaffolding, she appeared to be in perfect proportion. But, given the angle of slope from the wall to the vault of the ceiling, she looked distorted to a viewer standing below on the floor. A number of corrections were made, elongating the neck and body so that, from the artist's vantage, the cow is distended and unnatural. But from the floor, the image is in proportion. This level of sophisticated manipulation of an optical illusion is quite amazing and proves that, where artwork in other caves, and in Lascaux as well, was created as an intimate conversation between the individual artist and the spirits, often in cramped and remote places, this gallery was intended to be seen by others and seen correctly. Not publicly like the Hall of the Bulls, because it is much too confined a space, but rather for a select few or single individuals at any one time.

Beyond the Red Cow are horses and three more cows, completing the representation of the three mating seasons. Three cows and the second of three famous "Chinese Horses" meet head-to-head on the ceiling, the four animals seeming to spin in space like the paddles of a Casablanca fan.

Back around the chamber towards the entrance and very near the stag is the first of the "Chinese Horses", of particular interest for the choices the artist made in portraying it. The other two horses, each very different from the other, have distinctly drawn muzzles and ears, applied in detail with a brush to achieve a firm line. They are both energetic, prancing along the imaginary ground line where the wall begins to meet the ceiling. All of the anatomical features are present and clearly outlined in black. The extravagant length of the tails indicates they are wearing their winter coats. The third horse is actually quite shaggy, sporting the same coat as their modern-day descendants, the Przewalski horses, in winter. The central horse, with a black mane and the upper body a beautiful ocher yellow, is one of the most famous pictures of Paleolithic art. The artist used the natural white of the stone as the belly color and outlined the defined legs and hooves in heavy black. It is surrounded by signs; a grid, nested lines and others.

The first horse nearest the stag, however, is not nearly so solid. There is only a hint of a nose and no front legs. Instead, it is the hindquarters and belly that are drawn very carefully, using black brush strokes against the yellow belly to indicate shading and even the thick hair of the animal's coat. The rear hooves are clearly defined and the far hind leg is black as if in shadow, contrasting with the near leg, which is much lighter. A blank space at the top of the back leg sets it apart from the belly, a common technique used to achieve depth. The mane and neck, on the other hand, are outlined by a series of blown dots, black for the mane and red for the chest, that give an indistinct, sfumato finish to this part of the creature. The face is non-existent, disappearing in a blur. The pointillist feel of the spotted horses of Peche Merle, with dots both inside and outside the figures as if gathering into existence, continues here. A blush of light-yellow color forms the horse's back above the shoulder, fading into the natural white of the stone in a band down to the front right shoulder. Continuing the three-dimensional logic of the stags in the Hall of the Bulls, that the stag closest to the observer is most complete, the impression is that this horse is literally dropping from the sky, hind legs first. Or, in the shamanic sense, it is materializing

out of the membrane of the ceiling and the head, neck and front legs have yet to fully coalesce. The picture has a curious 'rocking horse' feel to it, with the weight on the back legs, the belly firmly set and a weightless feel to the indistinct head and chest and the invisible front legs. The decisions to create parts of this animal very clearly and others not at all was the choice of a highly talented artist with a clear vision who understood perspective 20,000 years before the Renaissance.

Beneath where the front legs should be runs an inverse arc of dots quite dark and distinct, with what appear to be wings of dots to each side. It is quite close to and almost a continuation of the line of dots underscoring the stag. The 'curly bracket', as it's called, follows the curve of the red dots forming the horse's neck and chest and extends toward the back hooves. Its shape, were the dots joined in a line, is reminiscent of the 'placquard-type signs' in other Solutrean caves. The curl, a concentration of five dots in a roughly circular pattern, appears where the front legs should be and the size of dots becomes smaller and less distinct under the hind feet, as if they are somehow involved in the materialization process; the more distinct the animal, the less impressive the dots.   Patterns of dots are one of the universal entoptic hallucinations to appear in trance. They are often incorporated into more intense visions, which materialize as deeper altered states are experienced. Many Paleolithic images are created by blowing dots of pigment close together to make a line and others, like the stag, are underlined by or decorated with dots. The curly bracket appears beneath the least formed part of the animal as if the front legs had yet to emerge. It seems to represent the raw energy of the Otherworld beyond the membrane, feeding like seeds through the veil to coalesce into the Chinese horse, as other dots have formed the mane and neck. Although some are made with a pad soaked in pigment, that these dots are formed by spitting pulverized material from the mouth onto the rock, the complimentary and creative role of human breath-as-spirit or speech and prayer cannot be ignored. The inspiration to bring an image to the surface is allowed to materialize by human agency. A sign of intense, red nested lines just touches the bracket, similar to signs found on lamps and spear points in Lascaux.

By now, perhaps the complexity and technical difficulties of creating art in this or any other underground sanctuary become apparent. The incorporation of the natural surface, whether it will accept paint or engraving or both, choices of color and placement

the horse's musculature is masterly. But the belly becomes less distinct and the rump is vague, the tail a mere glancing line arcing upward, and the hind legs appear almost as stains running down the wall. Like the Falling Cow, The Galloping Horse is off-balance and weightless, caught in mid-leap lunging out of the wall. She is frozen in time as she materializes from the Other World, the front of her body precisely gathered into form while her hindquarters are seen as if through old glass. As she slips through the membrane of the rock she becomes more clearly defined as her body enters this physical world. The motion and urgency of her leap is evident. At the left front hoof is a cruciform sign in red.

The animation of the animals pictured in this section of the luminous Axial Gallery is intense. Belligerent ibex, agitated horses, and tumbling cows contribute to an over-all sense of tense anticipation, transformation, and weightlessness, an evaporation of the laws of gravity that tie us to the earth. Yet here we are deep inside the earth, paradoxically enclosed within a cosmology where the walls are not really walls but a vast canvas of eternity spiralling through time. This spiritual spin cycle reaches its denouement at the Upside-Down Horse.

CROSSING OVER

Here, at the last constriction of the Gallery, a gifted artist chose to paint an astonishing yellow horse upside down and around a corner. The space narrows and the floor drops down. It is significantly constricted so that only a single person may enter, realizing the somatic sensation experienced during deep trance of one's body being squeezed into a tight space and venturing alone into the spirit world. The anticipation created by the swirling tension of off-balance, leaping and tumbling animals followed by the sudden dropping down of the floor and constriction of the threshold, the intensity of relatively large, excited animals packed into this small space all conspire to create a sense of weightlessness. The atmosphere is one of spiritual convection, of being simultaneously cast into the void and pulled into the vortex of the *axis mundi*, which is exactly what was intended. The architecture of the cave alters dramatically here, serving the shaman/artists' purpose perfectly. A channel runs down the center of the lowering ceiling, dividing the panels of the Galloping Horse and the battling ibex on the opposite wall neatly in two. Crevices open near the floor to the left as if the cave plunges down forever. Fissures reach up, dividing the left wall

and opening a wing-like 'V' on either side. Just beyond, the 'false pillar' is suspended, hovering more than a foot above the floor. The surface of this hovering pillar is where the artist chose to place the Upside Down Horse, the denouement of a panel of horses caught in a moment of transformation. Thirty-three signs that accompany the four animals mark the symbolic intensity of this threshold. We have liftoff.

The horses surrounding the Upside Down Horse are all leaping into the depths; the first two in particular have their ears pricked straight up in an attitude of intense alertness. The third, above the upturned hooves of the Upside Down Horse, is black and vaporous, less animated than the other two. Its shadowy head and chest are indistinct but darkly colored and a hint of the lower belly is shown but only the natural white stone breathing through gives volume to the side and flank. The legs are non-existent. Like a small rain cloud, it drifts forward and down toward the curve of the Meander. A disembodied black foreleg floats above the Upside Down Horse.

The first of the other two horses is vaguely located on a ground line, rising from a rough horizontal layer of rock pocked with holes that made the precise application of paint very difficult. Although all four feet are carefully and squarely painted in the spaces between the natural holes in the surface, it seems to be floating in space, emerging from an effervescent layer of rock, its head thrust forward. The hooves are round and hazy, as if they suffer no pressure from the earth. A horizontal line of blown red dots passes across its front legs just at the top of the layer of dark, pocked stone. Above, the white of the natural wall shows through blank spaces that define the inside of the far legs, adding to a feeling of airiness. But the firm black line of its back and mane keep it from floating away.

The horse above this one is, by comparison, unmoored entirely. Only the top third of the animal is here, its belly and hindquarters dissolving into the wall. The artist's magnificent use of rare three-color polychrome combined with the natural white wall, contributes to the sense of stratigraphic materialization. At the bottom, a hazy light yellow blown on the surface blends into the background, intensifying higher up the body. This is overlaid with red at the forward thrusting neck and then combined with black toward the back. The backline and mane are firmly defined by black. Its front feet are contracted upward and a swelling in the rock suggests the extended haunch tensed in a leap. But this horse has no face. The black mane, jutting forward, ends in a point just where the nose

should begin. The image has a propelled, forward motion that cuts bladelike along the wall. The ears are painted precisely with a brush and stand straight up in agitation. Something is definitely happening up ahead. This animal is rising up and forward, the back defined while the lower body remains indistinct and the face not materialized. It is leaping into the void that has already claimed the free-falling Upside Down Horse.

Two rough vertical fissures rise up from the dissolving chasm below, dividing the wings of this panel. The horses are positioned two on each side of this natural feature. The vertical expansion of the location encouraged the artists to imply a number of planes to achieve a three dimensional quality, the nearer horse being most complete and the polychrome and black horse less so. The contracted front hooves of the polychrome horse almost touch the left fissure and the ears of the Upside Down Horse originate in the right one. Between these pairs of horses is a sign found nowhere else in Paleolithic art. Two branching symbols, more than seven feet in height reach almost to the floor and stretch into the space above the polychrome horse. They appear to face each other as the branches extend outward from a parallel center. The left branch rises up in a single line through the effervescent dark layer of rock, touching the first of the red dots that pass through the lower horse's leg, creating a right angle. It continues upward in front of the first horse and passes into its neck, branching out to the left through the head and above into the belly of the polychrome horse. At the point where it touches the first horse's neck, the throat is a deep, glowing red. The right branch emerges between the two fissures near the bottom of the wall and passes through the hooves and mane of the polychrome horse, branching right and arcing over the Upside-down Horse without touching it. It reaches into the white, suggested belly of the black horse. They are deep red and echo the vertical fissures, further dividing this panel in two. This unique tree-like symbol overlays the first three horses and implicates them as part of a unit, binding them symbolically as they surround this intensely unique space. The complex, thematic symmetry of this panel, paralleling the cave architecture so closely, is highly provocative. A threshold has been breached. The bottom, shaky as it is, is about to fall out entirely.

Where the Galloping Horse and the off-balance Falling Cow, among others in this gallery, demonstrate the relative force of gravity that holds us on the path of the *axis mundi*, the Upside

272

Down Horse has been completely cut loose. Here, the laws of nature no longer apply; we have been drawn into the realm of the supernatural. The painting is, by any standard, an astonishing work of art. The animal is vibrant yellow, sprayed from all directions to completely cover the rough natural rock. The front hooves and mane are black. It is completely upside down, front hooves pointed straight up, the tail straight down, and the hind limbs aimed toward the back of the cave. Its body wraps around the false pillar as suggested by a natural feature of the rock that forms the back. The forequarters are visible from the Gallery but the hindquarters are in the Meander. It is anatomically complete in every detail and intensely present, certainly not, like others, fading off into the distance. The path is so narrow here one has to move carefully not to rub against it. It is literally in your face.

This is not a painting intended to be seen in a group setting, as were those in the Hall of the Bulls. This is reserved for a single visitor on the tight path around the false pillar. This is frozen motion, which can only be seen and appreciated while moving through this narrow threshold sideways, as the path descends. From no place in the sanctuary can this image be seen in its entirety and it cannot be photographed completely for the same reason. Yet it is in proportion, both front and back as well as to the other horses in the composition. The artist had to hold the complete image in his mind and execute it in sections. There have been many theories as to just why an artist from 18,000 years ago would have painted a horse with its hooves in the air; that it's dead, it's rolling on its back in imaginary grass, it has slipped and is falling. This last is the closest but seriously lacking in context. This horse is indeed falling but not on any icy Paleolithic hillside. It has, like the others behind it, leaped through the dividing red-branched symbol and is being drawn into the vortex of the labyrinth and into the Other World.

This is an iconic trance-struck horse tumbling into Eternity. The animation of the figure is agitated. The ears are angled back and its nostrils are flaring. It is painted into a concave curve around the pillar so that its hindquarters, deep in the Meander, are lower than its head and it seems to be sliding down around the wall, similar in this regard to the Falling Cow.

In this image of a horse falling through space we have the culminating experience of the consciousness-altering Axial Gallery. The Hall of the Bulls, with its seasonal symbols and fertile family groups firmly planted in their spiritual space announces the cycle of

social life and its sanctity. This successful tribal energy, herded into the narrowing depths by the otherworldly Unicorn and proclaimed by the bugling stag, becomes an individual quest in the funnel of the Axial Gallery. The narrowing space admits a single pilgrim to pass alone down the final stages of this inspired hall surrounded and finally overwhelmed by the increasingly disorienting images, entering into them like Jackson Pollock stepping into the fractal realities of his huge canvases on the studio floor. The spirit animals begin to spin and wheel in their white, luminous universe overhead like celestial objects. The tensions increase and, as the Great Black Bull takes his herd to the upper air, all sense of gravity slips away. Animals are falling, dropping from the sky like comets and those who maintain their footing are vigilant, attentive and tense with anticipation. Finally, the three horses at the end of the Gallery leap through the red branching symbols, across the dividing fissures, into the tight confines of the Meander. The trance journey has led through the red-symbol veil of transformation to the spiraling center of the labyrinth where the body, like the Upside Down Horse, is cut loose and the spirit freed. Here, the ultimate transformation takes place. The bonds of the physical world, defined by waking reality, time and the movement of the seasons have been completely left behind. The biological calendrics of horse-aurochs-stag give way to the Eternal as these horses of early spring leap and fall into the resurrecting potential of the vortex.

The Upside-Down Horse is possibly a mythic figure, or a metaphor at the very least, in the process of being taken through the tight confines of the membrane between life and death, to emerge into the spirit world beyond death and time. As the horse tumbles into the narrow twist of the Meander, so does the hero/shaman leave this plane of existence and enter into the fine-mesh funnel of the labyrinth. It is significant that the chosen animal is a horse. The people of Lascaux revered horses on many levels, as they are the first and most numerous animals represented in the cave. Aujoulet's research tells us the horse is a symbolic animal of early spring, of the return of life after the crushing winters of the Last Glacial Maximum. What better spirit to enter the vortex of the labyrinth than one that is promised to return?

At this underworld interface between life and death, when upper air seasons swung between desperate cold and relative lush warmth, at this constricted threshold of transformation on the edge of the Meander, were found stone chips and ocher in the soil as someone

prepared and left an offering. Three flint blades, showing traces of use on their edges and covered with red paint were left in a hole in the wall in front of the Upside Down Horse. Blades that were used for engraving images, and paint had, in ritualized circumstances, supernatural qualities, which released spirits from beyond the veil. They were magical tools in this context. Blades, bits of bone, and animal teeth have been found wedged into the walls of many Paleolithic caves. In Gabillou an ocher-covered blade was found. In Le Trois Frères, a cave bear tooth was left in a niche and in Elène hundreds of bits of bone were stuffed into cracks in the walls. In the deepest chamber of Lascaux, The Diverticule of the Felines, a horse tooth and a bit of bone were found, and a considerable amount of pigment, as if charging its spiritual battery in this potent place. This practice of leaving offerings in magical caves continues today from Scotland to India to Mexico. On ancient Crete where Ariadne's labyrinthine dance floor may have inscribed the first graphic labyrinth into memory, supplicants placed tiny symbolic golden axes or 'labyrs' in the recesses of cave walls. In a shamanic world where all existence participates in spirit, tools and bones possess souls. By reverently returning them as a form of seed to the membrane, passing them back through the veil, it may have assured their rebirth. The paint was a spiritual solvent enhancing the permeability of the cave surface and allowing spirit animals to emerge. Painting the blades and placing them in the wall allowed them to dissolve into spirit even more easily and pass through. The blades in Lascaux, placed intentionally at this threshold, sealed a contract with the spirit world that included them as roundtrip tickets, guaranteeing entry and return from the center of the labyrinth.

Aujoulat points to many graphic conventions; the way tails are attached, the spraying technique, and the shape of the hooves, from the Galloping Horse and Falling Cow to the Upside Down Horse, a space of a few meters. This suggests that a single artist may have envisioned and executed a significant stretch of the Axial Gallery containing some of its most breathtaking works. If that is the case, we are privileged to share in one person's inspired manifestation of a coherent, ancient revelation that still leaves us breathless. These are not isolated images but a contiguous mythological legend.

Let's ignore for a moment Aujoulat's advice to not let one's imagination run away with oneself. What are imaginations for, after all? And, I believe this is exactly what the painters of Lascaux intended; to create an environment that actively enhanced and

manipulated one's imagination to trigger a deep trance state. The question could be asked if these four horses, bound together in this tableau as they are by the red symbols, follow a form of progression deeper into the cave. They appear to be in the process of progressive transformation, moving into transcendence at the end of the *axis mundi*. The first horse emerges from the eroded ground layer, fully detailed. The polychrome horse drifts above, entangled in the red branches, partially disappearing and clearly leaping into the void. The Upside Down Horse has crossed over, falling through space and time while a vague black shadow horse floats above, its chest not quite touching the front hoof of the Upside Down Horse. The artist's intention was to view this panel while in motion through the narrow constriction and around the pillar. This contributes to the idea of these images as interactive iconic art, drawing the participant deeper into the cave experience. The Upside Down Horse literally cannot be seen any other way. These animals are, together with the cave architecture and the symbols in this panel, united in a transformative mythic moment of great import.

BEYOND THE VEIL

What does our shamanic spirit horse find beyond the veil, beyond the prayer of the red-painted flint blade offering? What is there to greet the weightless spirit horse in the Meander, that odd space just large and flat enough so a single person can sit at the end of the journey down the Axial Gallery? More to the point, what would a trancing shaman find there? The Red Panel, revealing three denizens of the Other World; all red, all oddly proportioned and distorted. There is a rawness about these figures that renders them a bit eerie. In the shamanic experience of teleportation to the Otherworld these weird images tell the spiritual traveler he has arrived. And it's crowded in here. The space is not quite 20 feet long and gradually closes down from about six to two and a half feet and comes to an end. The only bison in this section of the cave is here. It is the first image in the Meander, facing forward, head low and both horns visible. The visitor here is personally reenacting the man-versus-bull confrontation. The bull's sex is evident and tail raised in agitation or perhaps anger at the intrusion. He is a frightening, combative presence. If the seeker is to gain power from this dangerous journey, this aggressive spirit animal, a gatekeeper to the deeper secrets, must be confronted. But unlike the careful and accurate artistic detail so beautifully rendered in the rest of the gallery, like so many other images that are minutely defined and heavily painted, this bison is vague and lumpy, a cloud of red, with spindly legs that seem unable to support its massive body. It is composed of indistinct conjoined dots coming together in the shape of a bison. Although its body is shown in profile, its head confronts the seeker straight on and lowered. He must be met head-on if the seeker is to enter the Meander, the final stage of the journey.

Beyond the bison stands another horse, and a very interesting one. It too, is all red with the natural white of the wall giving shape to its underside. Its legs melt away into the eroded stone beneath it. But, although the body is in profile, the head is tipped to the right in three-quarter perspective. At least it appears to be. It could be in profile as well. The facility of Paleolithic artists to create marvelous optical illusions encourages consideration of an intended duality. Parallel marks at the top of the head could be the short ears of a horse in profile. Or two larger marks with what may be eyes between give one the impression that the horse is tipping its head toward the viewer with a rather quizzical expression. Looking at it long enough, like the picture of two vases that become faces in profile, this horse both looks away and then straight at you. The third figure, according to the experts, is another horse. But it looks remarkably like an elongated cat with a single giant paw. The conversation with the cave determined that this figure be made to fit in a channel of the wall, which dictated its bizarre appearance. There is only one last figure, a crozier shape facing the end of the Meander that may or may not indicate the beginnings of a horse's head. With the last two horses and possibly the beginning of a third, the cycle of life and spirit returns again with images of spring and renewal. If the final crozier shape is a horse, then it is the perfect bookend to the springtime horse's head that greets the visitor at the beginning of the journey in the entrance to the Hall of The Bulls; they face in opposite directions, Janus-like, as if symbols of an outgoing and incoming year. The bugling autumnal buck at the doorway of the Axial Gallery signaled the coming spiritual winter that has been navigated to this final symbol of a nascent spring.

The Red Panel, outshined so completely by the technically dazzling art of the other galleries, has been mostly ignored in the writings. Indeed, by comparison it seems almost an afterthought executed by an amateur with leftover paint. Yet when seen in the light of a labyrinthine journey it makes perfect sense. Here, beyond

the signpost of red tree-like symbols, one encounters creatures of a very different sort, linked by their color, placement, and strangeness. If, as Aujoulat states, Lascaux was planned and executed in a short period of time, the Meander, with its trio of unique spirits was an intended part of that plan. At the end of the tumultuous journey down the Axial Gallery, one has been compelled to confront the aggressive bison, to sit in this small space in the company of these peculiar red animals and commune with the spirits before unwinding back on the solitary journey through the events of the gallery; past the falling, tumbling, agitated creatures, into the comforting communal expanse of the Hall of the Bulls with its fat, sleek summer families presiding, and out to the upper air of time, life, and tribe. The labyrinth of Lascaux was brilliantly designed and created to instill the sacred lessons of the shamanic journey to the spirit world during a time of great climatic and cultural stress. In surviving the terrifying lessons of the vortex, an alternate reality has been encountered and a transformation complete, ordained by the spirits that dwell there. The spiritual Argonaut has confronted the bison/minotaur at the Center, conquered his fears and learned cosmic secrets. Now the work of integrating the rebalanced forces sought beyond the veil into the waking world of the uncertain Last Glacial Maximum must take place.

CHAPTER 14

WHEN ANIMALS WERE GODS

'When we walk to the edge of all the light we have and take the step into the darkness of the unknown we must believe that one of two things will happen. There will be something solid for us to stand on, or we will be taught to fly."
Patrick Overton

"It is the Minotaur who conclusively justifies the existence of the labyrinth."
Jorge Luis Borges

"A maze requires no Minotaur; it is its own Minotaur. In other words, the attempt of the visitor to find the way is the Minotaur."
Umberto Eco

GO FOR THE LIGHT

Light is an enigma of the highest order, the agent of all things visible. As in the Whirlwind Complex where the volitional power of the wind can't be seen except by its effects, the energy that illuminates all things is invisible in itself and impossible to catch. Physicists and mathematicians have tried and failed, although we humans today can travel faster than sound. Light too, is known only by its deeds, how it interacts with other things by caressing, bouncing off or passing through. Both wave and particle, we know light only by what it touches. Slanting rays of golden sunlight appear so solid they could be sliced like butter and put on a plate. Yet it is not the light we see, but the sparkling dust motes it strikes. Our world is made manifest by the paradoxical coexistence of light and its absence, darkness. Light, with nothing to touch, is darkness, pregnant with potential.

As visual creatures we harvest light and the bounty it reveals. We

have but to open our eyes, sift light from shadow and flood our lives, language and symbolism with metaphors. Our lives hinge on the deeds and sufferings of light that create a 'vision' of the world. What, then, are we to make of ancient people who intentionally descended to the most lightless place on earth to create visionary art? Purposely depriving themselves of natural light, they sought the entoptic sparks of hallucination, the dots and grids that signaled departure into another reality, the inner light of divine manifestation. In the caves, the visible world is extinguished and the invisible becomes apparent.

The cave-world was ripe with power and possibilities. In these protean sensory deprivation chambers they entered into trance communions with animal gods and opened portals to the spirit world by removing and adding stone and light. Lit only by fire, the darkness was a medium, a tool of revelation like a piece of magical obsidian, which could be sculpted with light into visible form. Controlling fire in lamps was an Upper Paleolithic invention, and communities of people who made lamps lived where cave art was most prolific. Elsewhere in Europe they were extremely rare. Lamps had a very specialized original purpose here; for use underground. There was an impressive spiritual impetus to invent a brilliant tool that allowed them to illuminate the depths. The control of paradoxical light and shadow made possible the revelation of the world of emergent chthonic spirits.

From ground ocher and manganese, flaked flint tools and carved stone lamps, to the soaring fluted chambers of deliquescent crystal that rang like cathedral bells when struck, stone was, in all its forms alive and malleable. Recognizing the latent power thrumming in the black corridors, entering into communion with this telluric interior, creating portals with handprints, releasing spirit guides with paint from the swells and folds of calcite, engraving a form over and over to renew and tap the power of the Being manifesting there, running fingers in patterns through soft clay, touching spirit, entering into the images, breathing the gods into visible existence with puffs of pigment from the mouth, then leaving an offering of fox teeth, wedging a blade into the walls, or placing a bear skull on a prominent rock, closed a circuit of power between the sky world, the earth, and the world below that ran through the *axis mundi* of the labyrinth.

The Ice Age masters of illusion, archaic Conductors of Souls, carried flickering torches like their later counterpart

Hermes/Mercury carried the healing caduceus, a magic wand said to be so powerful it could bring the dead back to the light of day. They released the enigma of the labyrinth from dreams and stone by navigating the strange realities of altered states. Trained in the mysteries of the hallucinatory world they initiated others, not only in the esoteric practice of shamanism, but also the making of art, the summoning and expression of ecstasy. The consistencies of style and material manipulation are so remarkable over enormous expanses of time that there must have been schools instructive in the shared aesthetic/spiritual vision. The artist/teacher's purpose would have been not only to teach the techniques of image creation, but the cultural imperatives behind them, passing along a cosmological tradition, relying heavily on a ritual relationship with caves, that was deeply consistent at its base, century upon century for 20,000 years. Seeking and experiencing visions was central to their lifeway, as was evoking those revelations in art, either at the time of revelation or more likely, later, after returning to a normal state of consciousness. For those without the artistic gift, or too far-gone in ecstasy, one could meditate on or re-engrave an existing image, or re-paint a grid pattern, renewing and participating in its power. Lewis-Williams has suggested that similar in intent to re-engraving, rather than defacing them, hatch marks over existing images may be interpreted as a way of re-releasing the spirit, and allowing the essence to bleed through once again.

At some time during the Last Glacial Maximum, on the borderline between the end of the Solutrean and the beginning of the Magdalenian cultures, under intense social pressures brought on by rapid climate change effecting their world in unpredictable ways, a communal decision nothing short of genius was made to design and create a magnificent time machine in the Axial Gallery; not to travel to different eras but rather to stop time altogether. Here, one physically entered and moved through the lessons of the mythic universe bound on earth by the fertile cycle of the seasons and simultaneously into the deep trance of the timeless vortex, overcoming terrible fear of this walk among the spirits. Finally, slipping out of time, the seeker embraced Eternity in the Meander and returned transformed.

The seasons, once so dependable, were now uncertain. They began or ended sooner, the snows not arriving as in the past or staying much longer than expected. Occasionally there would be an unusually mild, flower-strewn summer or blasting cold that buried

the land in impenetrable snow. Migrating animals like the aurochs that had appeared with cyclical regularity, harbingers of the seasons that reinforced the order of the cosmos now arrived sporadically or not at all. Seasonal hunger turned into desperate starvation at such times and life was brutal. When the life-giving regularity of seasonal progression descended into unpredictable chaos, one constant in their lives would have been the mythic social glue that gave them the strength to prevail. To recreate the journey to the land of the gods by invoking the iconic animals of the seasons was a brilliant supplication for cosmic order.

The execution of this plan was involved; the accumulation of resources, constructing and moving scaffolding, the weeks of preparation, painting, and engraving followed finally by the intense spiritual preparation and anticipation for those who were to make the journey, the expectations of friends and family, the descent into the charged labyrinthine chamber of the underworld driven by the rhythmic music of drums, flutes and chanting, the embracing of the weird, hallucinatory Otherworld and the final leap of faith across the threshold at the Upside Down Horse. They were honoring and summoning the gods and would expect to meet them and converse. To organize such a tribal undertaking required the leadership of exceptional people, a tribal leader perhaps working in concert with an artist/shaman who envisioned the unique possibilities of Lascaux, or perhaps one charismatic genius who incorporated all those talents.

The traveler must be worthy. Central to this spiritual journey was the willing sacrifice of the shaman; the surrender of the wounded healer to the terrors of the world of the spirits. Cultural and mythic information was indelibly branded onto their souls as the visions revealed their secrets and exacted their price. The hardwired hallucinatory, neurological journey into the vortex of deep trance had been recognized, cultivated, replicated and enhanced as the mythic labyrinthine fulcrum upon which shamanic journeying turns.

Most importantly, the interdependencies developed through the hallucinatory trance experience, the personal encounter with the spirits, and the mythological cosmic legends told about these journeys were recursive. The visions and the stories enhanced one another so that the sacred caves became a two-way gauze through which percolated prayers from this world and responses to how one should inhabit it; how the people were to adapt to the dramatic events of climate change occurring during the Last Glacial

Maximum. One observed the proper rituals before entering the cave, some participants possibly enduring significant preparatory sacrifice. Entering alone or with others, one simultaneously walked the pathways through the chthonic realm of the spirits accompanied by song, chant, and the powerful spirit paintings. On each journey, increasingly familiar experiences and beings were encountered. This does not suggest that the journeys became any easier and they were only partly predictable, dependent on the shaman's personal power and spirit helpers to engage with elements of this surreal world. The dangers of entering the spirit realm were real and terrifying, demanding great courage to persevere and maintain sanity. The stories of these journeys were told and their images subsequently manifested on the magical surface. In the retelling of the spiritual experience, and the application of the wisdom so gleaned, lay the healing power of the vision. And so meaning and myths grow, becoming embroidered with the electricity of profound experience. Having visited the realm of sickness and death, suffered mightily and learned much, the shaman returned transformed, self-healed, and able to bring healing to his people. Yet the generative powers of the spirit world continually introduce new challenges, as does the middle world, proliferating at times with devastating traumas of war, starvation, injury, sickness and emotional catastrophe. During the Last Glacial Maximum, with the climate changing radically within living memory, a pervasive sense of anxiety at the apparent disruption in the cosmic order would have prevailed. When suffering and misery gripped the people, the shaman, guided by the ancient stories, consulted the spirits.

Different shaman/artists and their initiates brought unique talents to the journey, which became incorporated into the stories of the divine. Although a wide unity prevailed in the art for eons, regional and perhaps ethnic visionary and mythic selectivity chose bears or horses or mastodons as most frequently portrayed. Felines and other predators, once plentiful in the art, became more rare and relegated to distant chambers. Select symbols have importance in one era but not in others. Some chambers were decorated entirely in black, while others are red and a very few others glow with multiple colors. These choices were not made randomly, but were dictated by the gifts of the earth in available resources, the inspiration of the spirits and the conversation with the cave. The mythology, reinforced by ritual journeys underground in the spirit world, integrated those experiences into life in the waking world above.

The art, in turn, reinforced the mythology, with neither art nor mythology assuming pre-eminence, while the shifting priorities in this religion, responded to and reflected changes over the centuries in culture and climate.

Once the spiritual seekers emerged again into the light of waking reality, their people knew them as cosmic travelers, bearing privileged information from the other side of illness and death that only select people dare experience. They carried about them the aura of the other world, an emanation of strangeness, and would have held a position of wary respect as the possessors of powerful knowledge, abilities and undaunted courage who trafficked with spirits. The incalculable value of the journey lay in passing on the spiritual labyrinthine route and purpose to the next generation and the one beyond, cultivating a relationship with the Otherworld over time, indelibly imprinting a cultural identity and religious discipline to guarantee their survival. The journey, experienced by the earliest modern humans to enter Europe had at Lascaux, become refined, religious high art, indelibly imprinted onto their neurological, mythic, and spiritual pathways. At a time when their world was disrupted by the upheavals of the Last Glacial Maximum and their culture may have been under the pressures of transitioning from Solutrean to Magdallenean, the people of Lascaux found a spiritual anchor in the formal creation of a labyrinth where they could talk with the gods.

DANCING AND DYING

Although the Axial Gallery is the premier example of uniquely talented people conceiving, designing and creating a purposeful, mind-altering labyrinth, it is certainly not the only one. All decorated caves, regardless of their depth or architecture contain the unavoidable essence of journeying into a charged, sacred space. There is another cave, a contemporary of Lascaux nearby, that is similar in purpose to the Axial Gallery although much smaller and very different structurally; Gabilliou. Like Lascaux, it has an unobtrusive entrance and roomy chamber where a small group could gather, with a single narrow branching tunnel extending sinuously 100 feet underground. During the Solutrean/Magdalenian interface, visitors would have had to crawl on their stomach, on hands and knees into its narrow depths, one at a time. It is not nearly as spectacular as Lascaux as little of its surface is suitable for painting. Yet people sitting or lying down engraved the entire length of the

cave. Horses, aurochs, bison, a hare and unusual 'stretched' creatures with long necks and horns or ears on the tops of their heads adorn the walls.

But most significantly, the tunnel ends by turning slightly to the left and the seeker is confronted by a minotaur, the final image in the cave. His bison's head is topped with horns, his arms are held out in front of his body. A tail dangles down in back and his legs are lifted as if in dance. His posture is very like other Paleolithic sorcerer figures that preside over chambers of ancient secrets. Here, at the end of the cave, after an arduous spiritual quest through a narrow, confined space consistent with a journey through the altered state of the vortex, the shaman opened a channel by creating a representation of his spiritual transformation, the bison-man, a being who was adept at slipping across the borderland between life and death. Beyond the confines of the physical world the protean power of transfiguration exists, where the human body is shed and replaced by a body of spirit, one with the strength and capability to navigate along the blade-edge of paradoxical existence with equilibrium. Only when this transformation to spirit-being is attained can the shaman move into higher cosmological realms.

An entoptic grid sign is connected to the dancing minotaur image of Gabilliou by a line that runs from his mouth across a crack in the rock, down the muzzle of his face, and along the lip line, and just touches the top of the grid, as if breath or sound of some kind were implicated. A purposeful connection has been made. In the section of Lascaux called "The Nave" exceptional entoptic grid signs are found. There are three, each composed of juxtaposed rectangular fields of color contained within engraved borders. The compositions, small squares of different dimensions of black and ocher set against a rare mauve, appear like ghostly predecessors of abstract expressionist painter Mark Rothko's color fields. Rothko intended his paintings to incite the viewer to experience a sense of transcendent awe beyond the purely aesthetic. 20,000 years earlier perhaps, the Nave artist was expressing the same experience. These Rothkoesque quadrangular signs are placed so they just touch the rear hooves and tip of the tail of the imposing figure of the Great Black Cow. She is purposely poised there, a floating zeppelin of spiritual energy tethered to symbolic grids of transcendence. Over seven feet long, the heavy black paint of the cow covers part of a herd of horses, including an exquisite, energetic image of a rearing horse.

Aujoulat comments that here is an extremely rare analogous connection among the association of figures in the Nave and those in the Panel of the Falling Cow. The repetition of a large female bovine in the company of herds of horses and grid signs suggests a thematic metaphor. The grid signs in the "Nave", between the edgy confronting ibex in the Axial Gallery, touching the muzzle of the Falling Cow, in Gabillou and elsewhere, link the entoptic hallucinations of trance with iconic animals, placing them in the same altered reality. Whatever else they may have meant to the artists, as a graphic expression of deepening trance the frequent appearance of grids in caves of the Solutrean/Magdalenian suggests a continued refinement of visionary expectations for the seeker. The occurrence of grids in visions and in art was a signpost on the borderland between worlds, an artistic semaphore that things were becoming quite different. In deep trance, grids appear during the full-blown hallucinatory departure from waking consciousness and entry into an alternate reality where ego loss signals transfiguration into a spirit being, a concept certainly borne out by grids, forming the entoptic gateway of the vortex. This metamorphosis takes place within the labyrinth, the transitional stage of entoptics, reported by trance journeyers as materializing grids meshed together in a gradually constricting and spinning tunnel that opens out into the world of spirit. As an indicator of trance and all that implies, the image of the grid, like the frequent appearance of entoptic dots, bears a fundamental symbolic weight of transformative and creative potential in Paleolithic art. This impressive continuity of imagery in Lascaux and other contemporary caves, combined with the consistent use of similar signs, such as broken lines on tools, weapons, and on the surface of the caves, emphasizes the importance of these messages as integral to a religious discipline.

It is believed that Lascaux was heavily used by spiritual seekers, its messages shared by many who found inspiration in the narrative genius of the art that had been created in collusion with the cave. Each section of Lascaux was decorated and used in very different ways, each expressing a different category of the sacred, each requiring a unique space to respond to those needs that were provided by the cave and the spirits available there. Together, the vital symbolism and transformative powers of the chambers of this magnificent underground cathedral created a unity of vision anchored in the symbolism of the labyrinth and was passed through the generations to be discovered and rediscovered. Let's descend

now into the innermost depths, by way of the most intimate of chambers, to confront an enduring enigma unique to Lascaux and quite literally central to the labyrinthine experience; the encounter with the minotaur.

THE SHAFT

From the Hall of the Bulls, if, instead of proceeding straight ahead into the Axial Gallery the visitor turns to the right, he will have a very different experience. A tunnel called the Passageway branches off the Hall of the Bulls. In the Paleolithic it was intensively painted and engraved but, because of corrosion over the millennia, many images have unfortunately been destroyed. Yet, the fragments of paintings and the engravings that have survived demonstrate a very active artistry, unique detail and animation. Beyond the Passageway, one approaches the Apse from below and enters up an incline into an unexpected 'profusion of animals and geometric motifs'. According to Aujoulat that would require a book of its own to fully explain. In the Apse a bewilderment of engravings, an astonishing jumble of lines one atop another slowly sort themselves into hundreds of signs and images. Yet there is a conscious, thematic consistency; horses populate the upper level, cervids or deer in the middle, and aurox near the floor. Placement on the surface was not random.

In the most remote section of the Apse is a rounded area crammed with a tangle of animals and diverse signs, including the 'Placard-type' found at other caves of this era and painted grids similar to those under the hooves and tail of the Black Cow. All of the surfaces in the Apse are crowded with images. Even those surfaces of undesirable quality that were ignored in other parts of the cave are here, covered with engravings. This chamber is thick with spirit. The collision of stags, horses, bison, grids, striations, and club-shaped claviform signs is a relentless swirl of chaotic energy. The careful order of the Axial Gallery, where each image was intended, very purposely, to be seen individually and as part of a process has, in the Apse, given way to an exuberant outpouring of activity. Discovering patterns and even following the lines of separate images is a feat of great patience for the most practiced eye using lateral light. The engravings, to be seen well, cannot be flooded with direct light, as mentioned before. Rather, their edges and shadows are picked out by angular rays. The intention here was not to create a unified whole of instructive, deathless images,

unsullied by others. Rather, the process itself seems to have been paramount, the physical execution of creation, regardless of relationship to other images for the most part, seems to have been the point. The furious, personal and emotive release of creating images was more significant than having them viewed by others. The feeling is one of intense invocation of ecstatic prayer.

At the lip of the Apse, the floor drops away into a chamber of awe-inspiring, singular spiritual commitment. A theme of confrontation between man and bison that appears in a number of underground Paleolithic cathedrals is reproduced in Lascaux, not surprisingly, with particular genius. In the last century this area, a 16 foot-deep well, called The Shaft, was enlarged and a metal platform and ladder were installed. Aujoulat has suggested that during the Paleolithic, this chamber may have had a separate entrance and been distinct from the rest of Lascaux, though this is still debated. If so, at some point in time that hypothetical entrance collapsed and access was only through a small aperture from the Apse. From here, access to the Shaft from above would not have been easy should someone want to enter it to shamanize. The ceiling drops down to meet the floor, leaving only a narrow passage that leads to a sheer drop into the Shaft. The only way to reach the edge is by crawling. The wall of the interior of the Shaft undercuts the ledge used to access it so, to escape from the Shaft one had to climb up a rope (or be hauled),while swinging in mid-air. The space is small, not large enough to accommodate more than a very few people at a time, or move around in.

Yet many artifacts were taken into the Shaft and left behind. A large number of lamps were found, possibly as many as two-dozen. This is an estimate, although, as some have been lost since their discovery. The cave surface here is a darker, light-absorbent geological layer that would have required a lot of artificial light to illuminate it. Some lamps were turned upside down probably to extinguish them. A particularly beautiful example of a pink sandstone lamp was engraved with two sets of nested lines identical to those found engraved on the walls of the Apse. A perforated seashell from the beach 120 miles away possibly worn as a pendant, pigment, clay from the upper levels of the cave, worked flint blades and ivory spears adorned with the same 'broken signs' that are painted in the cave, were left here.

If people who used the cave for spiritual pursuits could only access the Shaft from the Apse, it would have been very

challenging. That they crawled to the edge of a black 16-foot drop burdened with parcels of weapons, lamps, clay, pigments or tools and lowered themselves into this confined well, tells us that these people were compelled by a driving non-material purpose. They were descending from the upper chambers, already a trance-inducing environment, into a deeper cosmic level that could accommodate very few people, and leaving artifacts behind, some, like the shell and spears, that have no function, save ceremonial in a cave. This implies a very intense and intimate experience. The level of commitment and vulnerability is particularly evident; the willingness to not only endure, but also purposely seek out the overpowering potential for claustrophobia and surrender to the transports of shamanic experience is courageous in the extreme. Once one is lowered into the Shaft and enters into a trance state, getting back out again could have been problematic, requiring reliance on assistants or the recovery of one's own strength to climb out. This is especially dicey, as this deep recess tends to collect toxic carbon dioxide, the amount varying with the season but highest during summer and autumn. These fumes can cause great discomfort, an altered state, or even death.

MEETING THE MINOTAUR

Of all the animals represented in the almost 300 caves of France, the most frequently depicted is the horse. Second to the horse is the bison. Each of the relatively few different types of animals occupying a spiritual niche in the Paleolithic cosmos, compared to the teeming numbers existing at the time, embody a web of mythic spirit power unknown to us. The bison held a unique place, as it is the animal most frequently conjoined with a human's body to become a sorcerer figure. Why would the image of a bison, magically joined with a human's body, remain meaningful for 14,000 years, from Chauvet to Lascaux, and not a horse, bear, or mammoth, also numerously represented and powerful animals in their own right?

The Paleolithic bison, driven like its North American counterpart to near extinction by hunting and habitat destruction, survived just barely in the forests of Poland. As we can extrapolate Ice Age hunter-gatherer behaviors from ethnographies, we can similarly extrapolate Paleolithic bison society from the American buffalo. Buffalo bulls are obviously powerful and very persuasively male, but what else? In his fascinating study, "The Time of the Buffalo",

naturalist Tom McHugh explores his subjects with respect, affection and observational care. He describes them as capricious animals, which will attack, or just as intently ignore intruders, even packs of wolves circling for a kill. They are curious about anything out of the ordinary and will cautiously investigate what it might be, gradually drawing near to sniff or lick the unknown thing. This was a characteristic Native Americans used to great advantage, allowing them to get close enough for a kill. As is well known, buffalo, for the Plains Tribes, were the center of their universe, providing the raw materials for almost everything needed to survive and flourish, as well as significant elements of their cosmology.

Buffalo do not migrate in any discernable orderly pattern. Indians and buffalo hunters alike reported the plains, teeming one week with thousands of buffalo, would be empty the next for no apparent reason. Many tribes as a result chose to be nomadic at a moment's notice, packing up to follow the herd when it decided to move on. Others perfected involved ceremonies to find and call the buffalo to the hunters. Semi-domesticated buffalo are stubborn and intelligent, notoriously difficult to herd, and almost impossible to turn in a stampede. Like many wild animals bred and raised in captivity they can turn suddenly and attack their keepers. They can run like a freight train at a top speed of 35 MPH and turn on a dime. The stories of hundreds of thousands of stampeding buffalo thundering across the plains and tipping over trains to continue on, are unbelievable to us now.

One of the most impressive characteristics of bison, remarked upon frequently is their stoic stamina. Not only are they able to survive in deep snow and terrible cold, they have been known to climb high into the Rocky Mountains. A traveler on the plains reported a bison bull enduring attack after attack by wolves for what must have lasted several days, long past what seemed possible; his eyes and tongue eaten out, nose gone, legs torn to strings, and yet he persisted in fighting to defend himself.

Likewise, their unexpected aggression is well known. McHugh comments that any approach, however carefully executed, is risky in the extreme and a terrifying charge can come after either great fanfare of ground pawing and bellowing, or no warning at all. He suggests one always has a route of escape, even if up the nearest tree, if you can find one on the plain. He quotes another source as having successfully stopped a charging cow by smacking her hard on the head a number of times with the flat of a pitchfork when she

was 'just close enough'. One comment he makes is particularly interesting for our purposes; that when attacked by a charging bison weighing over 2000 pounds with no tree or pitchfork in sight, the best thing you can do is to confront him and hope he stops. McHugh's experience was that the buffalo would usually do just that. Running invites pursuit and a person could never out-run a determined buffalo. Yet facing one down requires great courage. McHugh describes this as a test of wills, but for a Paleolithic hunter who may, like a Native American, have related to the buffalo as part of an extended spirit family and personal will may not be the power in play. We saw in the discussion of the Whirlwind Complex how the bison is woven into a complicated tapestry of mystical logic that should assume no less of the Paleos.

As a hunter, one knows the quirks and personalities of one's prey. Reports of Native American buffalo hunts are hair-raising adventures, pitting the skill and raw courage of the hunters against intelligent, strong, and fast-moving creatures. Imagine swimming a frigid river alongside a herd of buffalo with a knife in your teeth until you could plunge it into his heart. Another story told of an exceptional hunter who killed three in one day; one by smashing it with a rock, another with an arrow and a third wounded animal he strangled! The level of athleticism, risk and bravado is stunning. Beyond that, the art of an animal well-taken that embodies complex spiritual metaphors is respectful in the extreme. That it will also feed your people and supply them with vital materials for life transforms a simple confrontation into a fierce dance of life. The bison's noble death becomes a sacrifice.

The implications of confrontation with bull-as-spirit-being are metaphorically fascinating and may help to answer the question, why a bison and, therefore, why a minotaur? And why examples of the theme of man confronting a horned bovine were found in the cave art of this time. Let's return to the Shaft of Lascaux and tie these threads up.

Sixteen feet down, at the bottom of this well is one of the most famous paintings of the Paleolithic. Although we cannot say that the walls of Paleolithic caves can be read as 'mythograms' provided we knew the key, as Leroi-Gourhan suggested, this tableau is a provocative exception. Only a small area of the available wall space was painted here. On one side of the Shaft is a rough, partial painting of a black horse, the chest line completed by the natural shape of the wall. On the other side is a composition that has

sparked endless discussion because of its unique narrative possibilities. Cave art, to our understanding, doesn't tell stories we can begin to approach. It is a bestiary of iconic animals, often the same animals repeated over and over, alone or in combinations and in the company of mysterious signs, parts of humans, and composite creatures. Yet, in this weird well of spirits called the Shaft, there is a story being told that arises from and has remained at the center of the labyrinth. On the wall opposite the horse, a rhino faces left, tail raised in agitation, with six black dots evenly painted in two rows of three under the tail. This identical pattern of dots, painted in red, appears once again as the very last image at the end of the most remote room of Lascaux, the Chamber of the Felines. It probably had some terminal significance. Leroi-Ghouran commented that the rhino is a back-cave or marginal animal and to find it at the bottom of the Shaft accompanied by aligned dots, is perfectly consistent. As on any journey, we are at the end of one thing and the beginning of another.

To the rhino's right, however, are figures not found anywhere else. What appears to be a vertical staff is topped by a bird facing left and above it is a stick figure of a man facing right, having a head and eye shaped exactly like the bird. He is falling backwards, arms outstretched with four spread fingers on each hand. His penis is erect and pointing at a bison. Below the man is an inscrutable sign called the 'spear thrower', a longer broken line with short branching lines on either end that is repeated elsewhere in Lascaux and on artifacts from the cave. A powerful bison confronts the man. The animal's head is lowered, his horns tipped aggressively toward the man, emphasizing the arch of the massive bristling hump, tail raised over his back and eye wide. A barbed line, interpreted generally as a spear passes from under the tail through the gut and beyond, and the bison's entrails are spilling out. Analysis has shown that the rhino mentioned above was painted at a different time from the other images and so, must be considered separately from the intention of the original signs/man/bird/bison tableau. That this original construct of images was created as a whole makes it a striking communication from the ancient world.

What is being portrayed? It is clearly an action involving a death in progress. Is this a hunting scene in which the man wounded the bison that now has turned on him? Are they both dying? This is far too simple an explanation and doesn't account for many elements of the image. What does the bird-topped staff have to do with a hunt?

Why does the man's head replicate the bird's exactly? The man is tipping backward, rigid as a board with an erect penis, not crumpled in a heap, as one would expect a casualty of a bison attack to be. And why would an artist go to the trouble of creating what must have been an unfortunate, but not unusual occurrence during the Ice Ages in a place such as this? That it is a completely unique narrative in Paleolithic art makes it especially significant. Placed in the context of the other purposeful, intensely decorated chambers of Lascaux, and located in the topographical labyrinthine heart of the cave, this should be seen as not the result of an isolated moment of genius, but part of a contiguous spiritual universe.

Taking a shamanic perspective deepens and broadens our understanding of this inscrutable image. If the man is interpreted as a shaman in a trance, the pieces of the puzzle fall into place. In a deep trance, people collapse and sometimes go into a rigid catatonic state as we saw with the San, requiring an assistant to help them to safety. Men in trance, as in sleep, often have erect penises and the Western assumption, because trancing is not a usual practice, that it indicates mere fertility is too simplistic. It appears this shaman has been 'struck' into such a state, losing control of his body. His hands are splayed open with only four fingers. He very clearly has an eye exactly like the bird, a simple solid black dot, indicating that it is open. Lewis-Williams believes that the broken sign below the man, referred to by others as a spear-thrower, represents instead a sort of caption, indicating the shamanic metamorphosis required before translation to other cosmological levels can be achieved. There may be a parallel idea represented by the branching lines that divide the horses leaping into the void in the Axial Gallery from the Upside Down Horse already tumbling into it, although those lines are much more organically derived, echoing the architecture of the cave.

Shamans in ecstatic transport fly to other realms. In the natural world birds have access to sky realms unreachable by man. Migratory birds mass in huge flocks and fly away to places unseen and, like magic, reappear at the turn of the season. In Siberia, for example, geese inhabit a mystical place in the cosmos, on the plains of North America it is the eagle, and in Greece it is the crane. Often, shamans report being carried on the backs of magical birds, flying in the company of bird helper spirits, or by shape, shifting into birds themselves.

It has been suggested that the man in the Shaft scene is wearing a mask, but this is an insufficient reading of the image. The shaman

has identified fully with and is transforming into a bird, the same bird represented below him. The use of feathers, wings, or the body of the entire bird incorporated into ceremonial clothing, as well as amulet carvings are common shamanic paraphernalia. Shamans commonly carry staffs adorned with sacred items, including spirit animals from, which they derive powers. Artifacts and carvings from the arctic region include staffs topped with birds, or sculptures of shamans holding bird-topped staffs. This may be such a staff that remains standing, beacon-like, while the shaman literally falls backward into a trance. Or it could represent the manifestation of his helper spirit that has appeared to guide him to a distant realm, a psychopomp to the shepherd, the man beyond the borderland of death, once he achieves complete metamorphosis. The man is not dead, as his eye, like the bird's, is wide open. He is seeing the visionary world, which includes the bison bearing down on him, as does his bird companion.

It has been suggested by Davenport and Jochim that the type of bird pictured is an extinct form of grouse called a capercaillie, an imposing bird the size of a turkey whose now rare modern male descendants can weigh up to 14 pounds with a wingspan over three and a half feet. They are highly territorial animals that perform elaborate courtship dances in arenas they make called leks, to vie for mates. They fan out an elaborate tail, spread their wings, raise their heads and emit exotic calls in four parts described as tapping, drum roll, cork-pop and gurgling. But what may have made the capercaillie most significant as a shamanic animal is that while in their courting display, they are entirely in thrall, as if in a trance, and cannot be diverted from it, even though dangerously threatened.

The shaman in this tableau is in the process of becoming a bird from the waist up, including his hands, which only have four digits as do bird's feet. His human body is being relinquished, and his soul has left or is leaving his body for another realm, one inhabited by this charging bison. Once his transformation is complete, he will be able to fly, transcending the domain of the bison.

It is particularly important to notice the artistic techniques employed in creating the image in the Shaft, as they are so significantly a part of Paleolithic man's conversation with the cave. The bison was intentionally placed so its outline encloses a dark patch of ocher-colored rock, which lends it additional bulk and presence. Its hindquarters run right to the edge of a recess in the wall. The man, dots, bird-staff and sign appear on a much lighter

field of stone dappled with white. The upper body of the man, the bird, signs and legs of the bison were painted in firm, defined lines with a brush. Yet the pelvis, legs and penis of the man and the belly of the bison were sprayed from the mouth. It would have been easier to use one technique or another but that was not the priority. The method of evoking the image was vital to its spiritual success, dictated by inspiration from beyond the membrane. The type of surface on which an image is created, some being appropriate for spraying or painting, others only for engraving, often determines the technique employed by the artist. This is not the case here as there is no significant variation in the makeup of the surface. Blowing paint from the mouth with sacred breath in certain areas and using a defining brush elsewhere was the appropriate way to evoke different types of power in different parts of the painting. The man is a shaman in the midst of transformation into a bird; his upper bird-half is brush-painted to correspond with the bird and signs. That the lower, clearly procreative half of the man, and the soft underbelly of the bison are sprayed, while the intestines spilling out are not, is purposefully significant, though the symbolism eludes us. It links them in an inscrutable magical conjunction revealed to and by the artist in the deep retreat of the Shaft.

SACRED HORNS

Each of the iconic animals that appear and reappear with extraordinary regularity for 20,000 years in Paleolithic art, embodied deep symbolic import that ran through the lives and mythology of the people who sought out and endured difficult conditions to evoke them. That there was a wide similarity of symbolism over distance and time is clear. The horse, the lion, the bear and all the rest occupied unique categories of spirit and those categories wove into others to create a complex tapestry that was the Paleolithic cosmos. Aside from Aujoulat's discovery of the seasonal attributions of horse/bovine/stag, we can only look for patterns that hint at the inscrutable interweavings of meaning. To posit symbolic significance on them as does Joseph Campbell in "the Way of the Animal Powers" by saying the Lascaux bulls represent the sun because that was their designation in myths around the ancient Mediterranean, is to deny the Paleos, their own reality and subsume it into another tradition entirely. In fact the bulls of the Mediterranean world, true to the multi-faceted generative capability of symbolism, also represented kingship, the weather, the earth,

storms, earthquakes and any number of other phenomena. There is no evidence to support such a random, pinpoint interpretation. Then what is the evidence for the minotaur?

The minotaur is nothing without his horns. George Frederick Watts painting of a minotaur is pathetic for many reasons, not the least of which is that his horns are so ineffectual and nested in soft, curly hair. Horns and virility are linked mythically in many cultures. Horned bovines and horns themselves were symbolically important throughout the Mediterranean world, as Campbell said, although their significance varied widely. Horned skulls were enshrined in great numbers at Çatal Huyuk and paintings of bulls adorned the walls, horned figures appear in North African rock art and so-called 'horns of consecration' decorate the architecture of Knossos. In Egypt sacred bulls and cows populate the cosmos. Once we can refer to a literary tradition, as we do in Egypt and Sumeria, which reveals the interpretation of the images, we can be certain of the intent of the symbolism. Even then, however, horns can indicate many things; the horizon, vitality, the new moon as well as the solar power. Indigenous art often portrays shamans and enlightened beings as wearing the horns of rams, stags, antelopes or bovines as an indication of the mystical flowering of magical power and wisdom; antennas, if you will, that link them to the deities.

In the Shaft, the man is literally knocked backward by the spiritual power of the bison. The bovines in the Hall of the Bulls are in family groups and at the very least, symbols of summer and possibly a fertile season of plenty. The bulls are imposing, even overwhelming, but not threatening. The images of confrontation between man and bovine, however, are of a decidedly different category. Some of the animals are bulls, one is a musk ox, another a bison. The important distinction seems to be that they are horned, aggressive animals, probably male and certainly in a different context than the bulls of the Rotunda. A carved block at Roc de Sers shows a naked man possibly running from a bison. He is turned away from the animal and his knees are bent as if he is propelling forwards, either in flight or after being struck. The animal's front feet are firmly planted and the head is lowered menacingly. The stance is remarkably similar to the foggy bison encountered in the Meander.

There are no bison in the first two galleries closest to the entrance, neither in the communal Hall of the Bulls nor the mind-altering Axial Gallery, although the first of the three peculiar red

animals encountered in the Meander just past the transitional Upside Down Horse, is a bison. There are apparently two in the chaotic engraving of the Apse, but it takes an expert's eye to find them. The Panel of the Imprint has one complete figure and possibly fragments of two more. The last image in the "Nave" is a very narrow constriction where the visitor must walk quite close to the paintings, is an unusual diptych called "Crossed Bisons', two fearsome bulls moving in opposite directions. Yet as their hindquarters intersect with the larger animal clearly in front, they are a single image brilliantly rendered using conventions of perspective to evoke dimensions of depth. They are painted in an alcove, one on each wing, enhancing the tense, animating effect of their aggressive natures. The bulk of their foreparts are enhanced a bit beyond what is the case in living buffalo, and the poses are tense and bristling, making them quite fearsome. One appears to be molting and the other's sex is quite purposefully painted in red against a purplish black coat. Having to move past these beasts in this narrow confine as an initiate, in an altered state of consciousness, knowing these images as aggressive spirits, would have been unnerving.

However, in the most remote gallery of the cave, the Chamber of the Felines, the bison are featured, being out numbered only by the ubiquitous horses. There are nine here, in the company of six lions, carnivores that are relegated exclusively to this very narrow and distant space. There are three on each wall, all facing into the deep chamber. The final animal image here is a deeply engraved bison, and on the opposite wall, the terminal pattern of six red dots identical to the black dots in the Shaft. The communal aurochs that dominate the Hall of the Bulls and many other galleries have not a single representative here. This is the most distant chamber housing predatory cats with a far different, yet inscrutable, spiritual function. And of course, there is the bison in the Shaft.

Second only to horses in number, bison seem to have occupied a wide mythic and artistic category. Clottes says, as one of the favorite themes of artists, second only to the horse, they were individualized, varying the eyes, coat, stance and horns. The frequency of their appearance in art, often in the company of horses, led Leroi-Gourhan to postulate his male-female theory of symbolic dichotomy. In Chauvet however, 14,000 years earlier, bison are relegated to remote or terminal sections of galleries. We find a number of them in the End Gallery, in the company of the magnificent minotaur. Clottes says of Chauvet the bison appears to

be a species that is not only rare but also limited to the deepest parts of the cave (2003; p.187). They are the only animal, aside from one owl, shown full-face. The rest of the bestiary is shown in profile or three-quarter. A line of these bison heads are stacked one on another along a vertical ridge in the End Chamber and a bison emerges frontally from a uterine recess in the wall, just opposite the minotaur and vulva. In Altamira, however, the ceiling is covered with bison in a plethora of moods and activities. In the Middle Magdalenian cave of Troi Frères, a minotaur dances at the center of an exuberant panel of animals, 30 of which are bison, over twice as many as the others combined. In the later Magdalenian cave of Niaux, bison are 'legion' and Clottes says each is unique, an individualized expression of artistic license not seen executed in any other animal. It seems that the bison moved, historically and artistically speaking, from the deepest parts of Chauvet to cover the walls of Niaux. Perhaps this suggests a growing appreciation for this iconic animal, one that encouraged a heightened sense of freedom, in Clottes' words, to express a more unique, personal relationship with its spiritual power, unlike the more formulaic images of horses or mammoths. Regional, climatic and mythic differences all play into how, and how many bison were represented in cave art. Although they were hunted, it was reindeer and not bison that constituted the bulk of the Paleolithic diet. Ultimately it can only be said that the bison played a vital part in the spiritual life of Paleolithic people.

This individualized relationship may have cast the bison as a more present, or accessible spirit animal encountered at the interface between the worlds. A shaman in deep trance who tapped into bison energy, morphing into a composite being half man half bison, would more easily flow between the worlds. There are no horse, cervid, mammoth, or rhino-headed beings in the caves, although these are the other commonly featured animals. There are exceptions, however, as there always are. In Troi Frères, the famous dancing 'Sorcerer' figure is a composite of cervid antlers, owl eyes, horses' tails and man. An enigmatic figure at Cosquer may be a seal, or a man, or both, and there are a few ibex-composite creatures. Other bird-headed figures occurring art Pech-Merle and Cougnac, contemporaries of Lascaux, may indicate a metamorphic thematic consistency. Yet there are more bison-headed figures than any other composite creature.

THE MYSTERY

In the Shaft a great mystery is revealed. The recurring theme in several caves of this time of man confronting a horned bovine, or being combined with one, demonstrates that this was a significant mythic event. These were swift, powerful and dangerous animals that could easily kill a man. While the aurochs in Lacsaux's Hall of the Bulls are enshrined as holy families, the animal in the Shaft is a deadly threat. His location, where only the most intense spiritual journeying took place, exposes the dangerous nature of the shamanic experience. The shaman who attempts to cross that ultimate border between life and death in the center of the labyrinthine vortex must confront the Paleolithic minotaur. If he is unprepared, weak, or hesitant, he will lose his soul to this being, returning (if he returns at all) a shattered failure. The minotaur in historical myth has always been a powerful, yet sacrificial creature. His existential purpose is only to await what will become his food or his conqueror/executioner, the shaman/hero and confront him. The danger involved in 'slaying' such a powerful creature translates into spiritual or heroic wealth incurred. The journeyer who enters the minotaur's lair at the center of the vortex stands in great peril of extinction and must be prepared to make the ultimate sacrifice himself. To succeed demands strength of purpose, unflagging courage, personal power, and strong spirit helpers.

Although the bison in the Shaft has been dreadfully wounded, the animal is far from debilitated. Paradoxically, this spirit bison's sacrifice increases his strength rather than depletes it. His aggression and vitality are palpable. For the shaman, there is tremendous power in the confrontation and conquest of terror and pain, his stock in trade. Like the agile hunter who had the courage and strength to strangle a wounded bison, the shaman must draw on his spiritual potency to overcome the mystical bison. However, the shaman depicted in the Shaft scene is not the slayer of the minotaur/bison. The spear, if that is what it is, enters the bison at the anus and passes through and beyond the animal's underbelly. The placement of the spear is precise and intentional, as is every element of this iconic work of art. The man cannot have thrown the spear, because it enters the animal from the opposite direction. Notions that the man threw the spear at the retreating animal, which then turned on him, are wrong-headed. Another reading to consider is that the spear has always been lodged in his body, in an ancient mythic counterpart to the mystical wound of the Fisher King of the Grail legend. The 'wound' of the King, healing the destitute land, and 'possession' of the Grail are inextricably bound together. To achieve all, the courageous hero must ask the right questions and be pure of heart, or he may join previous champions who hang dead in their armor from a tree outside the castle of the Fisher King. The bison's wound, like the Fisher King's, is its existential purpose. The nature of his being in the context of the Shaft and the center of the labyrinth is to be wounded and dangerous. The dual 'deaths' we are witnessing represent the clash and melding of spirit energies into a magical translation to the Otherworld, evoked on the sacred membrane of the deepest chamber of a cathedral cave. To successfully make that sacred journey to death and back, demands a sacrifice, and both the shaman and the bison together fulfill that purpose. There is a dynamic tension of equivalent potency in these two figures.

Shamans the world over, to gain power and spirit allies, must make this dangerous, sacrificial journey to the other world where they are 'killed', ritually dismembered and reassembled into a unique human who can traverse multiple universes, engage with dangerous beings, redress energetic balance between worlds, and heal illnesses. The bison is defined by his own pain. The shaman is not here to slay this powerful bison, but rather to be a worthy opponent; to see the wound for what it truly is and thereby 'heal' it and, in so doing, gain power and heal himself. He cannot be dissuaded from his purpose by fear of this aggressive magical being. As a 'wounded healer' himself, his knowledge of how to redress energetic imbalances, combined with increasing familiarity with this guardian of the border gained through many ecstatic journeys, will allow the shaman to literally take wing as a bird-spirit and move into higher cosmological realms. 'Wounded healers' shamanizing in the Shaft identified completely with the disemboweled bison, the best of them merging with that bison power to become minotaurs, dancing across the border between life and death at the center of the vortex.

The artist of the Shaft scene has captured the ecstatic multi-valenced moment of the experience of passing through the veil between the worlds at the center of the labyrinth, engaging a powerful spirit helper and transcending bird-like into another realm; precisely the experience a shaman would have sought in this mystical place at the heart of the sacred cave. In the Shaft scene of Lascaux we are a witness to the ultimate shamanic mystery; the

earning and bestowal of transformative power that allows the shaman to tap into the unformed pool of energy beyond the membrane to work his magic, to realign imbalance in the cosmos by placing himself between opposing forces of chaos and creation, and to remove the kinks from the web of life so that energy flows unimpeded, at least until the next 'sickness' arises. The minotaur is paradoxically, both door and key to the higher cosmological realms, and there can be no labyrinth without a minotaur. Where the pilgrim at the end of his journey down the Axial Gallery must confront the vague, foggy, red bison in the Meander, the master shaman in deep spiritual transport must merge with the enigmatic, brilliantly rendered and extremely aggressive wounded bison spirit of the Shaft. From the vantage of the Paleolithic shaman, Theseus's brutal slaughter of the Minotaur Asterius pales in comparison.

The enigmatic power of the minotaur is undiminished today, though it has gone through many permutations. He still embodies the raw sexual energy evoked in Chauvet, the liminal quality of having a foot in each world as in Trois Freres, and the mythic transformative capabilities and terrifying danger of The Shaft. Paleolithic hunter-gatherers, killed and consumed the middle world counterparts of these iconic animals that populate their interior sacred spaces, including bulls and bison, partaking of their animate souls to feed their own. Creativity implies necessary destruction and the opposite is equally true. Gods and monsters dwell together in the center of the labyrinth and the line between them is very thin. The Paleolithic minotaur is an epiphanic, shamanic channel through which flows the energies of life and death. At the center of the labyrinth is where all paradoxes collide, resolving into unity. Sacrifice is made, balance is redressed and life regenerated in the lair of the minotaur. In this lightless sensory deprivation chamber, shamans saw visions lit by the splendid sun of hallucinatory revelation, the inner light that illuminates harsh truths, undeniable death, and the raging beauty of life.

Around 18,000 years ago the earth quite literally shifted on its axis and the planet began to warm. For the next 10,000 years the erratic weather cooled and warmed dramatically. The freezing and thawing of the earth drove the engine of life to continually adapt, compelling humans and animals to migrate with the vegetation and water. Polar tundra, hammered by high winds and vicious dust storms gradually gave way in warmer years to the spread of shrubs and grasses, dwarf willow and artemisia crept up the rugged

hillsides. A whipsaw return of bitter cold brought a withering encore of the Ice Age, which again dissipated and warmed. Birches replaced juniper and by 10,000 BCE deep woodlands lay in a lush blanket across Europe. As the ice retreated, melting into foaming rivers and enormous lakes and filling the seas, the gigantic animals moved north to the cold and gradually winked out, extinguished by the warm hand of the Holocene epoch. The wild, untamed world softened; wild wheat seeds and grasses sprouted dependably by pleasant streams and the wildlife was plentiful. There was no need to pack the children and frail, old people and move to follow the herds. Tangled vines were trellised, dogs tamed, goats and sheep penned and bred. The people abandoned their rock shelters and spirit caves, moving into seasonal, then solid homes and villages surrounded by farms and lowing cattle. The lunar glow of the horned goddesses of Crete and the radiant echoes of the bull/sky god Asterius emerged from the mouths of caves into the light. Ariadne unspooled her magic thread in the sunlight on a labyrinthine patterned palace floor to guide the dancers. Young men and women still confronted bulls, vaulting gracefully between their horns in celestial ceremonies. Yet they kept their cave-consciousness; at the center of rough village or splendid city beats the heart of a man-made cave, a barrow, kiva, temple, or a cathedral with a labyrinth set into the floor. The call of those deep interior spaces, humming with the voices of gods, where the paradoxes of life are resolved in a moment of ecstatic transcendence has never left us.

In the valleys of the Dordogne and Vezere, the Loire and Rhine, gentle waters slowly buried abandoned campsites in silt. The forgotten weapons, the broken tools and lost jewelry, the dry bones of reindeer, the remnants of a body of ancient life were buried. The limestone portals to caves froze and thawed, cracked, slipped and slowly tumbled into rubble, sealing a world of spirit and art inside. Stones detached from the ceiling and fell, crushing the huge skulls of long dead cave bears, sending bones and teeth spinning in the darkness before eternal silence settled in like a black dust. Trees gained a foothold and grew, insinuating their roots through crevices in the splitting rock to emerge in the dark realms below where horses prance and bulls stand at sentry with their magical families. And the minotaur dances in grief and celebration, in joy and desperation, calling the gods and the people together across the threshold between the worlds, at the center of the labyrinth.

FINAL THOUGHTS

I began this book to resolve a paradox for myself, asking the questions how can one symbol comfortably contain both monster and god at its center and why now, in this modern world, is this ancient symbol re-emerging with such vitality? The answer to the first question lies at the heart of the labyrinth; how one defines the nature of the minotaur, inseparable from his labyrinth, and one's confrontation with him. He is both barrier and ticket to enlightenment; the guardian one must pass to enter the higher realms of deity. In the Paleolithic this was the province of initiates and shamans who sacrificed themselves to the raging hallucinations of altered states that set them in the realm of the spirits. Today, in our tame and comfortable world, the labyrinthine experience is understood as a life journey we all take. We venture into the fearsome darkness of unexplored spiritual terrain, and, disoriented, we hope for a guide and a light, and both dread and welcome the culmination of the journey. Whether facing down illness, coming to terms with trauma, surviving the death of a loved one or a nasty divorce, to welcome the better angels of our nature we must confront our personal minotaur and see him for what he is before we can sprout wings and move on. Walking a labyrinth as a meditative exercise gives us the sacred space and time in which to draw close both to our minotaurs and to our higher self, transform pain into strength, and integrate a small journey into the larger landscape of a life with integrity. Whether one is an Ice Age hunter or a housewife, this is the universal goal we all seek.

Why have so many modern people been captivated by the labyrinth? Why build this ancient symbol in schoolyards, hospitals, churches and gardens and invite perfect strangers to share the experience of walking it? Far from its Paleolithic origins, it is welcoming, fun and calming. The designs are beautiful and intriguing. And it is without judgment. People of all ages, backgrounds, religious persuasions, races and proclivities find comfort there.

As a species we are witnesses to the unprecedented destruction of our planet at our own hands. Daily reports detail the catastrophic results of wars, overpopulation, global warming, death of the oceans and the decimation of species. The specters of pandemics, massive storms and economic collapse hover ever closer. It is entirely possible, some would say probable, that our wanton destruction of planetary bio-diversity is irreversible. Outdated behaviors and beliefs, greed, ignorance, racism, sexism, intolerance and wanton cruelty are literally killing us. As the vital resources of livable land, food and water become increasingly rare, the pressures will only worsen. We have made the minotaur mighty and terrible and his thirst for blood cannot be slaked.

In the Paleolithic, people lived with no notion of the larger forces shaping global weather, yet they endured. Today, we are becoming tragically aware of the results of our success as a species and the consequences, and, like a flourishing virus in a shrinking petrie dish, we deny the limits of our tolerance. We face pressures not unlike the Paleos at the cusp of the Last Glacial Maximum, and ours, like theirs, threatens to sound the death knell of our way of life. But where the gradual end of the Ice Age led to the more temperate Mesolithic, and eventually agriculture and the formation of cities, our environmental crises appear to have no such silver lining.

The ceremonies growing up around the new labyrinth movement are inclusive, joyful, respectful of the planet, and encourage the work necessary to help save it. People who are drawn to it are caregivers, counselors, spiritual advisors, organic gardeners and landscape architects, but anyone with hope for the future is welcome. The labyrinth has reappeared in our midst and we have responded to it at a time when its power is needed, when the paradoxical issues of life and death must be addressed. Epiphany is momentary, but the journey is eternal. The labyrinth symbol has surfaced in our lives to help shatter a bulwark of old beliefs and to knit together the fabric of a new spirit, arising like gold cloth woven from straw in the space of a night.

1. Villars.
Man with arms upraised facing charging bison.

2. Lascaux. Shaft Scene.
Man in trance and confrontational wounded bison.

3. Le Roc de Sers.
Escaping man holding something over his shoulder,
pursued by bison.

4. Laugerie Basse.
Man knocked down by charging bison.

BIBLIOGRAPHY

Abuusch, Tzvi: <u>Gilgamesh, Hero, King, God, and Striving Man</u> in Archaeology Odyssey, July August 2000 Vol. 3 No. 4

Apollonios Rhodios, The Argonautika by Apollonios Rhodios, trans. Peter Green, Berkeley (CA) University of California Press, 1997

Attenborough, David. 1987. The First Eden: The Mediterranean World and Man. Boston: Little, Brown and Co.

Aujoulat, Norbert. 2005. Lascaux; Movement, Space and Time. New York: Harry N. Abrams Inc.

Bahn, Paul, ed. 2003. Written in Bones; How Human Remains Unlock The Secrets of the Dead. NY: Firefly Books, Inc.

Bahn, Paul G. , ed. 2000. The Atlas of World Archaeology. New York: Checkmark Books

Barber, Elizabeth Wayland. 1995. Women's Work; The First 20,000 Years. New York: W.W. Norton & Company, Inc.

Bauval, Robert and Adrian Gilbert.1994. The Orion Mystery. New York: Crown Publishers.

Bonnefoy, Yves. 1991, 1993. American, African and Old European Mythologies. Chicago: University of Chicago Press.

Bord, Janet. 1976. Mazes and Labyrinths of the World. New York: E.P. Dutton.

Budge, E. Wallis.
1969. The Gods of the Egyptians. New York: Dover Publications.
1978. An Egyptian Hieroglyphic Dictionary: New York: Dover Publications
1967: The Egyptian Book of the Dead; (The Papyrus of Ani) Egyptian Text and Transliteration and Translation. New York: Dover Publications

Bunson, Margaret. 1991. A Dictionary of Ancient Egypt: New York: Oxford University Press

Burkert, Walter. 1983. Homo Necans; The Anthropology of Ancient Greek Sacrificial Ritual and Myth. Berkeley: University of California Press.

Calasso, Roberto. 1993. The Marriage of Cadmus and Harmony. New York: Alfred A. Knopf

Castleden, Rodney. 1990. Minoans, Life in Bronze Age Crete. London: Routeledge.

Campbell, Joseph, 1983. Way of the Animal Powers, Vol 1 Hitsorical Atlas of World Mythology. London: Summerfield Press

Chippendale, Christopher and Tacon, Paul S. C. 1998. The Archaeology of Rock Art. Cambridge: University Press

Clark, R. T. Rundle. 1978. Myth and Symbol in Ancient Egypt. London: Thames and Hudson, Ltd.

Clottes, Jean & Lewis-Williams, David. 1998. The Shamans of Prehistory: trance and magic in the painted caves. New York. Harry N. Abrams, Inc.

Clottes, Jean. 2008. Cave Art. London: Phaidon Press, Inc.

Clottes, Jean. 2003. Chauvet Cave; The Art of the Earliest Times. Salt Lake City: University of Utah Press

Clottes, Jean. 1992. The Cave Beneath the Sea; Paleolithic Images at Cosquer. New York: Harry N. Abrams, Inco.

Clottes, Jean. 2003. Return to Chauvet Cave; Excavating the Birthplace of Art: The First Full Report. London: Thames & Hudson

Davenport, Demorest & Jochim, Michael A.; 1988. The Scene in the Shaft at Lascaux: Antiquity. Vol 62 #236 pp.558-62

Devereux, Paul. 1997. The Long Trip; The Prehistory of Psychedelia. New York: Arkana, The Penguin Group

Davis, Wade. 1998. Shadows in the Sun. Washington, D.C. , Island Press/ Shearwater Books.

Dickenson, Oliver. 1994. The Aegean Bronze Age. New York: Press Syndicate of the University of Cambridge

Discover Magazine. Flexing Mental Muscles, by Eric Haseltine. November, 1999. page 132

Discover Magazine. Paleolithic Protectress, staff. March, 1999. page 19

Dissanayke, Ellen. 1992. Homo Aestheticus. New York: U.of Wash. Press.

Doob, Penelope Reed. 1990. The Idea of the Labyrinth from Classical Antiquity through the Middle Ages. New York: Cornell University Press.

Dronfield, Jeremy. Subjective Vision and the Source of Irish Megalithic Art. Antiquity: #69, 1995

Fagan, Brian. 1999. Floods, Famine and Emperors. New York: Basic Books

Fagan, Brian. 1998. From Black Land to Fifth Sun. Massachusetts: Helix Books

Fagan, Brian. 2005. The Long Summer. Basic Books: New York

Farnoux, Alexandre. Knossos; Searching for the Legendary Palace of King Minos. Harry N. Abrams, Inc., Publishers

Elgar, Frank. 1963. The Rock Paintings of Tassili. London: Thames and Hudson

Fagels, Robert. 1991. The Iliad. Homer. New York: Viking

Fagles, Robert. 1996. The Odyssey. Homer. New York: Viking

Foley, Helene P. , ed. 1994. The Homeric Hymn to Demeter: Princeton, N.J. : the Princeton Univ. Press

Faulkner, R. O. 1993. The Ancient Egyptian Book of the Dead. Austin: The University of Texas Press

Frazer, Sir James George. 1950. The Golden Bough: A Study in Magic and Religion. New York: The Macmillan Co.

Gimbutas, Marija. 1989.The Gods and Goddesses of Old Europe. Berkeley: University of California Press.

Graves, Robert: 1955-60. The Greek Myths. New York: Moyer Bell Limited

    1970.The White Goddess; A historical grammar of poetic myth. New York: Farrar, Straus, and Giroux

Grimal, Nicolas. 1994. A History of Ancient Egypt. Cambridge, Mass. : Blackwell Publishers.

Hawkes, Jacquetta. 1968. Dawn of the Gods. New York: Random House

Halifax, Joan. 1982. Shaman; The Wounded Healer. London; Thames and Hudson Ltd.

Hayes, William C. 1965. Most Ancient Egypt. Chicago: University of Chicago Press.

Hayden, Brian. 2003. Shamans Sorcerers and Saints. Smithsonian Books: Washington

Hammmond, et al. 1988 Past Worlds; The Times Altas of Archaeology. London: Times Books Limited

Harner, Michael. 1990. The Way of the Shaman. New York: Harper and Row

Henderson, Joseph Land, Maud Oakes. 1963. The Wisdom of the Serpent: The Myths of Death, Rebirth, and Resurrection.Princeton, New Jersey: Princeton Universtiy Press.

Herodotus, The Histories.

Hesiod, 1974. The Homeric Hymns and Homerica. Hugh G. Evelyn-White, trans. Cambridge and London: Harvard University Press

Hesiod and Theognis: 1986. Hesiod: Theogony, Works and Days. Theognis: Elegies. Suffolk, Great Britain: Penguin Books,

Homer: 1990. The Ililad. New York: Penguin Books

Hopper, R. J., 1976. The Early Greeks: New York: Barnes & Noble Books

Hornung, Erik. 1990. The Valley of the Kings: New York: Timkin Publishers, Inc.

Hornung, Erik. 1999. The Ancient Egyptian Books of the Afterlife: New York: Cornell University Press

Hurwit, Jeffrey M. 1999. The Athenian Acropolis; History, Mythology, and Archaeology from the Neolithic Era to the Present. Cambridge: The Cambridge University Press

Johnson, Laurin R. 1999. Shining in the Ancient Sea; The Astronomical Ancestry of Homer's Odyssey. Portland, Oregon: Multnomah House Press

Jones, Prudence & Pennick, Nigel, 1997. A History of Pagan Europe. London, Routledge

Jordan, Michael. 1993. Encyclopedia of Gods. New York: Facts on File

Jordan, Paul. 2000. Neanderthal; Neanderthal Man and the Story of Human Origins. Glouscestershire: Sutton Publishing Limited

Katz, Richard. 1982. Boiling energy. Cambridge: Harvard University Press

Kern, Hermann. 2000. Through the Labyrinth; Designs and Meanings over 5,000 Years. Munich: Prestel

Kalweit, Holger, 1984. Dreamtime and Inner Space; The World of the Shaman. Boston: Shambhala Publications, Inc.

1987. Shamans, Healers, and Medicine Men. Boston, Mass.: Shambhala Publications, Inc.

Kendall, D.G., et al 1974. The Place of Astronomy in the Ancient World; A Joint Symposium of the Royal Society and The British Academy. London: Oxford University Press

Kerenyi, Carl, 1976. Dionysos; Archetypal Image of Indestructible Life. New Jersey: Princeton University Press

Krupp, E.C. 1991. Beyond the Blue Horizon, Myths and Legend of the Sun, Moon, Stars and Planets. New York: Harper and Collins.

Lajoux, Jean-Dominique. 1963 The Rock Paintings of Tassili. Cleveland: The World Publishing Company. (library # MCL 709. L19r - pp731 &73)

Lehman, Johannes. 1977. The Hittites; People of a Thousand Gods. New York: The Viking Press.

Lessa, William A. and Vogt, Evon, Z. eds. Reader in Comparative Religion; An Anthropological Approach: New York. 1965

Lewis-Williams, J.D. and T. A. Dowson. <u>On Vision and Power in the Neolithic; Evidence from the Decorated Monuments</u>: Current Anthropology 34, no.1 (February 1993)

2002. The Mind in the Cave; Consciousness and the Origins of Art. London: Thames and Hudson.

Mallory, J.P. 1989. In Search of the Indo-Europeans. London: Thames and Hudson, Ltd.

Mackenzie, Donald A. 1995. Crete and pre-Hellenic. London: Senate

Manetho. 1980. Manetho with an English Translation by W.G. Waddell: Cambridge, Mass.: The Harvard University Press.

Maspero, G. 1897. The Dawn of Civilization, Egypt and Chaldea. New York: D. Appleton & Co.

Maspero, G. 1968 The Dawn of Civilization, Vol II. New York: Frederick Ungar Publishing Co.

Matthews, W.H. 1970.Mazes and Labyrinths, Their History and Development. New York: Dover Publications

McGrath, Sheena. The Sun Goddess. Blandford

McHugh, Tom. 1972 The Time of the Buffalo. New York: Alfred A. Knopf

McKenna, Terrance.1992. Food of the Gods. New York: Bantam Books

Merlin, Mark David. 1984. On The Trail of the Ancient Opium Poppy. London and Toronto: Associated University Presses.

Mithin, Steven. 2004. After The Ice. Cambridge, Mass: Harvard University Press

Mithin, Steven. 2006. The Singing Neanderthal. Cambridge, Massachusettes: Harvard University Press

Morkot, Robert. 1996.The Penguin Historical Atlas of Ancient Grece. Avon, GB. The Bath Press

Murphy, Edwin. 1990. The Antiquities of Egypt, a Translation, with Notes, of Book I of The Library of History of Diodorus Siculus. New Jersey. Transaction Purlishers

Narby, Jeremy & Huxley, Francis, eds. 2001. Shamans Through Time; 500 years on the Path to Knowledge. New York.: Jeremy P.

Tarcher/ Putnam

Neumann, Erich. 1963. The Great Mother; An Analysis of the Archetype. Princeton, N. J. Princeton University Press.

Nur, Amos and Eric H. Cline. Earthquake Storms in <u>Archaeology Odyssey</u>. September/October 2001, Vol. 4 No. 5

<u>Parabola; Myth, Tradition, and the Search for Meaning: Light :</u> Vol. 26, Number 2. May 2001

Pausanias. 1971. Guide to Greece. Suffolk, Great Britain:Penguin Books

Pearson, James L. 2002. Shamanism and the Ancient Mind. Walnut Creek: AltaMira Press

Petri, Flinders.1932. Seventy Years in Archaeology. New York: Henry Holt and Company

Pfeiffer, John E. 1982. The Creative Explosion. New York: Harper & Row, Publishers, Inc.

Pindar. 1912. The Extant Odes of Pindar. Ernest Myers, translator. London: McMillan & Co.

Pliny.1962.Natural History, Vol 36-37. Massachusetts: Harvard University Press.

Platon, Nicolas. 1966. Archaeologia Mundi; Crete. Geneva: Nagel Publishers

Plutarch. 1931. Everybody's Plutarch. New York: Dodd, Mead & Co.

Pollan, Michael. 2001. The Botany of Desire; A Plant's-eye view of the World. New York: Random House

Puharich, Andrija. 1974. The Sacred Mushroom, Key To The Door of Eternity. New York. Doubleday

Ramos, Pedro A. Saura. 1998. The Cave of Altamira. New York: Harry N. Abrams, Inc.

Ransome, Hilda M. 1986. The Sacred Bee in Ancient Times and Folklore. London. Butler and Tanner Ltd.

Ripinsky-Naxon, Michael. 1993. The Nature of Shamanism: Substance and Function of a Religious Metaphor. New York: State University of New York Press, Albany.

Romm, James. 1998. Herodotus. Yale University Press, New Haven and London

Rowlands, Penelope (article) 1998. SF Examiner Magazine a section of the Sunday Examiner and Chronicle. December 13, 1998

Rudgley, Richard. 1999. The Lost Civilizations of the Stone Age.

New York: The Free Press

Ruspoli, Mario. 1987. The Cave of Lascaux; The Final Photographs. New York: Harry N. Abrams, Incorporated

Ryan, William and Pitman, Walter. 1998. Noah's Flood; The New Scientific Discoveries About The Event That Changed History. New York: Simon & Schuster.

Salomon, Anne. Rock art in Southern Africa: Scientific American, November 1996.

Schultes, Richard Evans and Hoffman, Albert; 1992. Plants of the Gods; Their Sacred, Healing and Hallucinogenic Powers. Rochester,Vermont: Healing Arts Press

Shanks, Herschel: Into the Labyrinth. Archaeology Odyssey, July/August 2000, Vol. 3 No. 4

Stiebing, Jr. , William H. : When Civilization Collapsed Archaeology Odyssey, September/October 2001, Vol 4 No.5

Strabo. 1967. The Geography of Strabo with an English translation by Horace Leonard Jones. Cambridge: Harvard University Press

Strehlow, T.G.H. 1978. Central Australian Religion; Personal Monototemism in a Polytotemic Community. Bedford Park, Australia: Flinders University Press

Stix, Gary. 2008. Traces of a Distant Past, Scientific American, July 2008 p. 56

Thiel, Rudolf. 1967. And There Was Light; The Discovery of the Universe. New York: Alfred A. Knopf

Thorpe, S.A. 1993. Shamans, Medicine Men and Traditional Healers, Pretoria: University of South Africa

Yates, Royden, et al. 1990. Pictures From The Past, Pietermaritzburg, SA: Centaur Publications

White, Randall. 2004. Prehistoric Art; The Symbolic Journey of Humankind, New York: Harry N. Abrams Publishers, Inc.

Thurston, Hugh. 1994. Early Astronomy. Vancouver, B.C.: University of British Columbia Press

Time Magazine. January 29, 2001. p. 59 Sharon Begley

Walker, Barbara G. 1983. The Woman's Encyclopedia of Myths and Secrets: New York: Harper and Rowe, Publishers, Inc.

Walker, Barbara G. 1988. The Women's Dictionary of Symbols and Sacred Objects: New York: Harper and Row Publishers, Inc.

Weil, Andrew. 1983 . From Chocolate to Morphine. Boston: Houghton Mifflin Co.

Whitley, David S. 2009; Cave Painting and the Human Spirit; The Origin of Creativity and Belief. New York: Prometheus Books

Whitley, David S. 2000; The Art of the Shaman; Rock Art of California. Salt Lake City; University of Utah Press

Wilson, Ian. 2001. Before the Flood; The Biblical Flood as a Real Event and How It Changed the Course of Civilization. New York: St. Martin's Press

Wong, Kate. 2009 "Twilight of the Neanderthals" <u>Scientific American</u>; August 2009